No Hope for Heaven, No Fear of Hell

No Hope for Heaven, No Fear of Hell

The Stafford-Townsend Feud of Colorado County, 1871–1911

by James C. Kearney, Bill Stein,
and James Smallwood

Number 1 in the Texas Local Series

University of North Texas Press
Denton, Texas

©2016 James C. Kearney

All rights reserved.

Printed in the United States of America.

10 9 8 7 6 5 4 3 2

Permissions:
University of North Texas Press
1155 Union Circle #311336
Denton, TX 76203–5017

The paper used in this book meets the minimum requirements of the American National Standard for Permanence of Paper for Printed Library Materials, z39.48.1984. Binding materials have been chosen for durability.

Library of Congress Cataloging-in-Publication Data

Kearney, James C., 1946– | Stein, Bill, 1954–2008 | Smallwood, James.
   No hope for heaven, no fear of hell : the Stafford-Townsend feud of Colorado County, 1871–1911 / by James C. Kearney, Bill Stein, and James Smallwood.
     p. cm. -- (Number 1 in the Texas local series)
   Denton, Texas : University of North Texas Press, [2016]
   Includes bibliographical references and index.
   ISBN 978-1-57441-650-3 (cloth : alk. paper) | ISBN 978-1-57441-659-6 (ebook) | ISBN 978-1-57441-711-1 (paper : alk. paper)
   1. LCSH: Vendetta—Texas—Colorado County—History—19th century. 2. Vendetta—Texas—Colorado County—History—20th century. 3. Criminals—Texas—Colorado County—Biography. 4. Colorado County (Tex.)—History—19th century. 5. Colorado County (Tex.)—History—20th century. 6. Texas—History—1846–1950. I. Title.

F392.C58 K43 2016
976.4/25306–dc23
                   2016022324

No Hope for Heaven, No Fear of Hell; *The Stafford-Townsend Feud of Colorado County, 1871–1911* is Number 1 in the Texas Local Series

The electronic edition of this book was made possible by the support of the Vick Family Foundation. Typeset by vPrompt eServices.

Contents

List of Illustrations After Chapter 5	vii
Abbreviations	ix
Preface	xi
Acknowledgments	xv
Introduction	1
1. The Murders of Bob and John Stafford at the Hands of Larkin and Marion Hope	5
2. The Seven Townsend Brothers (and One Sister) of Texas	21
3. Robert Earl Stafford	39
4. The Rise of Sam Houston Reese and the Assassination of Larkin Hope	61
5. The Killings of Sam and Dick Reese	77
Photo Insert	
6. The Terrible Affray at Bastrop and the Shoot-out at Rosenberg	99
7. The Interim	119
8. The 1906 Skating Rink Shoot-out	127
9. The Assassination of Jim Coleman	135
10. The Deaths of Marion Hope, Will Clements, and Jim Townsend	145
11. Postscript	151

Appendices
- Appendix A: Feud Biographies ... 161
- Appendix B: Goeppinger Interviews ... 181
- Appendix C: Ranger Captain Sieker Report ... 197
- Appendix D: Witness List Stelzig Murder Trial ... 203

Endnotes ... 211
Bibliography of Sources Used ... 265
Index ... 279

List of Illustrations
After Chapter 5

1. Colorado County map
2. Antebellum Plantation House (Tait House) Columbus
3. Black women Colorado County, ca. 1900
4. Colorado County cowboys on the Prairie
5. Wegenhoft brothers
6. Asa Townsend
7. Rebecca Townsend
8. Bob Stafford as a young man
9. Bob Stafford bank and residence
10. John Stafford residence
11. Stafford meat packing plant
12. Colorado County Courthouse
13. Sheriff J. Light Townsend
14. Marcus Townsend
15. Bob Stafford drawing
16. John Stafford
17. Larkin Hope
18. Sheriff Reese and Deputy Kollmann
19. Judge Mansfield and Commissioner's Court
20. Assassination of Larkin Hope drawing
21. The death of ex-Sheriff Reese drawing

22. Walter Reese
23. Keetie Reese
24. Hub Reese
25. Lillian Reese
26. Walter Reese and Lavaca County lawmen
27. M. H. Townsend in later life
28. Mrs. M. H. Townsend
29. Townsend Home, Columbus
30. Sheriff Burford
31. Arthur Burford
32. Jim Coleman and Walter Reese
33. Walter Reese and Texas Rangers
34. Poster announcing Mass Meeting
35. Newspaper drawing of 1907 Marion Hope trial
36. Ranger Captain John Reynolds Hughes
37. Ranger Captain John H. Rogers
38. Ranger Captain James Abijah Brooks
39. Ranger Captain Bill McDonald
40. Ranger Captain Leander H. McNelly
41. Ranger Captain Lamartine P. Seiker
42. Stafford men, ca. 1911
43. John Goeppinger at the time of his retirement
44. Ike Towell's tombstone, Columbus, Texas

Abbreviations

AG	Adjutant General
AGR	Adjutant General Records
ANML	Archives of Nesbitt Memorial Library
ATSL	Archives, Texas State Library, Austin, Texas
BCAH	Briscoe Center for American History, University of Texas, Austin, Texas
CCF	Criminal Cause File
GP	Governors Papers, Texas State Library, Austin, Texas
HTO	*Handbook of Texas online*
ms	Manuscript (unpublished)
NHT	*New Handbook of Texas*
NML	Nesbitt Memorial Library, Columbus, Texas
NMLJ	*Nesbitt Memorial Library Journal*
RG	Record Group
SWHQ	*Southwestern Historical Quarterly*
TSL	Texas State Library, Austin, Texas
UT	University of Texas

Preface

Bill Stein conceived the idea for this book in the 1990s. The project, however, sat on the backburner until the last year of his life when he took it up with renewed interest and dedication. He had approached the University of North Texas about a book-length treatment and received a green light.

After Bill's untimely death in 2008, his brother Chris Stein asked me to take up the project where Bill had left off. I was a friend, historian, and colleague of Bill. Moreover, like Bill, I also grew up in Colorado County and had that immediacy to the story that comes with being a native.

Upon examination of his papers, I discovered that Bill had compiled an exhaustive file of primary sources, written a set of research summaries of various episodes connected with the feud, and started a list of short biographies of the very large cast of characters involved in the story. I have made extensive use of all these resources, which were entrusted to me for this purpose. Bill had not, however, developed either an outline or undertaken the actual writing of the story beyond the research summaries and biographies mentioned. Thus, this very complex and involved story still needed to be organized, interpreted, and written from beginning to end. The finished manuscript, however, is thoroughly grounded in Bill's research as well as his scholarly writings about Colorado County, which appeared over several years in the *Journal of the Nesbitt Memorial Library*, which he edited and produced.

In 2011 the Nesbitt Memorial Library Foundation contracted Dr. James Smallwood to help organize the archives at the library. Dr. Smallwood, a renowned Texas historian, author of innumerable books, and recognized expert on Texas Reconstruction, spent over a year completing this task and in the process became intimately acquainted with Colorado County history. He also became very interested in the feud story. We had many valuable conversations concerning the story and the best way to organize it as a book. I often stood in amazement of his vast knowledge and was in general agreement with his points of emphasis and overall interpretation.

Dr. Smallwood, however, had a more ambitious vision, namely to embed and develop the feud story within the larger context of "private justice" in post-Civil War Colorado County—largely gratuitous acts of white on black violence—which he intended to catalog and discuss in depth, and he began a rough draft that reflected this vision. The story grew into something much larger than what Bill Stein had originally envisioned, as several colleagues noted, and after Dr. Smallwood's death in 2013, I decided, regretfully, to abandon this approach and refocus the book back on the feud itself.

I also had done extensive research on my own at one point, but what I most had to offer in this regard was a taped interview with John Goeppinger, which was conducted at his invitation in 1972. Mr. Goeppinger was ninety years old at the time and had a remarkably clear memory of the events from 1890 forward, events in which he had actively participated on several occasions. He realized full well the deeply disturbing and even self-incriminating nature of much of what he had to say, but he was striving plainly for some sort of redemptive effect through his revelations, as if a confessional. He realized, moreover, that he was the last living participant, the last to know what really had happened from first-hand experience. His only caveat was that he be dead when the tape was made public, and since the tape was made over forty years ago, that requirement has been met.

—James C. Kearney

Acknowledgments

Many people have contributed in various ways to the production of this book, but I wish to offer my special thanks to Tracey Wegenhoft, Roger Wade, Donaly Brice, and my wife Paulina. Tracey began the transcription of the Goeppinger interview. Roger Wade took up where she left off and finished the transcription, a long and arduous task, which forms such an important component to this book. Donaly Brice, at the time archivist at the State Library, sent me valuable documents from the Attorney General's files and the Governor's papers, which document the extensive role of the Texas Rangers in the feud. Donaly also volunteered to read a revised manuscript (one of several) and offer comments. He was meticulous and detailed in his observations, pointing out factual errors, identifying awkward phrasing and questionable punctuation, and sharing his thoughts on overall readability. I thank him for his warm support from beginning to end and for the many hours he spent reviewing the manuscript. And finally, I thank my wife for her patience. Those who have never put together a peer-reviewed book, suitable for publication by a major publisher, have no concept of the time commitment required, the many steps involved, and the frequent frustrations and setbacks that one encounters along the way. It can be a strain and I thank my wife for her patience and understanding on this journey.

Finally, I also wish to thank the three official peer reviewers of the manuscript: Bill O'Neal, Carl Moneyhon, and Kenneth Howell. Each offered valuable advice and suggestions, which I have endeavored to incorporate in the final version.

INTRODUCTION

Colorado County has a troubled past. The gun violence that wracked the county for decades had its immediate roots in the post-Civil War era. This situation was compounded by the fact that the Old South truly meshed with the Old West since the county's physical geography enabled both slave-based plantations and extensive cattle operations. Prior to the war, many large slaveholders from core southern states relocated their plantations on virgin soil along the Colorado River basin and, to a lesser extent, the Navidad River basin at the western edge of the county. After the war, large-scale cattle operations flourished on the wide-open prairies between the two river basins and supplanted the plantations as the predominant economic activity. Old attitudes associated with slavery did not permit an easy adjustment to emancipation of the former slaves, leading to much violence and mayhem, while the rapid rise of the cattle industry offered a fresh arena for friction and bloodshed.

Two family names have come to be associated with the gun violence that plagued the county for decades after the end of the Civil War: the Townsends and the Staffords. Their stories, however, cannot be separated from the larger picture that included habituation of generations of young men to violence and the evolution of a code of honor that tolerated and encouraged private justice. In *I'll Die Before I Run*, C. L. Sonnichsen wrote, "In Texas the folk law of the frontier was reinforced by the unwritten laws of the South and produced a habit of self-redress more deeply ingrained perhaps, than anywhere else in the country. The grievances and abuses of the bad days after the Civil War gave extraordinary scope for the application of the old ways of dealing justice."[1] The troubles in Colorado County offer an almost perfect case study for Sonnichsen's observation.

There was, however, an important corollary to the Southern code of family honor strongly evident in the troubles in Colorado County: namely, the determination on the part of the two prominent families to amass wealth and achieve status, and the resolve to hold on to it, once obtained, by whatever means necessary, including extra-legal means. Elected office was one of the paths to both, since political power often translated into financial gain and social standing. The sheriff's office, especially, was a very powerful institution in nineteenth century Texas, with little outside control to check excesses. It placed one in a position to cement lucrative deals at a time when the courthouse was very much the center of commercial activity in the county. Control of the sheriff's office, self-evidently, also gave one a decided advantage should the threat of gun violence arise.[2] The sheriff's office, therefore, became a focal point of conflict in Colorado County.

In those areas of Texas that had substantial black populations, such as Colorado County, the key to obtaining and holding on to political power for over thirty years after the South's defeat was the black vote, a volatile issue that fueled many of the fabled Texas feuds of the times, such as The Jaybird/Woodpecker feud in neighboring Ft. Bend County. But although they all emerged from the same fire, so to speak, each grew into something distinctive.

This book neither catalogs nor examines all the violence of the period; rather, it concentrates on those individual acts of private justice and extra-legality associated with the Stafford and Townsend families. During the same time-frame, the county also experienced an appalling string of mob-inspired lynchings, of tribal eruptions of white-on-black violence that continued to plague the county for decades. These are mentioned in the course of the narrative and form a disturbing background to the primary focus of the book.

It should be noted that this tale falls clearly into two distinct phases: the first phase beginning with an 1871 shoot-out in Columbus and ending with the deaths of the Stafford brothers in 1890; the second commencing, ironically, also with the deaths of the Stafford brothers, blossoming after 1898 with the assassination of Larkin Hope, and concluding in 1911 with the violent deaths of Marion Hope, Jim Townsend, and Will Clements, all in the space of one month. One of the main challenges for the author has been to disentangle the various strands and make clear to the reader how the two phases relate, how the one story evolved into the next, yet never completely separated from it, even as the cast of characters changed. It is a complicated story; the reader cannot expect a casual read and will have to pay close attention.

Finally, the Colorado County story represents the last of the major Texas feuds that have not received book-length treatment, at least, book-length treatment that rests on documentation and aspires to be unbiased.[3] This then, is the tale of the Staffords and Townsend families, and how their aspirations for wealth and status brought them into conflict with one another, and then, in the case of the Townsends, brought them into conflict with themselves.

CHAPTER ONE

The Murders of Bob and John Stafford at the Hands of Larkin and Marion Hope

As the new decade of the 1890s began, Columbus and Colorado County could look back on several years of unprecedented growth and prosperity. Old Columbus had undergone a complete facelift from the modest and sometimes makeshift wooden buildings that had once lined Milam and Spring streets, the main corridors of commerce. A row of stately two-story brick structures with impressive facades and other elegant touches denoting prosperity and optimism had supplanted the old structures. Among the many businesses that lined the courthouse square were two jewelers, three drug stores, five general merchandise stores, a butcher shop, several grocery stores, law and medical offices, a newspaper office, a saddle and harness shop, and eight saloons.[1]

The newly constructed Stafford Opera House and Bank stood out clearly as the crown jewel among all the new structures, while R. E. "Bob" Stafford's imposing residence, next door to the opera house, counted as the grandest new home in town. The opera house was the largest of its kind in the state for the period and offered a convenient overnight venue for the numerous theatrical groups and minstrel shows that regularly travelled the rails between Houston and San Antonio. Thanks to R. E. "Bob" Stafford, the town and its citizens now had a claim to elegance and status that it had not previously enjoyed. Columbus was on the map.

But one thing was missing. The old wooden courthouse, now woefully inadequate, looked out of place across the street from such an impressive array of elegant buildings. To remedy the situation, Commissioner's Court voted to construct a new courthouse in 1890 that would be sizable enough to handle the expanded business of the county and would also be equal in style and elegance to the other impressive courthouses being built across the state in this era of general prosperity.

A firm was engaged to draw up plans and bids were let out. A date was set for the laying of the cornerstone for the new showcase of the county: July 7, 1890. The county planned a large celebration replete with a parade, speeches, and a large public barbeque at the "grove," the large stand of majestic, moss-laden live oaks in the northern part of town.

As the day for the celebration rolled around, throngs of celebrants descended on the town from surrounding communities and across the state. It was a festive occasion for all to enjoy. No one foresaw the tragedy about to unfold, for the shocking finale to the long-standing state of ill will between Bob Stafford and the Townsends was about to play out in dramatic fashion in the midst of the celebration.

The Townsend family's rise to affluence and status in the county had played out over many years and several generations. Bob Stafford's ascension to fame and fortune in Colorado County, by contrast, was no less than breathtaking and had rapidly eclipsed all the Townsends put together. The roots of the bad blood between the Townsends and Bob Stafford lay in specific events, to be sure: in a shoot-out of January 1871 on the streets of Columbus (examined in a later chapter) and in various squabbles concerning cattle and grazing rights. But even more than this, Bob Stafford's rise had aroused envy, resentment, and fear, and not only in the methods by which he achieved wealth and prestige—a combination of shrewdness, determination, and outright ruthlessness—but in the sheer dimensions of his success. The enormous wealth of Bob Stafford—by some estimates a net worth of $2,500,000 at the time of his death—was a serious cause of concern to the Townsend faction and the political machine they controlled.

With the construction of the opera house and the establishment of a bank, both in 1887, Bob Stafford had shifted his power base off the prairies and located it literally across the street from the courthouse, which the Townsends had jealously controlled for years. This represented a substantial threat to Marcus (Mark) Townsend, attorney, state legislator, and power broker, and to Sheriff J. Light Townsend, Mark Townsend's uncle. The two had controlled county politics for a decade with the help of the large black vote that tended to vote as a block. The two men had profited handsomely from the many side deals that came with this arrangement, but with the November 1890 election looming on the horizon, there was no guarantee that this comfortable (and profitable) arrangement would continue into the future. Bob Stafford, easily the wealthiest man in the county, was their avowed political enemy and had made it known on numerous occasions how strongly he resented their manipulation of the black vote. The stage was set for a confrontation.

Bob Stafford knew that his son Warren would be present at the festivities, attendant to the laying of the cornerstone of the new courthouse, and he also anticipated that he would, as usual, get drunk and become disorderly. Although married and a family man at this point, Warren Stafford had a serious problem with alcohol and a bad temper, which was exacerbated by his chronic drunkenness. Anticipating trouble, Bob Stafford approached Larkin Hope, the newly elected city marshal of Columbus, before the festivities began. Stafford wanted assurance from Hope that, should his son became unruly and disruptive, he would be discreetly whisked from public view.

Stafford was particularly concerned because the "calaboose"—the term used at the time for a kind of holding cell separate from the county jail—stood in the middle of Spring Street just to the east and in full view of the Stafford home. It was usual practice to put drunks and other disorderly people in the calaboose rather than the county jail until they sobered up and faced a judge. Above all, he did not want his wife Sarah to have to witness the public humiliation of her son Warren at a time of general celebration.

Larkin Hope and his younger brother Marion, who served as deputy city marshal, were the nephews of Sheriff Light Townsend. Their mother, Mary (Townsend) Hope was Sheriff Light Townsend's sister. The previous city marshal, Ike Towell, was an ally of the Staffords who had attempted to aggressively enforce a new city ordinance requiring segregated seating at the Columbus train station. This had alienated the black electorate, which was substantial and tended to vote as a block. Larkin Hope had capitalized on the backlash to win the election, which heightened resentment against the Townsend machine in certain quarters.

Larkin Hope, at thirty-five years of age, had already garnered a nasty reputation for violence, with numerous fights and at least two murders under his belt.[2] Several years before, he had shot and killed a black man in Oakland who had confronted him after discovering that Larkin had seduced his daughter.[3] Later, he had killed a semi-paralyzed Mexican on the streets of Columbus who, he claimed, had threatened him with a knife. Neither murder had resulted in a conviction.[4]

He had also been involved in a serious incident in Columbus in 1889 that nearly cost him his life. He had threatened Ike Towell, his predecessor as city marshal. But before he could pull his gun, Towell pinned him up against an iron pillar, pulled out his knife, and practically disemboweled him. (See Goeppinger interview #3) According to the newspaper report in the *Weimar Mercury*, Hope was not expected to recover, but somehow managed to survive his wounds and then defeat Towell in the election for the marshal's office.[5]

Over the years Hope had drifted in and out of jobs. Similar to many lawmen of the period in Texas, he had also made the transition from lawbreaker to lawman seamlessly, as if this were a natural progression. Tax rolls of the period confirm that, although married and with four children by 1890, neither he nor his brother owned a house or any real estate of taxable value.

Larkin Hope seemed to exemplify the classic "Napoleon" complex: short of stature, anemic, and with a baby face. He compensated for his inadequacies with swagger and a big gun. But until this day there was no documented history of bad blood between Bob Stafford and the Hope brothers. Lillian Reese maintained that Stafford had lent the chronically penniless Hope money on more than one occasion with little prospect of being paid back.[6] If true, Stafford felt justified in asking a favor and apparently had received assurances that his son would be treated with deference.

Marion Hope was four years younger than Larkin. He too was married and had a family, but unlike his brother he had no record of violence prior to 1890. Marion and Larkin were very close and Marion always looked to his older brother for guidance. Marion was also slight in stature, but cut a much more urbane figure. A later newspaper account described him as a snappy dresser with a neat dark moustache and handsome, well-proportioned features.[7]

The day of celebration arrived and the festivities commenced. Warren Stafford, true to his nature, became drunk and created a scene at the public barbeque at the "grove" on the north end of town. Accounts differ as to exactly what happened next, but all accounts agree that Larkin and Marion Hope arrested and handcuffed Warren and then marched him straight down Milam Street through the throngs of celebrants to the intersection with Spring Street, then took a left turn past Bob Stafford's house in full view of his mother, and then locked him in the calaboose that stood in the center of the street. It appeared to many to be an act of intentional provocation.

This duty completed, the Hope brothers then walked back up Spring Street to the Nicolai Saloon, which stood on the corner of Milam cattycorner from the Stafford Opera House and also in view of the Stafford residence. Larkin took a beer while Marion lit up a cigar. The two placed themselves in the doorjambs of the two doors that opened out onto the sidewalk where they could keep watch over the street. The time was about three o'clock in the afternoon. It did not take Bob Stafford long to find out what had transpired and that the Hope brothers were in the saloon across the street from his bank and opera house, as if waiting for him.

Although unarmed, Bob Stafford marched across the street and confronted the brothers. Eyewitness accounts reproduced in great detail in several newspaper articles as well as court document offer a precise picture of how events unfolded. Stafford began cursing Larkin and his brother Marion for their treatment of his son Warren, calling them, among other things, a "goddamn set of worthless curs."[8]

At six-foot four and of a large frame, Bob Stafford towered over Larkin, and as he cursed him, he shook his fingers angrily in his face. About this time, Larkin's wife, hearing of the altercation, drove up in a buggy and tried to persuade Larkin to go home, but he refused her entreaties and ordered her to leave, which she obliged.

He then turned and walked back to the saloon with his pistol drawn. About this time, John Stafford, hearing of the affray, approached the saloon carrying a package in his hand. He walked into the saloon and placed the package on the bar, and then he turned to walk outside. Several witnesses testified that John, who was known to be mild-mannered, never raised his voice and attempted rather to persuade the parties to separate before the confrontation escalated out of control. Also two other men attempted to intervene, but Bob continued his tirade, growing ever more vociferous, and giving full vent to his anger.

Alluding to the Townsend control of the black vote, his last words were, "you are a nigger loving son-of-a-bitch."[9] Larkin Hope replied that that was more than he could take, cocked his pistol and fired three shots point-blank at Bob Stafford. Stafford collapsed mortally wounded without uttering another word. At this moment, Marion Hope, who had followed John Stafford inside the saloon, pulled his pistol and shot John Stafford, who then settled to the floor clutching his wound next to the doorjamb in an upright posture. Larkin then walked up to John, cocked his revolver, and aimed it at his head. John pleaded, "I am killed, don't shoot again," but Larkin replied, "Take your medicine like a man, you son-of-a-bitch," and calmly delivered the *coup de grace*, the blast causing horrible burns to the skull of Stafford. Death was instantaneous.

In the confusion that followed, Larkin remained at the saloon but Marion, fearing reprisal, fled to the residence of his uncle, Sheriff Light Townsend, who, due to a supposed indisposition, had remained in bed at home throughout the festivities. He quickly roused himself and hurried up the street to the saloon and placed both Larkin and Marion into custody.

The shootings shocked the community and created a sensation throughout the state, for "Colonel" Stafford—as he was now universally addressed—had a very high profile across the state and beyond. In terms of cattle owned outright, he was most likely the largest cattleman in the state.[10] In addition to his cattle, he had established a bank capitalized solely from his own resources, started a mercantile business, opened an opera house, and built a large refrigeration and meatpacking house. He had also platted a new town in 1888 on his land south of Columbus, initially named Stafford Station, but later changed to Altair in order to secure a post office.

The fallout to these events was immediate. On July 14 Larkin Hope resigned his position as city marshal and on September 9, 1890, the fall term of the Colorado County Grand Jury returned indictments of first-degree murder against both Larkin and Marion Hope.[11] The prosecution argued successfully that a change of venue was necessary for a fair and impartial trial.

> the fact that the sheriff of this county [*sic.* J. Light Townsend], who is charged with their [*sic.* Larkin and Marion Hope] custody and who must serve all orders issued by this court is an uncle of the accused – a man of large influence and condition in this county.[12]

Friends, family, and supporters of the Staffords were absolutely convinced that the shootings were nothing less than premeditated assassinations orchestrated from behind the scenes by either Sheriff Townsend or Mark Townsend, or both. Lillian Reese stated unequivocally that the murders were planned and she suggested a clear motive, namely that Sheriff Townsend had received word through the grapevine that Bob Stafford had planned to have him assassinated and thereafter orchestrated an elaborate preemptive strike using the Hope brothers.[13] According to this scenario, the supposed indisposition that had kept Sheriff Townsend at home in bed was a mere ruse in order to distance himself from the appearance

The Murders of Bob and John Stafford

of involvement. (See Goeppinger interview #1) Other more dispassionate observers also felt that the sad turn of events could only be explained in terms of a conspiracy. One of these accounts, a written report to the governor of Texas outlining the history of the troubles in Colorado County, serves as a succinct summary of all that heretofore had taken place and is worth quoting at length:

> Thirty years ago two factions were prominent in the county—the Stafford faction and the Townsend faction; and collisions between them were tolerably frequent, chiefly on account of conflicting interests on the prairies—the grazing land. The Townsends finally sold out their stock interests to the Staffords and for some years comparative peace reigned between them. The Stafford's growing in wealth but declining in family strength; while the Townsends were comparatively poor but being a fruitful people gained in family strength. It is perhaps twenty years since J. L. Townsend laid his plans to become sheriff of Colorado County—cultivating the Negro vote which together with his family connections carried him into office easily. He speedily assumed an attitude of marked antagonism to the Staffords, especially Bob Stafford, who was at the head of that family and rapidly becoming very wealthy. As Townsend was repeatedly elected to the sheriffalty his confidence grew and he became more arbitrary in his bearing, which aroused Stafford's ire and rendered personal collision between them imminent. Matters were in this condition when Robert and John Stafford were killed on the 7th day of July 1890. These homicides were perpetrated by Larkin and Marion Hope, kinsmen of Townsend; and while ostensibly the

result of a personal altercation, were almost beyond a question of a doubt the result of premeditation and deliberate plans as the testimony on the trial in one case showed conclusively—notwithstanding the jury brought in a verdict of acquittal.[14]

In September the call for a public meeting went out, which quickly turned into an anti-Townsend rally. It was after all an election year, and Light Townsend had once again placed himself on the ballot as an independent for reelection in the upcoming November general election. A large number of citizens turned out and authorized the committee sponsoring the meeting to publish their resolutions in the *Colorado Citizen*:

> Resolved: That this is an anti-Townsend meeting ... We protest his candidacy because: first, the said J. L. Townsend has heretofore never affiliated with the Democratic party; second, that the said J. L. Townsend is at this time the party to a feud existing in this county, and that said feud cannot be settled as long as he remains in office; third ... he prostituted the high office of Sheriff, for the benefit of two murderers; fourth, that he is attempting to control not only the sheriff, but every other constable and marshal's office in the county for his own purposes.
>
> Committee (September 1890) [15]

Light Townsend responded to this proclamation with an open letter of his own to the citizens of Colorado County published in the *Colorado Citizen*. Alluding to his support among the black electorate, he conceded in a masterful exercise of fence straddling that (true) he had always run as an independent, but this should not be construed to mean he was not at heart a dedicated Democrat who wholeheartedly subscribed to the party platform and who faithfully endorsed party candidates at the state and national level at every election.[16]

Townsend also addressed the question of the "feud" to which he supposedly had been a party. He denied vehemently that such a feud had ever existed and, if it had, he had never been a party to it.[17]

Despite town meetings and lingering suspicions, when voting day rolled around the first Tuesday in November 1890, Light Townsend won reelection in a spirited contest where the majority of the white electorate opposed him. Once again, however, the combination of the large Townsend family plus the black vote carried the day.

In the meantime the murder case against Larkin and Marion proceeded through the courts. In the October 2, 1890, *habeas corpus* trial before Judge McCormick at Columbus, the judge refused to grant bail for Larkin Hope and remanded him to the county jail in Austin County. Marion was granted bail in the sum of $5,000, which was quickly made by Mark Townsend.[18] In an important development, the two cases were separated so that each man faced trial separately. Larkin Hope's case came up first and was scheduled for January 1891, but was later continued at the prosecution's request until July 1891.[19]

When trial day finally arrived, scores made the trip from Columbus to Bellville, either as potential witnesses or curious spectators. It was reported that Bob Stafford's widow spared no expense to try to get a conviction, including hiring private attorneys to assist with the prosecution. Despite the fact that much of the sworn testimony strongly supported the belief that the homicides were the result of premeditation,[20] the jury quickly brought in a verdict of acquittal.[21] Mark Townsend and the battery of lawyers he had assembled to defend Larkin Hope had prevailed.[22]

Marion Hope's trial was scheduled for January 17, 1892, but was continued twice at the request of the prosecution,[23] and finally dismissed July 5, 1893. In the petition for dismissal the district attorney justified his request by stating,

> because at a former term of this court a companion case to this involving the same facts, was tried and the defendant acquitted; that by reason of said acquittal this case has been so weakened that I deem it impossible to secure a conviction at least in this county where the case has been considerably discussed and the sympathy of the public is entirely with the defendant.[24]

Thus, after a long and protracted legal fight, in a disturbing pattern that was to be repeated many more times in the years to come, the Hope brothers avoided any legal consequences for the deaths of Bob and John Stafford.

Mark Townsend not only defended the Hope brothers successfully, but he also supported their families during the yearlong hiatus. The Townsend faction appeared to emerge unscathed from the whole affair and poised to continue in control of the county for years to come, for both Light and Mark Townsend were still in their best years, while their formula for political success had proven unassailable.

The historian is left with unanswered questions in regard to the Stafford murders on the part of the Hope brothers of July 1890. Certainly a consensus emerged in many quarters that the Hope brothers had acted merely as pawns in a larger Machiavellian conspiracy on the part of Mark Townsend, or Light Townsend, or both, to retain control of county politics through premeditated murder. Nevertheless, despite the admittedly strong circumstantial evidence, it has never been proven beyond a shadow that there was, in fact, a conspiracy.

It is equally possible that commentators of the period might have underestimated the degree of personal animosity that existed between Bob Stafford and Larkin Hope growing out of the recent election for town marshal. Under this scenario, the murders could well have been a simple spontaneous eruption of personal hatred between the two men, but one that played out within the larger context of Stafford and Townsend animosity that had existed for years. Bob Stafford's last words, which alluded in no uncertain terms to Larkin Hope's support among the black electorate, serve to reinforce this interpretation.[25]

The bottom line is at this belated point the historian who yearns for objective truth will never know for certain which scenario best explains the facts. But in a real sense objective truth did not matter at the time; perceptions did. Friends, family, and associates of Bob and John Stafford firmly believed that Mark and Light Townsend were behind the murders. For his part, Mark Townsend lived in constant fear that his enemies were biding their time and awaiting the right opportunity to seek revenge.

The historian is also left with the question as to whether a *bona fide* feud had actually existed between the Staffords and the Townsends prior to the deaths of Bob and John. Light Townsend, as noted above, claimed that no such feud existed. Bill Stein believed that no such feud existed prior to 1890 and most historians would agree with him. Undeniably, a long-standing condition of distrust and even hatred had prevailed between Bob Stafford and various Townsend men, and this situation had heated to the boiling point in the lead up to the 1890 sheriff's election. Over a nearly twenty-year span, however, only one shooting had occurred, in 1871 between the families with no follow-up reprisals; by most metrics, this was not enough bloodshed to qualify for an actual feud. However, as Ranger Captain Lamartine Sieker astutely observed in an 1899 report to the governor, the murders clearly set the stage for the next round of troubles that blossomed into a real feud, and this because the old Stafford crowd became a bedrock of support for the Reese faction. (See Appendix C for the full text of Captain Sieker's report.) Seen in this light, it becomes appropriate to use the term Stafford/Townsend feud, although no one with the Stafford name remained to carry on. Thus, the shootings were both beginning and end: for the Stafford brothers and their high profile prominence in the county 1890 certainly marked a definitive conclusion; for the larger story, however, the shootings became the starting point for a whole new round of troubles.

In respect to R. E. "Bob" Stafford, his demise at the hands of the Hope bothers was so abrupt and unexpected that it deprived him not only his life but his legacy as well. With only a dissolute son to briefly carry on the Stafford name—Warren died in 1893—memory of Bob Stafford's important role in the post-Civil War Texas cattle industry seems to have perished along with his person. To underscore the point, a well-known book on Texas cattle barons of the nineteenth century did not even mention Bob Stafford's name in the index much less offer an extended tribute to his accomplishments,[26] a man who might well have been the largest cattleman in the state at the time of his death.

In a real sense, the deaths also deprived Columbus and the county of an alternative and more deserving legacy. How ironic that the killings of the Stafford brothers occurred on the day set to mark the laying of the cornerstone for the new courthouse: this symbol of the rule of law and of promise for the future. The new courthouse seemed to say that the community had now transcended the years of gun violence and private justice that had plagued Colorado County and other areas of Texas in the years following the Civil War and that the county was now poised to enjoy a new period of peaceful prosperity. Sadly, the celebration, as it turned out, both commemorated the new courthouse and set the stage for a renewed cycle of private justice and lawlessness in Colorado County.

To understand both the events of July 1890 as well as the subsequent violence, it will be necessary to examine the history of both the Townsend and Stafford families in the county. This will be the subject of the next two chapters.

CHAPTER TWO

The Seven Townsend Brothers (and One Sister) of Texas

Seven Townsend brothers (and one sister), the progeny of Thomas and Elizabeth Stapleton Townsend of Florida and Georgia, made the move to Texas in the early decades of the nineteenth century. With one exception, all the brothers and the one sister eventually settled in Colorado County, which at the time of its establishment after the Texas War of Independence was considerably larger than it is today, embracing portions of present Fayette and Lavaca counties. As their father and grandfathers before them, the new generation resolved to carve a future on the shifting frontier, but this time the frontier was in far-away Texas.

During the nineteenth century an unmistakable restlessness characterized the family, and this restlessness drove them to pick up stakes and relocate every decade or so, first to Georgia from the Marlboro District of South Carolina, then to Florida, and finally to Texas. But there was method to their uprooted life: often taking advantage of bounty lands for military service, they positioned and re-positioned themselves on the leading edge of the frontier to profit from the inevitable growth to follow as land hungry masses followed in the footsteps of the vanguard. At least three Townsend generations followed the formula.

The Townsends were also surprisingly well educated considering the families were often far-removed from the local country schoolhouse, not to mention institutions of higher learning. Judging from extant letters and other documents of the period, most had progressed well beyond rudimentary literacy while demonstrating an ingrained appreciation for Anglo-Saxon common law and custom, which formed the basis of local government and regulated commerce at all levels.

The family was thoroughly Protestant (Methodist or Presbyterian) and most of the menfolk were dedicated Masons, which in turn presupposed a certain familiarity with pen and paper. Indeed, the Townsend men often established new lodges as they moved on to virgin territory and frequently occupied higher offices within the organization.[1] To be a Mason, it would appear, was a kind of unspoken requirement for any position of prominence throughout the South and was an obvious plus in both business and politics.

Rather of the yeomen freeholder class than to the manor born, the family remained nonetheless fiercely proud of their status and ever eager to advance their standing a notch. Ambitious, yes, but also dedicated family men who successfully sired extraordinarily large families generation after generation. They also had the unsettling habit of marrying within their own extended family. Over and over again we encounter relatives of the second and third degrees of sanguinity joining hands in marriage. Widely accepted at the time, the custom is now frowned upon. Nonetheless, the practice had advantages. A move invariably included a large contingent of the extended family, uncles, in-laws, cousins, etc., which offered a self-contained community from which to draw mates even while on the move.

Upon hearing that Mexico had passed a liberal colonization law in 1825 that encouraged Anglo-American colonization in Texas, two sons, Thomas Roderic and Spencer, travelled by horseback to Texas from Florida in 1826 to assess the situation first-hand. They scouted as far as the northwestern boundary of Austin's colony, which was still very much frontier and beset with Indian troubles.

Undaunted by the Indian threat, the brothers took a fancy to the area to the west of the Colorado River basin and above the gulf prairies to the south. Along the river and creek bottoms they found fertile soil for cultivation with abundant water for man and beast while upland areas offered unlimited pasturage for their animals. The favorable mixture of open and wooded land also presented sufficient timber for the construction of homes, sheds, and fences without, however, being so densely forested as to require a stupendous amount of labor to clear. The landscape was gently rolling and well drained for the most part which freed it from the damp odors characterizing the prairies to the south that were universally considered to be the source of fevers and disease.

Anglo-Americans began filtering into the area as early as 1821. The district, in fact, was one of the first sites of Anglo settlement in Texas. By 1823, 159 people in 49 households had located in the district.[2] These settlers formed the vanguard of the colonization enterprise begun by Moses Austin and continued by his son Stephen F. Austin. Many present citizens can trace their roots back to this period and point proudly to ancestors who were members of the original 'Old Three Hundred.'

In 1831 Thomas Roderic returned to Texas with another brother Steven. This time they undertook the long and arduous trip by wagon train from Florida to Texas accompanied by wives, children, slaves, and outfitted with supplies, tools, and seeds for planting. Along the way, Spencer and cousin William Stapleton joined them. Thomas Roderic preferred to settle a league of land granted to him in Burnett's colony in present Anderson and Houston counties, but Steven and the others moved on to the point where the old La Bahia Road crosses Cummins Creek about fifteen miles north of present La Grange.[3] To the family then goes the honor of settling the spot that many years later took the name "Round Top," although it was known for many years simply as "Townsend's Settlement." Eventually several others members of the extended settled nearby. The cemetery of Florida Chapel on the south side of Cummins Creek harks back to the Florida roots of the family.[4]

Records from the period indicate that many of the settlers had brought slaves along with them, but the numbers were usually small and the farmsteads on which they toiled bore little resemblance to the large slave plantations that later would come to line the Colorado River.[5] This description fits the Townsends. Indeed, with the exception of the slaves, the pre-independence society in the area had an unmistakably yeoman stamp.

The pre-revolutionary phase provided a true frontier experience for the intrepid settlers of the area. Danger was a constant presence and luxuries were unknown. According to a common saying of the time, "Texas was a great place for men and dogs but a miserable place for women." In July 1823 the murder of the elected *alcalde* of the district, John Tumlinson, by a raiding party of Indians who had swooped down from the upper reaches of the Brazos underscored the danger and even prompted Stephen F. Austin to relocate his headquarters to San Felipe twenty-five miles to the east, which was considered safer.[6] The Townsends of Cummins Creek found themselves exposed and vulnerable and suffered several raids. On one occasion, a slave woman was filled with arrows while washing clothes in the creek.

The discontent that had brewed for many years among the Anglo settlers came to a head in 1835 after a series of incidents and skirmishes escalated into open conflict with Mexican authorities. Austin's Western District became a central stage to this unfolding drama. Most male citizens of the area answered the call to arms, but all were caught up in the wild and panicky retreat known as the "Runaway Scrape," which was precipitated by the twin disasters of the Alamo and Goliad. As Santa Anna moved eastward with large armies in pursuit of Sam Houston and the Texan army, the fledgling community of Columbus stood briefly in the crosshairs of the struggle. The two armies faced each other across the river for two days—a literal Mexican standoff. But Houston, taking counsel only with himself (and to the dismay of his men who were clamoring for a fight), decided prudently to withdraw to the east, closer to the border with the United States. One has to wonder what would have happened had Houston decided otherwise? To Columbus would have gone either glory of San Jacinto or the ignominy of defeat. As it was, General Houston, practicing a "scorched earth" policy, ordered Columbus burned to the ground before crossing the river to deprive the Mexicans of anything useful as spoils of war.[7]

The Townsend clan was already sufficiently numerous and established to field a sizeable contingent once hostilities broke out. Stephen organized a company of rangers largely manned by Townsend settlement members.[8] Both Spencer and Steven appear on the roles of those who fought at the Battle of San Jacinto, while two other brothers, Moses and William T., missed out on the momentous fight through no fault of their own—they had been assigned to guard the baggage train at Harrisburg. To the in-laws Joel Robison and Scion Bostick go the honor of capturing Santa Anna and returning him to the camp of Sam Houston.[9]

Santa Anna's defeat at San Jacinto April 21, 1836, not only secured independence for the Anglo colonists, but also set into motion that train of events that eventually brought most of Western North America, including California, into the United States. For the settlers who had made their homes in the district, however, the future significance of the battle did little to compensate for the immediate catastrophe that confronted them. Not only were most of the farmsteads destroyed or looted, but also much of the valuable livestock was gone: either consumed by the passing armies or estrayed. Little but ashes remained of what once had been Columbus. The situation was so dire that many chose not to return at all. Those who did return had to start over from scratch.

The Townsends chose to remain and start over. After the war Asa, Spencer, Moses, and Steven Townsend all received headright grants from the Republic of Texas in Colorado County.[10] Over time several communal clusters of Townsends took shape in the area, each associated with one of the brothers. Present Round Top, as noted, traces back to Steven and his extended family. Spencer Townsend chose to settle about forty miles to the south at the point where the Gonzales Road crossed the Navidad River. Moses Townsend took possession of a quarter league of land, a bonus grant for his service during the revolution, further down the Navidad River in present Lavaca County. Asa settled on a branch of Harvey's Creek between present Weimar and Columbus.

Several Townsend men are closely associated with the formative years of Colorado County and with Columbus, the new county seat.[11] Steven was elected the county's first sheriff while brother William T. served as the first district clerk. Spencer, unfortunately, had the distinction of serving as the first inmate of the new jail, which Asa and William T. had contracted to build in 1841.[12] He had been charged with attempted murder.

But of all the brothers, Asa Townsend is most closely associated with Columbus. He and his brother Spencer are also the most important of the original Townsend siblings to this story.

Asa Townsend

Born on December 14, 1795, in the Marlboro District of South Carolina, Asa was the oldest of eight sons born to

Thomas and Elizabeth Stapleton Townsend and the next to the last to make the move to Texas. He arrived in 1838 with his sizable family and five slaves. Already a man of property and influence in Florida, he was able to liquidate his estate to finance his new start in Texas. He immediately purchased 320 acres of the William Bell headright on Harvey's Creek near the Borden community between present Weimar and Columbus where he set up his farmstead.[13] After a three-year wait, as required by law, he applied for and was granted an additional 640 acres by the Republic of Texas, which he conveniently located next to the other property.[14] Over the course of the following years, other members of the extended family settled close-by, including his wife's brother William Stapleton and his sister's husband Sion Bostick and their respective families.[15]

In addition to the usual crops of corn and cotton, Asa is said to have been a breeder of fine racehorses.[16] In 1841 an Indian scare led Asa to purchase a home in Columbus for himself and his ever-expanding family, and from this point on he divided his time between his farm and the new town of Columbus, which was reconstituting itself from the ashes of war.[17]

Except for the warrior component, Asa exhibited all the traits typical of the clan. Alone among the brothers, there is no record of him ever having participated in an active military conflict, at least during his years in Texas.[18] Asa's Columbus residence allowed him to serve on various public commissions and committees over the years—activities that would have presupposed residency in the town.[19] He also served a brief term as county coroner and is said to have filled in on one occasion for the sheriff during an extended absence.[20] In addition, he helped to establish both the Masonic lodge and the First Methodist Church in Columbus.[21]

The US censuses of 1850 and 1860 both list Asa as a farmer, but there is a good deal of evidence to suggest that real estate was at least as dedicated (and lucrative) an avocation for him as farming. Deed records of the time show a long list of transactions, especially the buying and selling of city lots in the town of Columbus.[22] The old Townsend appetite for deal making was well represented by Asa.

As the years ticked by, Asa prospered financially, rose socially, and emerged as the undisputed patriarch of the Townsend clan. By the 1850 census he had an estate valued at $6,000, which including five slaves.[23] By the 1860 census, his slave count had grown to sixteen while his net worth had increased markedly to $30,000.[24] With over forty head, he was also the largest horse breeder in the county. Although his holdings placed him below the handful of large plantation owners who had moved into the county in the 1850s, he still stood far above the average head of household. His stature and influence in county affairs also grew as the years passed by.

Eventually Asa and his wife Rebecca had fifteen children of whom, remarkably, twelve lived to adulthood. One of his nephews reminisced years later that Asa was fond of saying, "I'll be fired if I can't feed twelve as easily as I can feed six."[25] Of these, eight were sons: Lynn, Jack, Moses Salon, Thomas, Sumner, James Light, Hampton and Matthew, the latter two being twins. Of these sons, Moses Salon and James Light are the most important to this story, although Sumner and Thomas play minor roles. One daughter Mary is also important.

Asa Townsend died in 1876 at the venerable age of eighty-seven. His first wife Rebecca had predeceased him by fifteen years. He remarried but had no children with his second wife. By the time of his death, all of Asa's sons had long since reached manhood and cast about for ways to carve a place in the world commensurate with their status as Townsends. The frontier, now reduced to scattered pockets in the far west, was diminishing rapidly, and the old formula for success and wealth followed by their father and grandfathers before them no longer made sense. The sons would need to seek their fortunes closer at hand, and where better than in the continued growth and prosperity of the county? And by all accounts, the economic tide was still rising in the 1850s and capable of floating yet another generation of Townsends to acceptable levels of affluence and status.

Spencer Townsend

Asa Townsend's younger brother Spencer Burton Townsend (1806–1857) arrived in Texas before the Texas Revolution. Upon arrival he immediately signed up with a unit of Texas Rangers in East Texas under Eliza Clapp and participated in several Indian campaigns before the war. During the war he fought with Clapp's rangers at San Jacinto where he lost a little finger from an enemy bullet.[26] Samuel Luck Townsend, a nephew, wrote in his memoir that his father Stephen had to beg Spencer to stop killing Mexican prisoners after the battle was over, which provides an interesting insight into his character.[27]

Although he received an unconditional headright grant from the Republic of Texas for his service during the war, Spencer never adopted the staid life of a farmer; at least there is little evidence to suggest he did, and due to his unsettled habits, the exact course of his life is harder to reconstruct than that of his elder brother Asa. His focus was more to the west in Lavaca County, which was carved out of Colorado County in 1844. Paul Boethel mentions Spencer during this period in several books about Lavaca County and the picture he paints is not very flattering.[28] According to Boethel, Spencer had shot a man in the back in Houston after the war and fled west to avoid prosecution. The criminal casebooks of both Colorado and Lavaca counties also reveal that he had many run-ins with the law in these counties and most of these were of a violent nature, including charges for assault and murder.[29] The man obviously had a quick temper, a ruthless nature, and did not back down easily from a fight.

During this period Spencer Townsend also bet heavily that the fledgling community of Petersburg five miles south of Hallettsville would become the new county seat of Lavaca County. In anticipation of its coming importance, Spencer contracted to build a two-story log building to serve as courthouse and he also operated a mercantile store and tavern in the town.[30] The election to decide between the two towns became heated with Spencer emerging as spokesman for the Petersburg partisans. When it looked like Hallettsville would win the election, the Petersburg crowd appropriated and burned the ballot boxes.[31] The county was forced to hold another election but once again Hallettsville prevailed. The affair, one of the more colorful stories associated with Lavaca County, left hard feelings that survived for many years.

Despite his unsettled ways and penchant for violence, Spencer also sired a very large family. He died of natural causes in 1857 well before the troubles commenced that are the subject of this book. Four of his children, however, became involved either directly or indirectly on both sides of the feud and thus continued a legacy of private justice and violence for which the father had became notorious.

James Light Townsend

By far the most important of Asa Townsend's sons was James Light Townsend. "Light," as he was known, was born November 12, 1845. He served as the Colorado County Sheriff from 1880 until his death on his birthday in 1894, a total of fourteen years. Although only seventeen years old at the time, he volunteered as a private in the Civil War, was captured at Yellow Bayou, Louisiana, and exchanged as a prisoner in 1864.[32]

After the war, Light worked on his father's farm at present Borden for a while but grew weary of it. He moved to Tennessee for a wile then returned to work at various occupations including a stint on the railroad. With little to recommend him other than the good name of his father and his former military record, he decided to run for sheriff in 1880 at the age of thirty-five.

John Goeppinger maintains that several business and civic leaders in an around Columbus, including his grandfather Seymour, recruited Townsend to run because they believed he would be able to control the black vote. (See Goeppinger Interview #1, "The Townsends and Staffords") In his first election, he ran as a Republican but declared himself to be a Democrat at heart. Subsequently he ran as an independent and, in his final election, he ran as a Democrat. As one commentator of the period put it, "Townsend knew how to both howl with the wolves and run with the hounds."[33]

To win and retain control of the sheriff's office is a central theme of this story and with each successive election, Light Townsend solidified his control of the office, winning successive elections by comfortable majorities. As he lay unconscious and dying in November 1894—the result of food poisoning—the tallies came in and confirmed he had handily won his final race for Sheriff.

By most counts Light Townsend was a competent sheriff. He certainly looked the part with a sturdy bearing, rugged good looks, and piercing blue eyes. Several dramatic episodes illustrate his fearless dedication to duty when circumstances called for it. In November 1886 he attempted to arrest a man by the name of Bob Johnson for horse theft in front of Kaufmann's store in downtown Columbus. When he put his hand on

Johnson's shoulder and told him he was under arrest, Johnson jerked a pistol from a saddlebag he was carrying and fired at the sheriff, the bullet passing through the calf of his left leg. The sheriff took cover behind the iron pillars of a store while the horse thief sought protection behind a hackberry tree. As they exchanged shots, the sheriff continued to call out for the man to surrender, assuring him that no harm would come to him and that he had no desire to kill him. The man replied, as several witnesses testified, "I'll die before I run or allow myself to be captured."[34] By the time the smoke settled, he got his wish; Townsend proved the better shot.

Sheriff Light's most dramatic encounter occurred in January of 1894. A notorious outlaw by the name of Dee Braddock from the Flatonia area had been arrested and placed in the Weimar jail. A young deputy by the name of Moses Townsend, a nephew of the sheriff, was apparently careless while attempting to serve a meal to the inmate. The desperate man succeeded in jumping the deputy and stabbing him with a concealed ice pick. He then bolted the jail, stole a horse, and made his getaway. The wound proved fatal for the young deputy. A few days later Sheriff Townsend received a telegram from Sheriff Hamilton Dickson of Wharton County to the effect that Braddock and several other outlaws had holed up in a remote thicket in Wharton County. Townsend and his then deputy Sam Reese from Colorado County quickly joined the sheriff and his men. They attempted to sneak up and get the drop on the party of desperados in their hideout but the plan went awry. Braddock had been tipped off and ambushed the officers when they entered the thicket. A general shoot-out ensued. Braddock was killed in the melee but not before Sheriff Dickson fell mortally wounded. A short time later, Sheriff Townsend in the company of Deputy Reese met H. H. Moore, a notorious killer and alleged hired gun of Bob Stafford, on the prairie near the scene of the previous shoot-out. Moore had concealed Braddock and was on the way to the hideout when he encountered the officers who were on the lookout for him. Moore decided to try and shoot it out, but Townsend quickly raised his Winchester and fired first. Moore fell from his saddle dead. Once again, Townsend had come out on top.[35]

These episodes solidified Light Townsend's reputation as a fearless lawman, but it must also be mentioned to his credit that individual acts of gratuitous violence as well as mob action against blacks fell off sharply during his term as sheriff. On more than one occasion Townsend stood firm or took evasive maneuvers against mobs intent on lynching black prisoners. There is no question that the Townsend political machine on occasion resorted to bribery (or the "boodle" as it was universally termed) to sway the black vote, but he also proved himself a genuine friend, an official who endeavored to enforce at some rudimentary level the equal application of the law, and this fact was not lost on the black electorate.[36]

Despite continued electoral success, Light Townsend was never an overly popular or beloved county official, especially among the white electorate. Many criticized his habit of appointing close relatives as deputies. Above all, however, his willingness to court the black vote as a means of gaining and retaining public office raised the ire and hatred of diehard conservatives and unreconstructed ex-Confederates, including the Staffords.

Light and his cousin Mark apparently used their influence to sway other elections as well, which gave them a virtual lock on all aspects of law enforcement in the county. In a 1900 retrospective to the governor on the roots of the violence in Colorado County, the attorney general observed that Light and Mark had come to control three of the county's power centers: the Sheriff's Office, the Columbus Town Council, and the Columbus City Marshal's Office.[37]

One other fact needs to be stressed. When Light Townsend was first elected Sheriff, he was a common laborer;

when he died in 1884, he was a wealthy man by the standards of the day, the owner of over 5,000 acres of land and several properties in Columbus, with no debts of substance.[38] Such an astonishing increase in wealth in fourteen years was certainly not due to his salary, which was modest, but rather the consequence of his position as sheriff, which he and his nephew Mark exploited in various ways, especially in real estate dealings. Both were obviously astute businessmen, but together they became a formidable team, and the numbers speak for themselves.[39]

Marcus Harvey Townsend

Marcus (Mark) Townsend (1859–1915) was one of those people who demonstrated from an early age the uncanny ability to focus on a goal and walk a straight path through all of life's distractions. He also had a definite Machiavellian bend. Mark's clear goal was money, power, and status, and he apparently realized early on that in the post-frontier era, education was the key to obtaining these things.

Mark's father, Moses Salon (1830–1867), was the oldest of Asa Townsend's sons. After he left home, he purchased a farm near Oakland in the 1850s. In addition to farming, he ran cattle and turned out hogs seasonally to roam the Navidad River bottom. But similar to his father, he also was a speculator, buying and selling land and horses.[40] But unlike his father and rather more akin to his uncle Spencer, he was quick of temper, which landed him an astonishing nine separate indictments for assault and attempted murder, one of which included his uncle Spencer as co-defendant.[41] There were also other indictments for gambling and breaking and entering. One suspects he spent a good portion of his time defending himself in both Colorado and Lavaca County courts, where the charges originated, and a substantial portion of his income paying the fines that were the usual penalty for such delinquencies.

Perhaps because of his aggressive nature, Moses Salon rose to the rank of lieutenant in Griffith's Brigade during the Civil War. Moses Salon survived the war only to drown in 1867 while fording a swollen Creek north of Columbus.[42] Though married and with a growing family, his unsettled nature had led him to cast about for a change. He was returning from a trip to Victoria County where he was contemplating a move and a new start. He left a widow and several children. His estate consisted of three hundred head of cattle valued at three dollars a head, which the probate judge set aside for the care of the children. One W. W. Bonds brought suit against his widow, Annie E. Townsend, to recoup money owed to him by Moses Salon, but without success.[43]

Experiencing both the fractured example of his father, Moses Salon, and the inspiring model of his grandfather, Asa, in whose house he spent most of his youth after the untimely death of his father, Mark determined to become a lawyer. Major Robert Foard, a Confederate veteran who had opened up a law firm in Columbus after the war, took the young man under his tutelage. Townsend began reading law while still a teenager. After graduation he spent a couple of semesters at Baylor and successfully passed his law examination whereupon he joined the law firm of Foard and Thompson in Columbus, quickly rising to become a full partner. He never forgot the warm support and encouragement he had received from Major Foard and in 1891, introduced a resolution to have a newly formed county in the Panhandle named after his mentor.[44]

In 1882 at the age of twenty-four he stood for and won a seat in the Texas House of Representatives. In the Eighteenth Legislature he authored a resolution to purchase the Alamo building, which was in ruins, and chaired the committee to oversee its purchase and restoration. In 1888 he was elected to the State Senate from the Eleventh District, which was composed at the time of Lavaca, Wharton, Gonzales, and Colorado counties.[45]

In addition to his legal and elected duties, Mark was a shrewd businessman, always on the lookout for investment opportunities. His achievements in this regard will be explored at a later date.

In 1883 he married Annie E. Burford, daughter of Will Burford, a prosperous farmer in the Osage community northeast of Weimar in Colorado County.

Although nine years younger than Sheriff Light Townsend, his intellect, drive, and willingness to use a gun put him on an equal footing with his uncle, and the two presided over the Townsend domination of county politics as equals until the untimely death of Sheriff Light Townsend in 1894 whereupon he emerged as the undisputed head.

From that point on Mark called the shots behind the scenes, especially in the troubles that commenced after 1898 with the assassination of Larkin Hope and which continued for a decade thereafter. He had the power to anoint or expel from the machine he had helped to create: a complicated nexus of political, business, and family relationships. Initiation into the "family" could translate into prestige and wealth; expulsion could spell financial decline and social exile.

On many scores Mark Townsend's life and career present a textbook example of the classic rags to riches story: of rising from a disadvantaged childhood to become a successful lawyer, honored state representative and senator, author of the bill to preserve the Alamo, successful family man, and, finally (at the time of his natural death in 1915), of departing this life a very wealthy man.[46] He was eulogized in all the major newspapers of the state as prominent and esteemed in the best circles of South Texas society.

In conclusion, one can stand in amazement at the collective vigor of the Townsend clan and admire a legacy writ large across the pages of Texas history. One can also note that continued proximity to violence and war was the trade-off that at least three generations of Townsend men (and women) embraced as part of their frontier formula for success. This proximity engendered an unmistakable warrior ethos that had been honed and refined over the generations. It is not surprising that the family counted among its members a host of Indian fighters, Texas Rangers, sheriffs, and other men of the badge. Likewise, when war came, they were often first to heed the call for military service, a legacy reaching back to the American Revolution.[47] In the period of turmoil and mayhem following the Civil War it also unfortunately predisposed them to seek private justice as a means to redress their grievances.

For the purposes of this study, Spencer and Asa are the two most important of the original Townsend brothers to settle in Texas, not as principals themselves, but merely for being the progenitors of those most closely involved. Generally speaking, the first phase of troubles arose between the children of Asa and Spencer Townsend, on the one side, and the Stafford clan, on the other, whereas the second phase exploded among the many grandchildren of Asa and Spencer and their respective allies, which included many former friends and associates of Bob and John Stafford.

Four of Asa's sons, one daughter, and three grandchildren became involved in one or both phases of the feud. Two of Spencer Townsend's sons, two of his daughters, and several of his grandchildren also had roles. Interestingly and sadly, both Asa and Spencer had children and grandchildren on opposite sides of the feuds.[48] The 1906 shoot-out on the streets of Columbus stands out as emblematic of this fact, for it took place exclusively among the grandchildren of Asa and Spencer Townsend.

Both Light and Mark Townsend were extremely ambitious and determined to amass wealth and attain social status, and both saw elected office as a means to achieve these goals. Although thoroughly Southern in sentiment—Light was after all a Confederate veteran—both put expedience over ideology in respect to race, and were willing to court the large black vote to gain and retain elected office. This brought them into bitter conflict with those die-hard ex-Confederates and Negro haters who bitterly resented the black franchise and who were determined to put an end to it.

CHAPTER THREE

Robert Earl Stafford

The Stafford side of the story, unlike the Townsend chapter, is essentially the tale of one remarkable man, Robert Earl "Bob" Stafford. In order to grasp the dramatic events of 1890, when Bob and his brother John Stafford fell mortally wounded at the hands of Larkin and Marion Hope, the reader needs to gain an appreciation for the astonishing rise of Bob Stafford in the Texas cattle business after the Civil War and the methods by which he achieved success.

Bob Stafford was born in Glynn County, Georgia, March 27, 1834, to Robert and Martha A. Stafford. Like the Townsends he had several brothers and, similar to them, the brothers decided to seek their fortunes in Texas. The Staffords were tall and fair-haired, reflecting their Anglo-Saxon roots. As an adult, Bob, similar to his brother John, stood well over six feet tall and, in later years, with his flowing red beard, cut an imposing figure, which he used to full advantage to intimidate others. He received his education at an academy in Waynesville, Georgia, but even with schooling appears only to have mastered the rudiments of reading and writing, as his extant letters reveal.[1] On December 27, 1854, he married Sarah E. Zouks of Liberty County, Georgia, who blessed him with seven children, but only two lived to adulthood.[2] The Staffords were never as prolific as the Townsends, which, as one commentator noted, contributed to their political disadvantage.[3]

Bob Stafford moved his family to Texas from Georgia in 1859 after sensing the economic opportunities to be found there. He settled his family initially on the Navidad River near the border between Colorado and Lavaca counties at Prairie Point (Oakland). He came to Colorado County to join his cousin, Robert Frederick Stafford, the first of the Stafford clan to make the move to Texas. Robert Frederick had bought 477 acres in adjoining Lavaca County early in 1859. Within a few weeks, Bob Stafford arranged to buy 354 acres in Colorado County, near the tract that his cousin had purchased.[4] Over time, three brothers, Benjamin "Ben," William "Bill," and John; a sister, Mariba; as well as an uncle, Richard Ratcliff, joined Bob in Colorado County.

The Staffords were relative latecomers to Colorado County. Bob Stafford arrived a full thirty years after the first Townsend presence. Nevertheless, the two families shared many similarities. They both came from old English stock that had detoured to Northern Ireland for several generations before making the move to the New World. Along the way both had become Presbyterian (and later Methodist) and both counted many members active in the Masonic Order. Such a family trajectory was more common in the South than the North and one that, some scholars maintain, laid already in the Old Country the foundations of a code of honor that demanded private justice in matters of family honor.[5]

Both families had also arrived in the New World in time to participate in the American War of Independence and had settled in Georgia when it was still frontier and beset with Indian troubles. They both were primarily planters and breeders and both were small slaveholders. Indeed, the wife of the one Townsend brother who stayed behind in Florida, Light Stapleton, had a family connection through his wife to the Staffords. His son, William Wallace, moved to Texas after the Civil War and apparently took employment with

Bob Stafford as a brand inspector because of this connection. His son, E. E. Townsend, renowned as father of the Big Bend, could later relate to his biographer many hair-raising stories of his childhood spent at Rancho Grande, the headquarters of the Stafford Ranch near present Nada.[6]

Although they may have thought of themselves as planters, the Stafford brothers had learned the cattle business from their father, a prosperous farmer who developed cattle herds on his land in Georgia. With the knowledge of the stock business he brought with him from Georgia, Bob Stafford's eyes turned quickly to the open prairies to the east and south and his mind began to contemplate the possibilities they held.

The early settlers of Colorado County settled mainly along the river bottoms and principal creeks that offered land suitable for cultivation and easy access to water and timber. The large slave plantations had located exclusively in the river bottoms. Meanwhile, between the Colorado and Navidad river valleys, vast unsettled expanses of prairie stretched between the river basins and remained in the public domain. The transition was often abrupt between the prairie and the river bottoms, and so it was at Prairie Point where Stafford had initially settled.

After less than a year, on November 20, 1860, Bob Stafford sold his farm to William Austin for $4,238 for a tidy profit.[7] He took the money in gold and began at once to invest in cattle, which at this time were often to be had for a pittance. Stafford was a visionary throughout his life, and, at this point, he gambled big on the future of the cattle business. As he later remarked, why put money into land when there was hundreds of thousands of acres of public land on which to graze your cattle for free.

The Civil War disrupted the lives and plans of nearly everyone and Bob Stafford was no exception. When war came, he volunteered first for a home guard unit, the Rovers, and was elected an officer.[8] But with the imposition of conscription in 1862, he soon found himself a private in a company raised by John Cunningham Upton of Colorado County that subsequently was attached to General John Bell Hood's Texas Brigade. Within a couple of months, however, and before seeing any action, he had an altercation with another soldier who shot and wounded him so severely that he was able to apply for and obtain a medical discharge for the remainder of the war.[9]

His early discharge put Bob Stafford in a good position to get the jump on competitors, and he used this to full advantage. Stafford bought out other herds, but he was also keen to put his mark on hundreds of so-called mavericks, or unbranded cattle, that were mixed in with the branded cattle and roamed the prairie and brush free for the taking. He was also not at all averse to incorporating other people's cattle into his herds when he thought he could get away with it, as numerous accounts testify.[10] The phenomenon of "drift" undoubtedly helped Bob Stafford as well as other Gulf Coast ranchers to augment their herds. One old-timer summed it up as follows:

> The most fortunate ranchers in the increase in herds in those open range days were, I think, those bordering the Gulf Coast. Cattle drifting from the north before winter storms could drift no further and I have often been told that some of the greatest fortunes there were based on drift cattle.[11]

In 1868 Stafford also bought a large stake in the cattle owned by James F. Wright, a large plantation owner and cattleman from Columbus who had suffered losses during the war. Wright owned 3,700 head of cattle valued at $8,000 and Stafford owned 1,800 head valued at $5,900.

Each man took half interest in the partnership to which Stafford also contributed $2,100 in borrowed money, most likely the first and last time Stafford ever took out a loan. The deal proved to be very favorable and helped to launch Stafford into the business in a big way.[12]

In the spring of 1869 Stafford, Wright, and Mary Pinchback, widow of John Pinchback, gathered their herds together for a drive, but they contracted with T. J. Groin and R. J. Hoskins to herd the cattle to Kansas. The following year, however, Bob and his brothers joined up with Robert and Henry Johnson, the later being a brother-in-law, to organize their own trail drive to Kansas. Bob, Ben, and John Stafford all went along.[13]

Both of these drives proved to be highly profitable and launched Bob Stafford on the path to enormous success in the cattle business.[14] He returned flush with cash at a time when hard currency in Texas was scarce and this he reinvested in more cattle and more brands.[15]

Annual drives of Stafford cattle continued for the next twenty years or so, until the Western trail finally closed for good in 1893.[16] We read, for instance, in 1879:

> Capt. R. E. Stafford is now engaged in gathering up 9,000 head for the spring drive to Kansas. A "bunch" of 3,000 has already been started.[17]

Or again:

> Capt. R. E. Stafford of Colorado County has disposed of about 15,000 beeves this spring and his stock of meat cattle is not yet exhausted.[18]

In the case of the drives to the railhead in Kansas, the herds would have consisted almost exclusively of one-, two-, and three-year-old steers. However, as Western ranges opened up and grazing became available for cattlemen after the Plains Indians had been subdued and pushed into reservations, Stafford began to put together herds of breeding stock—cows, bulls, and heifers—and to trail them to Eastern Colorado, Wyoming, Montana, and other points west.[19] We read one example of this from 1884:

> Cheyenne Livestock Journal—R. E. Stafford sells to the Durbin Land and Cattle Co. of Sweetwater Wyoming 2,000 cows and two-year old heifers at $20; 1,500 two-year old steers at $20 and 1,000 one-year old steers at $16.[20]

Bob Stafford was not always above board in these dealings when he sensed the buyers were "green" with little cow-sense and not able to distinguish between young and old stock. E. E. Townsend, whose father worked for Stafford as a brand inspector, has left an amusing account of one of these "deals." In 1881 Stafford contracted to deliver 14,000 cows of breeding age. He scoured his range and culled his herd of every old cow and flat-mouthed mossy back his cowboys could find and delivered them to the buyer who was new to the cattle business and unaware that he had been hoodwinked.[21]

Some of Stafford's trailing adventures still excite our imaginations. We read the following report from the *Colorado Citizen* (Columbus) from 1887:

> Last Tuesday Captain R. E. Stafford and his force of cowboys crossed over about 3,000 yearlings to be delivered to Messrs.' Moore and Allen at Rosenberg with others held by George Little of Eagle Lake. As they crossed over the bridge [sic. East River Bridge at Columbus] they raised a roar like distant thunder and many of our citizens went down to see them over.[22]

Over the years, Stafford moved in and out of partnerships as the need arose. Subsequent to the early Wright association, mentioned above, Stafford entered into an arrangement with Samuel Allen of Galveston of the firm of Allen, Poole, & Co. The company specialized in slaughtering cattle for their hides and meat and had facilities for this purpose in Galveston and Tres Palacios Bay in Wharton County. Their main market was New Orleans and to this market they delivered many thousands of live cattle annually by barge and specially outfitted steamships owned by the Morgan Shipping Lines of Galveston. The cattle were loaded at company docks on the Matagorda Bay at Tres Palacios and Indianola. Allen, Poole & Co. also owned extensive herds of cattle themselves in several coastal counties as the following newspaper article from 1871 enthusiastically relates:

OUR CATTLE KINGS

> Texas supplied New Orleans with 85,355 head of cattle during year just closed. And now comes the *New Orleans Times*, without regard to the modesty of the parties, and says that chief among these monarchs of the prairies, and by far the wealthiest and most enterprising, are Messrs. Allen, Poole & Co. and their four ranches are said to feed 146,000 head.[23]

Messrs. Allen, Poole & Co., however, was soon to be supplanted by Bob Stafford. A financial panic struck the country in 1874 and Samuel Allen, Stafford's erstwhile partner, had acquired a large number of cattle on credit for the New Orleans market.[24] In consequence of this "tight," he was forced to liquidate assets in order to extricate himself from financial embarrassment. Stafford took advantage of this to buy out the firm's holdings in Colorado, Lavaca, and Jackson counties.[25] With this purchase, Bob Stafford became the largest stockman on the Gulf Coast and one of the largest, if not the largest, stockman in Texas, a fact almost completely forgotten by historians of the Texas cattle business.

Stafford, unlike Allen & Poole, demonstrated an uncanny knack for avoiding the pitfalls suffered by most large cattlemen of the period. The Western Trail and Chisholm Trails were in themselves perilous enough. The drovers had to deal with raging rivers, sudden blizzards, nighttime stampedes, as well as thieves and Indians, all of which carried the risk of serious loss. In addition, periodic panics in the market, such as in 1874, increased the peril of those who operated on credit, which was by far the majority of cattlemen. But not Bob Stafford. After the Wright deal that launched him into the business in a big way, he always operated on a cash basis with an uncanny sense for market timing. His star was always on the rise and the misfortunes that periodically beset others in his profession seemed only to play into his hands.[26] Others attempted, belatedly, to join the game, including several Townsends, but Bob Stafford got the jump on nearly everyone else in Colorado, Jackson, and parts of Wharton and Ft. Bend counties, and he never relinquished his advantage.

As Stafford expanded he also put in place the cattle crews and infrastructure necessary for branding, sorting, and driving enormous herds of cattle. In 1884 alone, Stafford's crews branded over 25,000 calves in Colorado and Jackson counties.[27] It took many crews, hundreds of horses, and scores of cowboys to accomplish this feat. Stafford conveniently located his headquarters for these operations, which he called *Rancho Grande*, at the edge of the prairie on the west bank of the Colorado River near present Nada in the southern tip of Colorado County.[28] He also expanded his range to the prairies on the east side of the river in the area between Eagle Lake and

Spanish Camp. It was possible to easily ford horses and cattle across the river from the eastern side at the *Rancho Grande* location when the river was at normal levels.

In 1881 the *Colorado Citizen* of Columbus touted Stafford's achievements:

> At the end of the late war, R. E. Stafford had an estate worth $5,000. Today [1881] he has $100,000 invested in pastures alone and 175,000 head of cattle, estimated value $1,500,000 and is at the present time increasing his stock and wealth at the rate of 33% a year. All this Mr. Stafford has done since the war, and by the raising of cattle alone, he never being engaged in any outside venture.[29]

Later Stafford joined forces with the legendary Ike Pryor of San Antonio. Indeed, it was reported that he rescued Pryor financially by fronting him money after a series of reverses in 1884 and 1885.[30] The two subsequently owned herds jointly in South Texas and in the Indian Territory in Oklahoma. In 1895, after Bob Stafford's death, Ike Pryor sealed the relationship by marrying Myra Stafford, the only daughter of Bob. He subsequently assumed presidency of the Stafford Bank in Columbus and control of his cattle interests.

Open range plus valuable cattle became a sure prescription for violence during the period. Cattle represented both cash and food for the hundreds of defeated soldiers who made their way home in groups or individually from the battle grounds of the South only to find their fortunes diminished or evaporated by the liberation of the slaves and/or the collapse in value of Confederate currency. Many found the temptation irresistible to parlay stolen cattle into hard cash or simply to use somebody else's property for food. Individual thievery became rampant but rustling on a large scale by organized bands became an even greater threat after thieves developed networks for disposing of stolen herds.

One of these gangs, the notorious "Mixon Creekers" in neighboring Lavaca County, were holed up in a scrubby brush area a few miles southeast of Hallettsville. Their criminality graces the pages of the Lavaca County criminal minutes from 1876 until 1881.[31] The gang, in turn, had connections with similar bands in DeWitt and Gonzales counties, including the Taylor clan, famous for their involvement in the Sutton-Taylor feud of that area. The network of criminality extended as far west as Kimble County, where a notorious collection of outlaws and desperados known as the Kimble County Confederation had found refuge beyond the reach of the law.[32]

The turmoil of Reconstruction exacerbated this situation. Law enforcement broke down almost completely once federal military authorities began disqualifying elected sheriffs, constables, and county officials from office and replacing them, more often than not, with less qualified men. Until Governor Davis established the State Police in 1870, effectively no police force existed greater than the counties, which made it easier for law-breakers to simply cross county lines to avoid prosecution. Even after the state police were in place, implacable hatred on the part of many ex-Confederates toward the force, which included among its members both ex-Union men and blacks, undercut their authority sharply.

In this witches' brew of open range, general criminality, and post-war chaos, Stafford earned a reputation for a fierce determination to come out on top and an above average ruthlessness in dealing with thieves, rustlers, and anyone else who had the audacity to stand in his way. In one story, passed down anecdotally to the author, Stafford's men caught a thief in the act of skinning a steer. They killed him on the spot and then sewed him into the carcass of the dead animal as a warning to other thieves.[33]

In another story, Colorado County native Elizabeth Schoelmann related how Stafford's men had killed her grandfather, Henry Ilse. He had been summarily shot when he resisted the "assimilation" of his cattle into a Stafford herd being driven up the trail.[34]

It had taken foresight and guts on the part of Bob Stafford to jump into the cattle business when few foresaw its potential, but it now called for unrelenting vigilance and a willingness to use extra-legal means to hold and build upon what he had started. It was survival of the meanest and wiliest in the general disorder and chaos of post-war Texas, and on all counts Bob Stafford emerged as one of the meanest and wiliest, for it was within this atmosphere that he put together his cattle empire. He not only became merciless in safeguarding his property but he also began to consider the vast prairies that were still in the public domain to be his private turf from which it was acceptable to expel or kill interlopers and to appropriate the cattle of others that might wander onto his turf.

The prairie turf wars, early on, brought the Staffords into serious rivalry with another noted cattle baron, Abel H. "Shanghai" Pierce, one of the most colorful figures to ever grace the pages of the Texas cattle industry. The two men actually had a lot in common. Pierce was the same age as Bob Stafford and was similarly tall and imposing in appearance. He was also possessed of an extraordinarily loud voice, which "could be heard a half a mile off even when he whispered."[35]

Pierce had carved out his territory generally south of Stafford's range along the southern reaches of the Colorado and Tres Palacios Rivers to Matagorda Bay, but the two ranges overlapped and this was the source of the friction.[36] In 1877 Pierce had the following notice printed and posted in public places all through the lower country:

NOTICE TO ALL STOCKMEN

You are hereby notified not to work with or for Allen and Stafford under the penalty of the entire destruction of the grass as we are determined they never raise any moor cattle in the State of Texas no man in the lower country will be permitted to have any business transaction with them moov your cattle south of Mustang this is warning in time bare in mind

Committee of 35 Navidad
Organized August 4, 1876

Stafford responded with an announcement in the *Colorado Citizen*, as follows:

This notice could not have emanated from any but a cowardly and dishonest hand. It is doubtless the work of some parties who have been prevented from following their nefarious avocation of killing and skinning other people's cattle, and who are chagrined because they are prevented in their business of robbery. We have no idea if it was done by a committee, as alleged ... The threat of burning the prairies and inflicting a hardship on innocent citizens shows that no gentlemen were engaged in it ... We do not propose to be driven from the pursuit of a legitimate business by the threats of a set of cowardly cattle-skinners and thieves ...

Very Respectfully,
R.E. Stafford
Columbus, July 14, 1877[37]

Similar to Stafford, Shanghai Pierce gained a reputation for ruthlessness. One unfortunate event in particular came to be associated with him, namely the lynching of five men for rustling in June 1871, including the three Lunn Brothers. Due to lack of evidence, Pierce avoided indictment, but he found it prudent to remove himself to Kansas for a year until matters settled down.[38]

In this situation, where lawlessness held sway, many noted gunmen and desperados drifted into the area and hung out around the cow camps and small settlements that had sprung up to support the cowmen and their cowboys. Both Pierce and Staford were willing to utilize the services of these desperados when the need arose. The noted Johnny Siringo gives a good description of this class of ruffians in his famous autobiography, *A Texas Cowboy*. Siringo worked a spell as a Gulf Coast cowboy for Shanghai Pierce and nearly lost his life on more than one occasion.[39]

The rivalry between Pierce and Stafford persisted and in its latter phase evolved into the classic open range vs. barbed wire conflict, with Pierce playing the role of the fencer and Stafford that of the free–range advocate. Indeed, the hatred between Pierce and Stafford reached such a pitch that upon the murder of the Stafford brothers in 1890, Pierce forwarded $1,000 to the Hope brothers to pay for their defense as a gesture of gratitude.[40]

Many sources point to the fact that Bob Stafford had a less than charitable attitude toward the freedpeople. One particularly bloody and dramatic episode, which even made the *New York Times* in 1876 under the headline, "Horrible Murders in Texas,"[41] illustrated both his ruthlessness in respect to cattle thieves and his deep-seated prejudices. In July and August 1876 scattered acts of violence, which had their roots in conflict over rustling near Eagle Lake, escalated into a race war. James Underwood Frazar and his brother, Newton Ford Frazar, who ran a store in the Eagle Lake bottom, had come under suspicion in the recent murder of two black men, and a number of area blacks had threatened to attack the store in retaliation. Bob Stafford seized upon the volatile dispute as an opportunity to punish those black people in the area whom he suspected of rustling. Together with a number of cowboys who worked for him and a number of men from Eagle Lake, he rallied to the Frazar brothers' defense. Meanwhile, the escalating situation led many of Eagle Lake's terrified women and children to flee their homes for temporary accommodations in Columbus.

Over the next several days in a series of shoot-outs over a wide area, six black men were killed. Two of them, Bony Cotton and Lewis Evert, were regarded as notorious cattle thieves, but the others were simply in the wrong place at the wrong time. There were no casualties on the Stafford side.

Finally, on August 9, 1876, Sheriff Toliver took a posse to Eagle Lake to investigate. The same day he was joined by a posse of men from Weimar led by Constable Larkin Secrest. Confronting the combatants where he found them, Toliver ordered everyone to return to their homes.

The last skirmish occurred on August 10, as Stafford and his cowboys were leaving the area. One account has it they were ambushed by five black men, another that they encountered two black men riding near the river. The Staffords opened fire, wounding one man and killing a horse. Again, neither Stafford nor any of his cowboys were wounded. Having successfully separated the warring parties, Toliver, with twelve men, remained behind to count and identify the dead.[42]

Though none are specific as to time, place, or persons involved, many sources allude to the fact that the Staffords and Townsends had run-ins over cattle during this period as well. One newspaper article even led with the sensational title, "A Texas Steer Responsible for Feud in which many Lost Lives."[43] Likewise, Judge Mansfield of Columbus stated in a 1900 memorandum written for Governor Sayers on the causes of the violence in Colorado County:

> Thirty years ago two factions were prominent in the county—the Stafford faction and the Townsend faction; and collisions between them were tolerably frequent, chiefly on account of CONFLICTING INTERESTS ON THE PRAIRIES—THE GRAZING LAND." [Author's emphasis][44]

Lillian and Walter Reese also state outright in *Flaming Feuds of Colorado County* that, "One of the reasons for this feud was CATTLE."[Their emphasis][45] Though the Reese book concentrates primarily on the subsequent altercations and killings, it nevertheless offers interesting insights into the earlier troubles between the Stafford and Townsend families.

Which of the Townsends were involved in these "conflicting interests on the prairie?" It seems obvious that it should have been the Townsends whose properties most closely bordered the prairies, and this would have been Asa's sons, Thomas (Tupp), Sumner, and Light. Thomas bought his Uncle Moses's quarter league on the west side of the Navasota River near present Vienna and later partnered with his younger brother Light. The farm was only a few miles from the edge of the vast prairie that covered the lower half of Colorado County and extended south, east, and west over Jackson, Wharton, and Victoria counties as far south as the coast, all home turf of the Staffords. And indeed, Lillian Reese states in her book that these were the Townsends most closely connected to the "conflicting interests on the prairies."[46]

Another incident, unrelated to cattle, clearly became an added flash point for disagreement between Bob Stafford and the Townsend clan and may have precipitated the first shoot-out between the two families. This occurred on the streets of Columbus in December 1871. In July 1867 Lavaca County court issued a warrant for A. Stapleton Townsend (son of Spencer Townsend) for stealing two horses and conspiring to steal two more. Two days later a posse confronted Townsend near his house at Oakland and, when Townsend attempted to flee, shot and mortally wounded him.

The general consensus was that the shooting was unnecessary, since Townsend made no threat against the arresting officers. Four men in the posse were indicted for the murder and eventually were found guilty of manslaughter and sentenced to two years in the state penitentiary. Two days later, however, the defense attorneys asked for a new trial, citing among their grounds that they had only just discovered that one of the state's witnesses held exculpatory evidence for the defense that had been withheld at trial. That witness, Bob Stafford, claimed to have visited Townsend on his deathbed, and heard Townsend state that, because he was running from them, he did not know who had shot him. The defendants got their new trials and on July 15, 1871, were exonerated.[47]

Stafford's testimony evidently infuriated the Townsend clan. On December 5, 1871, some five months after the trial, Bob Stafford and Sumner Townsend, son of Asa and cousin of the slain Stapleton, met on the streets of Columbus and heated words led to drawn pistols. The *Colorado Citizen* reported:

> Disgraceful Affray—Our usually quiet town was thrown into a flurry of excitement on last Tuesday

evening. It seems that Sumner Townsend and Bob Stafford having some difficulty. A crowd collected at the concrete corner. Words brought pistols from their scabbards, and pistols, brought firing, and the six or seven shots resulted in the serious wounding of Sumner Townsend in the arm and shoulder, and of B. F. Stafford in the ankle severely. We do not pretend to say who was to blame in this matter. We know these men were upon the street among a large crowd, where peaceful men, women, and children were passing and that they were allowed to violate the law and endanger the lives of our people with impunity. The greatest want of this people is officers who will command their respect and enforce the laws under all circumstances.[48]

One can only infer that Bob Stafford's testimony was the source of the dispute since neither the newspaper accounts nor the court documents stated the exact cause of the affray, but all underscore that the quarrel arose between Bob Stafford and Sumner Townsend. Four days after the incident, State Police Captain Leander H. McNelly and one private arrived in town. They arrested the brothers Bob, Ben, and John Stafford, their cousin Richard R. Ratcliff, and Sumner Townsend. Apparently it had been four against one. All were subsequently indicted either for carrying weapons or for assault. Subsequent court documents make clear that although Ben Townsend and Richard Ratcliff had fired the shots on the Stafford side, the heated argument that participated the affray was between Bob Stafford and Sumner Townsend.[49]

In judgments handed down in June 1872, February 1872, and February 1874, Ratcliff was fined $150, Ben Stafford $50, and Bob and John Stafford one cent apiece for their part in the affair. The charges against Townsend were dismissed.[50] Interestingly, in one of the court documents filed in the case, John Stafford stated that he had only pleaded guilty to a charge of assault in an effort to, "keep down the feud and allay the ill feelings between his brother [Bob] and Mr. Townsend [Sumner]."[51] This is the first mention of the existence of a feud, but it also suggests that it was confined to Bob Stafford and Sumner Townsend. The lop-sided encounter, whatever its cause, must have had the effect of expanding rather than "allaying" ill feelings on the part of the Townsends.

Throughout all these episodes the star of Bob Stafford (and to a lesser extent that of his brother John) continued to rise, In 1878 Bob relocated to Columbus while John took up residence about three miles south of Columbus on the Eagle Lake road where the prairie commenced and Stafford land began. John Stafford had also prospered, but his wealth never approached that of his brother. Documents from the period also make it clear that he never was in partnership with his brother Bob, but rather served as his trusted right-hand man, an employee, as it were, albeit an exceedingly well-rewarded one. Bob Stafford's other brothers, Ben and Bill, had little or no connection to Bob's businesses after the earlier drives of 1869 and 1870. In later years, Ben served as the foreman of a road crew while Bill, in an application for a Confederate veteran pension in 1900, declared himself to be indigent.

In 1884 Bob Stafford moved his wife and family into a new, two-story house on the south side of the courthouse square while in 1887 John had an even larger, three-story house constructed south of town. (Illustration 2) In 1887 Bob commissioned the noted Galveston architect, Nicholas Clayton, to design and build a large two-story brick structure next to his house on the corner of Spring and Milam streets. (Illustration 3) The building served both as an opera house (upstairs) and a combined bank and retail space (downstairs), the bank being chartered and opened for business that same year as the Bob Stafford and Co. Bank.

The "opera" house was for a number of years the largest of its kind in the state of Texas, but it should be clear what this meant.[52] An opera house was a common term of the period for a public venue that hosted travelling troupes of entertainers who staged theatrical presentations, musicals, and minstrel shows. Columbus proved to be a convenient stop on the circuit that followed the railroad from New Orleans to El Paso.

Perhaps the most ambitious of Bob Stafford's initiatives was the construction of a large refrigerated packing plant in the northern part of town in 1885. Once again, Bob Stafford had shown himself to be a visionary who foresaw the changes inexorably altering the Texas cattle business due to the demise of the Western Trail, the disappearing public domain, and the resurgence of Texas Tick Fever, which had led to a quarantine of Texas cattle in several midwestern markets.

Stafford argued before his colleagues in various conventions and gatherings that refrigeration, coupled with the ever-spreading network of railroads, offered the key to the new challenges facing the cattle business. And he backed up his claim with his own money, building perhaps the first refrigerated packinghouse in the state with the capability of filling several refrigerated railroad cars per day with frozen beef. Stafford even commissioned his own cars to be built. In 1890 he landed a contract worth $300,000 to supply frozen beef to Liverpool, England, which seemed to confirm his predictions.

But throughout this extraordinary rise to wealth and prominence, which has no parallel either before or since in the history of Colorado County, one thing had remained out of Bob Stafford's reach: any degree of effective influence over county government. He had tried beginning in the 1870s to influence the sheriff's race, but had only met with frustration. Once the Townsend faction secured the Sheriff's office in 1880, he was not able to break their grip since their control rested solidly on the black vote over which he had little influence.

This was a concern for Bob Stafford. The ambitious Townsends were serious competitors in all business matters, and their lock on county law enforcement gave them certain business advantages. More importantly, nearly all the Stafford brothers had experienced serious run-ins with the law over the years, and an unsympathetic sheriff did not help things in these cases.[53] To make matters worse, Bob Stafford's only son Warren had turned out to be a pathologically violent individual who was constantly running afoul of the authorities. He also was a hopeless alcoholic, whose serial drunkenness inflamed his already belligerent nature. As the son of Bob Stafford, he also appeared to believe he was beyond the reach of the law. Doubtless the example of his father had reinforced this perception during his formative years.

In November 1879 Warren had started an affray that led to the lynching of two black men west of Columbus on the Hallettsville road.[54] In 1882, on the way to a dance at his uncle's new home south of town, he passed a camp of a man, J. W. Stedham, who intended to homestead with his family on the prairie. Stedham was categorized as a detested "nester," one of a group whom Stafford henchmen had expelled or killed on more than one occasion in the past. An altercation led to a fight and Stafford was slightly wounded in the arm by a pistol shot. Stafford rode to his uncle's house where he gathered a gang intent on revenge, including his uncle John. After getting sufficiently liquored up, they returned to the camp and shot the unfortunate homesteader in front of his wife and children and then hanged him from a tree.

After a protracted legal struggle, the murder cases against both John and Warren Stafford were eventually dismissed, but there was no guarantee that the next event would have such a favorable outcome.[55]

By 1890 the pressure had built to the bursting point. The rumor was that Bob Stafford was determined to use whatever means necessary, legal or extralegal, to unseat Light Townsend in the next election and thereby cancel the Townsend stranglehold on county politics.[56] This constellation of factors set the stage for the dramatic and tragic events of July 7, 1890, but the legacy of Bob Stafford continued beyond his death. Although nobody with the Stafford name took up the torch—Warren died in 1893—Bob Stafford left many friends and business associates who shared his intense dislike for the Townsends and their political machine and who were willing to wait patiently for an opportunity for revenge.

CHAPTER FOUR

The Rise of Sam Houston Reese and the Assassination of Larkin Hope

Sheriff Townsend appointed his kinsman Sam Houston Reese to be his chief deputy soon after the deaths of the Stafford Brothers in July 1890. Sam Reese had already acquired law enforcement experience as a constable, was known to be a solid family man, and was considered untainted in respect to the Stafford difficulties. His appointment, therefore, was greeted favorably in most quarters. Light Townsend apparently intended to groom him to be his successor.[1]

At the time of his appointment, Sam Reese was thirty-one years old, married, with five children: two sons and three daughters. Like the Townsends, the Reese family came from an old-line Texas family. Sam's father had settled initially in Austin County when Texas was still a republic, but after the Civil War had moved with his growing family, which came to include six sons, to Lavaca County. The family befriended Spencer Townsend, who had also established himself in Lavaca County although his home base was at Oakland on the Colorado County side of the Navidad River. Through this association, young Sam Reese made the acquaintance of Keron Blanche (Keetie) Townsend (1858–1944), one of the many children of Spencer Townsend. The two married in 1876 when he was just seventeen and she was eighteen.

Keetie was the sister of Stapleton Townsend, who was killed by a sheriff's posse at Oakland in 1867, and a first cousin of J. Light Townsend.

The young couple made their home in Oakland for many years where Sam supported his growing family as a farmer and stockman in the Navidad River bottom. Other sons and daughters of the elder Reese also married local families in the area so that, over time, the Reeses grew into one of the most influential and politically connected families in Lavaca County.

In 1886, when Sam Reese was twenty-seven years old, he was also elected constable for Oakland, and thus embarked on a career in law enforcement. Reese, however, aspired to be more than a farmer and constable on the fringes of the county where educational and cultural opportunities were limited for his growing family. When the railroad bypassed Oakland in favor of a more northerly route in 1873, the fate of the little hamlet of Oakland, whose star once shown so promisingly, was sealed and, like many similar towns throughout the state, began a slow but inexorable decline. Consequently, when Light Townsend offered Sam Reese a position in Columbus, which was emerging as a vibrant commercial, educational, and cultural hub for all of South-Central Texas, he jumped at the opportunity. For his wife Keetie, it also meant enhanced prestige within the extended Townsend family. And with the possibility of her husband becoming sheriff one day, it also promised that she might rise to become the matriarch of the extended family. Life was looking up.

Sam and Keetie Reese were devoted to each other and to their five children. In *Flaming Feuds of Colorado County*, John Walter Reese and his sister Lillian paint a touching but romanticized account of how close-knit and self-contained the family was.[2] Although not lacking in friends, the family preferred to keep company with themselves. Theirs was an exceedingly musical family. Sam Reese was an accomplished violinist and regularly played on an instrument that had been handed down in the family for generations. All the children mastered musical instruments and all could carry a tune as well. On special occasions the family would hold recitals for their own amusement and entertainment. Lillian, especially, cultivated her talent for the piano and for song, performing publicly and supporting herself in later years by giving lessons.

The Reeses did not take insults, real or imagined, lightly and appeared only to trust their very close friends, who were few in number. They were suspicious of nearly everybody else and always supported their own in any controversy that arose. One incident related boastfully by Lillie Reese in her book illustrates this lack of balance. According to her, when Hub Reese was a child, he insulted an adult, who responded by slapping him on the cheek. Hub ran to tell his father. While some parents might have been angry with their child, and apologized to the other adult for their son's insolence, Sam Reese confronted the man and hit him in the jaw with his fist.[3]

Although his main duty was to administer the jail where he initially took up residence with his family, Sam Reese had stood at Sheriff Townsend's side during the 1894 shoot-out with the notorious outlaw Dee Bradshaw and had performed coolly under fire and duress on this and several other occasions. There was a general consensus that he was a stalwart and competent lawman.

In 1894 Sheriff Townsend once again placed his name in the hat for a fifth consecutive term as sheriff. The shoot-out with Dee Bradshaw and the subsequent dispatch of the notorious H. H. Moore in the summer of 1894 had given him a welcome electoral boost by solidifying his reputation as a no-nonsense officer of the law. The rise in esteem that came in the wake of this affair seemed to sweep away at least some of the lingering hard feelings associated with the Stafford killings.

But then the unexpected happened: on election day the sheriff ate a tin of contaminated oysters and came down with a deadly case of food poisoning. The best doctors were summoned but could do little. Sheriff Townsend lingered long enough to hear that he had won reelection by a comfortable majority, but he soon slipped from consciousness and died shortly thereafter.

What to do? The commissioner's court cast about and, finally, on the basis of his established record as well as the influence of the Townsend family, voted to appoint Sam Reese as interim sheriff until a special election could be called. By the Texas constitution, all county officials serve four-year terms with the exception of constables and justices of the peace, who serve two-year terms. Because of this discrepancy, the county is obliged to hold elections every two years. In order to avoid the considerable expense of holding a special election, the commissioner's court ordered a new election for the sheriff's office to coincide with the regularly scheduled election of 1896, with the elected sheriff then serving a truncated two-year term. This would then reestablish the regular rotation of elections for the sheriff's office in 1898.

In the two-year interim Sam Reese grew comfortable in the role of sheriff and eagerly placed his name on the ballot for the 1896 contest with the blessing of Mark Townsend. The contest was spirited and became a three-way race between Reese, W. E. Bridge, and Step Yates, but once again the black vote proved decisive. Prior to the election, black leaders held a rally to decide whom to support. They eagerly endorsed Reese and even rode their horses, two hundred strong, down Milam Street in Columbus with a large banner proclaiming their support.[4]

Sam Reese settled in as elected sheriff, albeit for a reduced term. But he had every confidence that he would be able to solidify his support and maintain the office for years to come just as his predecessor and mentor Light Townsend had done.

Reese had also observed how Light Townsend had used his position to snare profitable business deals when they came his way. Reese's greed, however, soon caused him to overstep himself in a way that Light Townsend never had. He too began speculating in real estate in a big way (and apparently successfully) for he shortly came into possession of two river bottom farms as well as a nice house in town with several servants to perform all the duties of cooking and cleaning. To quote Judge Mansfield's report, "Reese was amassing money very rapidly, perhaps more rapidly than his predecessor had done."[5]

One deal in particular raised eyebrows and brought a charge of malfeasance that became an unwelcome distraction in the upcoming 1898 election. Seemingly with the complicity of the county treasurer, Joseph Burttschell, Sheriff Reese took payment for $20,000 from the county for a tract of land two miles east of town that they did not yet own, although they had an option to purchase the tract for $10,000. The county purchased the land to set up a county farm where the prisoners of the county could work and subsequently appointed August Burttschell as supervisor. This sleight of hand alone netted the partners $10,000 clear profit with no risk, the equivalent of about eight years' salary as sheriff. It also earned both Reese and Burttschell indictments for selling property to the county, a misdemeanor offense, but they both escaped with a light fine.[6]

We see already in this affair, it should be noted, the beginnings of a strong political alliance between the extended Reese and Burttschell families that became very important for subsequent developments.

In the meantime, the Hope brothers had not gone away. Earlier, in 1892, just two years after Larkin and his brother

Marion had killed the Staffords, Larkin hoped to rejoin the lawman's trade. He threw his hat into the ring for a constable's position in a precinct that included Columbus. In a tight race, he narrowly defeated Step Yates, but subsequently won reelection in both 1894 and 1896 by wider margins.[7]

By 1898 Larkin Hope felt prosperous enough to form a partnership with his brother Marion and open a grocery store and saloon on Milam Street, just west of the courthouse, and directly across the street from the Nicolai saloon where the two had gunned down the Stafford brothers.[8]

Surprisingly, the backlash for killing the powerful and rich Staffords had not coalesced into any meaningful political opposition: the Townsend machine, despite all, still controlled the outcome of elections. With Mark Townsend's support, Larkin Hope conducted a spirited campaign, including announcements in the *Colorado Citizen*, whose editor pointed out his previous experience in law enforcement and called him a "cool-headed officer, honest, industrious, and assiduous in the performance of duty," adding that he was a man who "is strictly sober, is not excitable, and is conversant with the duties of the office to which he aspires."[9] There was no mention of the men he had killed or of the past indictments for murder that grand juries had handed down.[10]

The glowing report in the local paper, however, contradicts in every particular other observations of Larkin Hope from this period. Accordingly, Larkin was a frequent visitor in the many saloons that lined Milam, Spring, and Walnut streets and was given to braggadocio, bullying, and threats, which naturally, in view of his violent history, had to be taken seriously. And once alcohol loosened his tongue, he would alternately rail against Sam Reese and Mark Townsend, his putative supporter, whom he accused of not following through on certain vague promises for the killing of the Stafford brothers. His saloon talk spread and reinforced the general perception that the Townsend clan in general and Mark Townsend in particular had indeed been behind the Stafford killings.

Indeed, whiskey could be considered another actor in this drama. There was definitely a saloon culture in Columbus, to which the large number of establishments testify, and it is no coincidence that several confrontations originated in saloons and spilled out on the street from there. This situation was aggravated by a habit that had developed in the town. Gun control laws, dating back to 1872, were actually quite restrictive at the time, permitting only officers of the law to legally carry firearms in public. This led to the practice of private citizens stashing pistols, shotguns, and rifles in the various saloons and other establishments where they could be retrieved and put into use at a moment's notice. And similar to urban gangs of the present, the different factions in town had preferred localities where it would be considered a provocation for a rival gang to trespass. This situation was compounded by the common practice of officers of the law—city marshals, deputies, constables, etc.—of drinking while on duty. Despite what the newspaper claimed, Larkin Hope was no exception to this practice.

This witches' brew of factors led to an atmosphere where a chance encounter or a loose remark could lead to a confrontation that could quickly escalate into violence. John Goeppinger has provided an account of just such a situation that resulted in the killing of Robert L. Foard, Jr. by Brack Smith in 1897. (See Goeppinger Interview #5.)

Heated elections only inflamed this situation and as the election of 1898 approached, Sam Reese suddenly faced a much stiffer opposition than he had anticipated.

During the campaign, a serious rift developed first with Larkin Hope and then with Mark Townsend. In the case of Hope a disagreement over fees collected and the respective roles of sheriff and constable was the putative cause.

It should be remembered that although the sheriff is the chief law enforcement officer of the county, constables are also elected in their own right, and are more officers of the court than subalterns of the sheriff. Constables can, and often do, go their own ways.

Mark Townsend had also grown uncomfortable with Sam Reese on a number of counts: he was too independent, strong-willed, and aloof. Moreover, both his financial missteps and his habit of ill-treating blacks had undercut the Townsend machine in general. But underlying the growing rift was a more ominous development, namely Sam Reese had begun to curry support among the erstwhile friends and associates of the Stafford brothers. Ike Towell, Dick Byars, and Frank Auerbach, to name three, were men who still nourished a deep hatred for the Hope brothers, the men who had pulled the trigger on the Staffords, and also for Mark Townsend, whom they believed to be behind the murders.

Meanwhile, the ill-will between Sam Reese and Larkin Hope finally escalated to the point that Reese, with the encouragement of his new-found allies among the old Stafford crowd, persuaded his son-in-law, Dr. Joe Lessing, Jr., to enter the constable's race against Larkin.[11] This, apparently, was the final straw for Mark Townsend. True, Larkin Hope was something of a loose cannon, a man who often bad-mouthed him in his saloon talk, but one thing was beyond doubt: past history dictated that Larkin Hope would always stand between him and the former friends and supporters of Bob and John Stafford.

Mark Townsend obviously still feared these people and suspected that they were biding their time and waiting for the right opportunity to seek revenge. But as long as the political machine he directed from the sidelines controlled law enforcement at different levels in the county, his enemies would be much less inclined to act. Mark Townsend was not about to let anyone cozy with the Stafford crowd take over both the sheriff's office and constable's position. This dynamic was well understood by most people at the time, but as the years have passed, has become less clear to historians, yet it is surely the key to understanding much of what followed.

With the encouragement of Townsend, Larkin Hope suddenly withdrew from the constable's contest and threw his hat into the sheriff's race. It was a dramatic and unexpected turn of events that caught Sam Reese and his supporters completely by surprise. For him and his family, it signaled no less than ex-communication from the Townsend machine with serious political, social, and financial implications. For those who had sided with the Staffords, it was like rubbing salt in the wound.

With the onus of the Stafford murders, not to mention other miscreant behaviors, it seems incredible in retrospect that Larkin Hope would have stood any chance whatsoever of winning a county-wide election, but such was the strength of the Townsend machine (now solely directed by Mark Townsend) that it was not only feasible, but odds on likely that Larkin Hope would win in the upcoming election. (See Goeppinger interview #6) And to insure that he would win, Townsend, by one account, was prepared to spend as much as $5,000, an enormous sum of money by the standards of the day.[12]

Sam Reese, however, enjoyed being sheriff. His family also liked him being sheriff and had grown comfortable with the prestige and standing that attended the office. They also had clearly relished the monetary rewards that had happily come along with the position, and looked forward to a continuation of these presents. None in the family could stomach the thought of being shut out from what they regarded as rightfully theirs by such a crass political maneuver on the part of Mark Townsend and Larkin Hope.

It was an affront and an indignity that was especially difficult for Keetie Reese and her sons and daughters to endure. Mark Townsend had spoken and now they were the black sheep, the has-beens of the Townsend clan. And to add insult to injury, the torch had been passed to someone whom they despised, namely Larkin Hope. Seen in this light, the intense hatred that developed within the Reese family toward other descendants of Asa and Spencer Townsend who remained loyal to Mark Townsend becomes more coherent and comprehensible. With the encouragement of his mother, Walter Reese and his siblings resolved early on not to accept passively the humiliation visited upon them. Their sense of Townsend family honor, now turned inside out, demanded that they strike back against those who had wronged them. Sullen resignation was not an option; private justice, if called for, would be.

There was only one way to avoid defeat and that was to get rid of Larkin Hope. As August 1898 dawned, the Hope brothers were planning to move their grocery store into a brick building that was under construction on the corner of Milam and Spring streets, directly across the street from the saloon in which they had killed the Stafford brothers. Things were looking up all over. The city's electric company was installing new and much better streetlights. However, as a follow-up in late July, they shut down the system for a month, making the city, once again, completely dark at night.

The evening of August 4, 1898, Larkin Hope received word from a black messenger, Tom Shine, that some men wanted to speak with him at the Brunson saloon, which was located on the west side of Milam Street just south of the railroad tracks. His wife urged him not to go, but he replied that he needed to meet with them and see what they had to say. He made his way down the darkened street toward the saloon. In the meantime a rider had tied his horse behind Auerbach's Meat

Market and the Gegenworth store on the west side of Milam Street and made his way stealthily up the dim alley between the two buildings where he positioned himself to watch the street. As Larkin approached, he was greeted by the blast from a double-barreled ten-gauge shotgun, both charges of buckshot taking effect in his upper body and neck. Larkin fell to the ground and, as he did so, he emptied his revolver wildly. The nearby saloon emptied and several men rushed to Hope's assistance. They carried him into a nearby drugstore and sent for a doctor. They also sent word to his wife to come as quickly as possible. Larkin Hope lingered for about twenty minutes before expiring in the presence of his wife and children—three daughters and a son. He was never able to speak or offer any indication as to who had shot him, but he seemed aware that his family was there. As he lay there dying, his wife Mollie wept and moaned.[13]

After the shotgun blast the assailant had calmly walked back to his horse, mounted, and ridden a wide circle to the north and then back to the east river bridge, which he then crossed in the direction of Alleyton. Sheriff Reese arrived on the scene shortly, but it took him about half an hour to get up a posse and mount a pursuit. But the late hour, the darkness, and the delay made it impossible to follow the assailant much less catch up with him.

Suspicion quickly fell on Jim Coleman (1876–1906) because eyewitnesses had placed him in Columbus the night of the murder, because he was a known friend and ally of the Reese clan, and because he had a reputation as a killer who preferred a shotgun. Coleman lived with his mother in Alleyton, a small neighborhood about three miles east of Columbus. She was the town's postmistress. He was also connected through marriage with the family of Joseph Burttschell, the county treasurer and political ally of Sam Reese, and with former Constable Jake Burttschell, who had owned a saloon in Alleyton before his death in 1894. Both men had married Coleman sisters. In his role as county treasurer, Joseph Burttschell also had been implicated in the dubious financial dealings of Sam Reese, discussed in a previous chapter. Burttschell and Reese, it seems, had forged a strong alliance in county government as well as a personal friendship that both wanted to continue. Jim Coleman was especially close to sons Walter and Herbert "Hub" Reese and passed time with them at the jail in Columbus or at their home.[14]

Jim Coleman's appearance belied his true nature. Photographs of the period reveal an almost impish, youthful freshness and playful demeanor. He liked to ham it up in front of a camera with his pistol in hand, as one of his pictures shows. He sported a nice mustache and dressed snappily. Underneath this exterior, Jim Coleman was a killer. His first murder was a revenge killing of a man named Tuck Hoover who had killed his brother-in-law and constable, Jake Burttschell, in a bar room altercation in Alleyton in May 1894.

Constable Burttschell was sitting peacefully in the saloon, which he owned, when Tuck Hoover, who also lived near Alleyton, rode into town, dismounted, hitched his horse, and walked toward the saloon with a cocked revolver. Once inside, he pointed it at the lawman and said, "Jake, I understand that you have threatened to kill me." Hoover then fired and the bullet went into or near the constable's heart. When Burttschell fell, the killer fired again, putting a second round into him. The victim died at the scene. Then, covering the clerk, Hoover backed out of the door. After mounting his horse, he directed it to the door of the saloon and fired yet another shot at the constable's dead body. About forty years old, Hoover had been considered as a quiet and peaceable man, but apparently something snapped and he wanted the constable's life.

A Weimar newsman related this news, adding that Hoover had only had trouble once before, about 1888, when he was in a gunfight wherein both parties were wounded but survived. After killing Burttschell, Hoover rode to Columbus, found the sheriff, gave the lawman his weapons, and admitted what he had done. A Weimar newsman opined that it had been a bad year for constables in Colorado County. In addition to Burttschell, the desperado Dee Braddock had murdered Constable A. M. Townsend of Weimar and an assailant had killed Constable D. L. Sutton in Houston.[15]

Hoover stood trial for the killing and was convicted of manslaughter and received twenty years in the state penitentiary for the deed. But on appeal the court reversed the decision and granted Hoover a new trial. Jim Coleman, who was Jake Burttschell's brother-in-law, swore revenge. On February 17, 1896, Hoover and his wife were in Neal's grocery store in Alleyton, next door to the saloon where Burttschell had died. Hoover was bartering with the owner when Coleman came out of a back room of the store armed with a double-barreled shotgun, one barrel having large buckshot and the other having small. Coleman emptied both barrels. The round of large shot came first and hit Hoover from the front. The round of small shot entered his back as he was falling to the floor. Hoover had his Winchester next to him propped against a counter, but he did not have a chance to use it. He died at the scene only a few minutes after the shooting. A news account said that Hoover lay dead within thirty feet of where Burttschell was when he died. A lad of twenty-one, Coleman rode to Columbus and surrendered to Sheriff Reese, while also turning in two pistols and the shotgun. Coleman was duly charged and tried for murder, but the case was eventually dismissed on a technicality and once again a case of private justice in the county went unpunished

According to John Goeppinger, Coleman had supper with the Reese brothers on the night of August 17, 1898, at the county jail the night of the assassination. Lillian Reese and John Goeppinger were also present, but both were teenagers at the time (Goeppinger was sixteen and Lillian was seventeen), and did not know exactly what was going on until an hour or so later when it became clear. The two Reese boys had conspired to assassinate Larkin Hope and Jim Coleman had agreed to perform the deed. When the meal was over, Goep (as he was called) was asked to go saddle Coleman's horse. Jim then stepped outside and Walter Reese handed him his ten gauge, double-barreled shotgun, the same one he had used to kill Tuck Hoover two years before. They opened the gate and Coleman headed toward town. In the meantime Goep had gone over to the house of a neighbor to visit a young lady, Jesse Stringer, who was staying there. To get out of the house, the two walked over to the East River Bridge, sat down and began to swing their feet off the bridge when they heard the blast of the shotgun and the responding reports of Larkin Hope's six-gun. The girl asked Goep what was going on. Goep replied he did not know for sure, but in his own mind he had a good idea. Directly the two heard Coleman's horse approaching and recognized it. As Jim passed by, his horse shied and he jerked up his shotgun. Goep called out, "Look out there, Jim, it's me Goep, don't shoot me." According to Goep, Coleman then rode on to the Burttschell home and later one of the ladies provided an alibi by swearing he had been there all along. (See Goeppinger Interview #6)

Coleman was duly arrested and charged with the crime. But the case against Coleman was circumstantial and never proved, or at least never resolved. It dragged on years with several continuances and two changes of venues and, eventually, simply disappeared in San Antonio district court where it had finally landed.

The John Goeppinger interview provides for the first time an inside account of the cast of characters responsible for the shooting. His revelation strongly suggests, moreover, that the sons of Sam Reese, John Walter and Herbert, hatched the plot on their own in concert with Jim Coleman, though this point cannot be claimed with absolute certainty. Accordingly, Sam Reese was unaware that his sons were planning a murder, which, if true, puts an extraordinary twist on the story that no one had suspected until the Goeppinger statement revealed it.

Whether a party to the conspiracy or not, the removal of Larkin Hope did not achieve the desired political result for Sam Reese and family. Mark Townsend quickly persuaded his brother-in-law, Will Burford, to fill the place of the slain Larkin Hope as a write-in candidate. The election became one of the hardest and bitterest in the history of the county with both sides spending enormous sums of money. When the day of election arrived, however, the Townsend machine once again prevailed.

The assassination of Larkin Hope in August of 1898 heralded the second stage of troubles. From this point on, the Stafford/Townsend dispute became a budding feud between different members of the extended Townsend family and their respective allies, but it did so in a way that never severed its connection with the previous troubles, which lived on as a kind of shadow feud in the background. Sam Reese not only lost the election, but he became a marked man as well. His death the following year at the hands of Mark Townsend, Will Clements, and Marion Hope, as well as the assassination of his brother Dick Reese, made it clear that the era of private justice was far from over and that the town now faced the possibility of a full-blown feud.

CHAPTER FIVE

The Killings of Sam and Dick Reese

In the general election of November 1898, Will Burford received 1,952 votes, Sam Reese 1,391, and a third candidate, James Shropshire, 871. Burford outpolled his opponents handily in Columbus, Weimar, and Eagle Lake. Perhaps most painfully, he soundly beat Sam Reese in Reese's hometown of Oakland.[1] Black voters played a pivotal role in the race and although at first they were unsure of whom to support, in the end they went strongly for Burford.

Their uncertainty resulted from the fact that both Sam Reese and Will Burford claimed to be the rightful heirs of Light Townsend and deserving of their loyalty. On September 3 black activists met in Weimar to sort things out and discuss the upcoming election.[2] Two things swayed them to support Will Burford: first, Mark Townsend appealed to them personally and, according to multiple sources, sweetened his appeal with generous amounts of cash;[3] secondly, Sam Reese had not shown the same deference and respect toward the black community during his tenure as sheriff as had Light Townsend, and this fact came back to haunt him.

Two contemporary observers held that the "Reeses were pretty tough about Negroes ... [and] if a Negro got out of line, he better watch out." The witnesses said that Sam Reese's wife, Keetie, "had been raised on a slave plantation and resented the loss of slaves to do all the work; whereas, the Townsend party always courted the black vote."[4]

Sam Reese did not accept political defeat graciously. Embittered, he walked away from his office the day after the election. The county had to call in the city marshal from Weimar, Henry J. Insall, to temporarily run the jail. Not that it was easy. Reese never turned over the keys and a rumor spread that he had thrown them into the river.[5] Further, he allegedly destroyed many of the records of the sheriff's office. Burford was forced to advance his timetable for the move to Columbus and take over the responsibilities of the office before his term officially began on January 1, 1899.

Sam Reese settled into a new routine soon enough, however, that included a morning ride out to his farm three miles northeast of Columbus. In the afternoons he would return to town around five o'clock and often take a swing through downtown to take care of business or to stop for some refreshment at the Brunson saloon before returning to his home, which was located a block north of the east river bridge. He was a man of regular habits and his routine became predictable.

Neither Walter nor Herbert Reese, the sons of Sam Reese, appeared to have much of a profession at this time although Walter, at twenty-one, was of an age to set out on his own. The brothers divided their time between the Reese house in town and the farm, or they just kept company with their friends in town. The whole family seemed to be biding their time and awaiting a chance for a rematch at the next election.

The incoming sheriff Will Burford was widely regarded as a man of personal integrity. He was also noted for his devout Methodist beliefs and for his stature as a prominent Mason. His large and prosperous farm was located near the Osage community on the west side of the Colorado River about six miles northeast of Weimar. His good name and community connections stood him well in the election, as the final tally showed, but he had been by his own admission a reluctant candidate who lacked both law enforcement experience and a forceful personality.

Although civic-minded and well-intentioned, given the circumstance of factional hatred existing in the county, Will Burford turned out to be a poor choice for sheriff. Burford, to quote Adjutant General Scurry's report, "... allowed himself to be managed by M. H. Townsend, and ... has shown bad judgment in the appointment of deputies ..."[6] The sole purpose of the appointment of these partisan deputies, it would appear, was to supply the legal protection Townsend desired.

Mark Townsend had retired from the Texas State Senate in 1900 to devote himself fully to his substantial business investments. Foremost among these was the Red Bluff Irrigation Company. In 1898 Captain William Dunovant had planted forty acres of rice at the lower end of Eagle Lake in Colorado County, the first rice west of Houston. His experiment attracted much attention.

Together with another investor, T. A. Hill, Mark Townsend and Will Burford formed the Red Bluff Irrigation Corporation in 1900 to capitalize on this new interest. Large swaths in the southern part of the county seemed ideally suited for the cultivation of rice. Their corporation purchased rights to river water from the State of Texas, built a pumping station, dug a system of delivery canals, and purchased thousands of acres of land to lease to potential rice farmers—an enormous and ambitious endeavor.

The investment demanded Townsend's full attention and constant presence in the county at the very times the events in question were playing out. In 1901 the corporation also platted the town of Garwood and applied for a post office that was granted that same year.[7] Mark Townsend, moreover, still maintained his principal residence in Columbus, one of the more impressive homes in the town, located just a block and a half west of the courthouse square. (see illustration)

What Mark Townsend desired above all in this time frame and context was a legal firewall between himself and his enemies, and with the election of Will Burford and the appointment several partisan deputies, he seemed to have justified the time, energy, and money he had expended in the recent election to achieve these ends.

Foremost among these partisan deputies was Will Clements (1876–1911). He was one of several children born to the union of Louise Florida "Lou" Townsend (1847–1886) and Augustus D. "Gus" Clements (c. 1844–1900) of the Oakland community. Lou (Townsend) Clements, Keetie (Townsend) Reese, and Jim Townsend were all siblings, the children of Spencer Burton Townsend, brother of Asa Townsend, and one of the original Townsend brothers to settle in Texas. The Clements siblings seemed to have little affection for one another, but curiously one of the sons, Spencer (1879–1906), preferred to live with the Sam Reese family. He was sickly and possessed of a milder temperament than his siblings. His aunt Keetie took him in and, over time, came to regard him as almost one of her own. To the great sadness of the family, he died at the young age of twenty-seven in 1906 in the Reese home, probably from pneumonia.

The fracture line that spread through the Spencer Townsend family, we note, produced a bizarre configuration of loyalties, revealing that close family ties can sometimes intensify ill will as well as nurture strong affection.

In contrast to Spence, Will Clements was loud and aggressive. He was also firmly allied with his second cousin, Mark Townsend, which deepened the crosscurrents of conflicted loyalties. Sam Reese regarded it as a personal affront when Sheriff Burford appointed Will Clements to be his first deputy.[8] He had a very low regard for the man and the ill will was mutual. According to a report of the period, "Mr. Reese, stinging over the result of the election, became very aggressive toward Clements, and serious trouble was only averted by the intervention of third parties on several occasions."[9]

On the afternoon of March 16, 1899, the bad blood between the two came to a head with tragic consequences for two innocent bystanders as well as for Sam Reese. Sam Reese, a man of regular habits, rode into town around five o'clock, as was his custom, from his farm across the river. He rode up Walnut Street then turned north into Milam where he stopped, dismounted, and tied his horse in front of the barbershop where he intended to get a haircut. After Reese's electoral defeat, Columbus City Marshal, W. R. "Bob" Walker, a friend of Reese, had deputized both Reese and his son-in-law, Dr. Joe Lessing, giving both the right to legally carry pistols.

Accounts differ in the particulars, but all agree an altercation between Will Clements and a man named Ed Scott had developed in a nearby establishment and spilled out on to the street just as Reese rode up. Scott was an acquaintance of ex-Sheriff Reese and the Burttschell clan. He had just been released from the county jail where he had been a cellmate of Jim Coleman for several months. This association apparently triggered the altercation. Will Clements, who was armed, was abusing and bullying Scott, who was not armed. Scott told Clements that if he also had a pistol, it would be a different story. Reese intervened in the argument and, according to one account, offered Scott his pistol. Clements barked that Reese should use his pistol himself whereupon both men drew their pistols and started shooting. At this juncture, Mark Townsend, Marion Hope, and A. R. "Gunger" Woolridge, another deputy sheriff, emerged from the drug store where the argument had originated with guns drawn. On the other side, City Marshal Walker and several men exited the Brunson saloon, some also armed.

A general shoot-out ensued with, by one estimate, over twenty shots being fired in all directions. Reese was initially grazed across the forehead and fell to the ground, still shooting. A second shot entered his neck and ranged down, severing the carotid artery—a fatal wound. Remarkably, Clements and his supporters emerged unscathed, but half a block down the street Johnny Williams, the six-year-old son of Columbus merchant and city alderman, Henry S. Williams, was hit with a stray bullet in his left hip. He had been standing in front of his father's store.

Another errant bullet struck a German farmer from the Bernardo community in the chest. Carl Boehme was in town shopping with his family when the gunfight broke out. He was driving his wagon in front of the Juergen saloon when struck. Still clutching the reins and a whip, he fell from the seat into the street. His pregnant wife Bertha and two of their eight children were in the wagon with him. As Boehme fell, the team broke and ran, taking the wagon and his terrified family careening through the streets. Joseph Gloger, who made furniture in a store nearby, stepped into the street and stopped the wagon. Boehme died where he fell, perhaps not ever knowing exactly what had happened to him. Bertha Boehme, realizing that her husband had been killed, collapsed in a dead faint.

According to a pro-Reese account published in the *Colorado Citizen* the following week, Walter Reese, who was across the street in the Brunson Saloon, stepped out just as the confrontation escalated and when he saw that his father was in trouble called out, "Look out Papa, they are trying to kill you."[10] Although unarmed, he ran to his father's aid as bullets whizzed around him and attempted to stem the flow of blood from his father's neck with a handkerchief. Not long thereafter Keetie Reese and her younger daughter Lillian, having heard the shots, rushed to the scene just as Sam Reese expired. As this was happening, both Walter and his mother, according to the pro-Reese account, faced abuse and threats from the Townsend crowd, which now included

Sheriff Burford, who appeared on the scene shortly thereafter. This charge was repeated in *Flaming Feuds of Colorado County*, where Lillian Reese stresses this abusive behavior as one of the acts that cemented their family hatred. In fairness to Sheriff Burford, however, other accounts explicitly contradict the Reese version of events, especially the assertion that he was often inebriated while on duty.[11]

Dr. R. H. Harrison, who had heard the shots, was quickly summoned to the scene. He noticed that the fatal wound was of a caliber no larger than a .38 whereas Clements possessed a .45 Colt, a larger caliber. Mark Townsend, known as a crack shot with a pistol, possessed a .38 Smith & Wesson. Although most accounts agreed that Clements had fired first, the Reese family placed the blame equally with Mark Townsend. They believed that the altercation had been a planned setup strikingly similar to the confrontation that had led to the shooting of the Stafford brothers nine years earlier, and that this time Mark Townsend not only orchestrated the confrontation from behind the scenes, but most likely fired the fatal shot as well. John Goeppinger echoed this version of events in his interview, while the presence of Marion Hope, who had also taken part in the shooting of the Staffords, reinforced the perception of a premeditated and staged confrontation. (See Goeppinger Interview # 7)

Once again the historian is left with unanswered questions, for there is only circumstantial evidence, however compelling, to suggest that there was, in fact, a conspiracy to kill Sam Reese. A contemporary expressed it this way: "It is a somewhat extraordinary coincidence that some five or six members of the Townsend/Burford faction, all armed, should be congregated at a point and at about the hour at which he [Sam Reese] was expected."[12]

But the real truth did not matter, and verily in this episode a *bona fide* feud was born. Each side became firmly convinced that they were in the right and that the wickedness of their antagonists justified any and all means to redress their grievances, including extralegal means. This filled all involved with a moral fury that obscured the real tragedy of this shootout (and others to come), namely that an innocent bystander had been killed and that a young boy had been so severely injured that he would remain crippled for life. Self-righteous indignation was especially evident on the side of the Reeses, and, as Ranger Captain Lamartine Pemberton Sieker later observed, Sam Reese's widow, Keetie, was the high keeper of the flame.[13] Her habit of displaying the bloody handkerchief used as a bandage on each anniversary of her husband's death reinforced this perception.

The shoot-out on the streets of Columbus created much excitement and further trouble was feared. The Reeses had quickly wired their numerous relatives in Lavaca County and elsewhere. Armed men began arriving daily, including several brothers of Sam Reese and a nephew, ex-Lavaca County Sheriff Jim F. Houchins. The Townsend faction, including the sheriff and his deputies, gathered at their end of town, and as the two crowds swelled to over twenty men apiece, the confrontation began to take on the aspect of a war between Lavaca and Colorado County, with current and former lawmen on both sides. In truth, however, the Reese faction also enjoyed solid support among the former friends and associates of the Stafford brothers in Columbus, men who saw clear and disturbing parallels between the death of Sam Reese and that of the Stafford brothers nine years before. The presence of Marion Hope at both shootings certainly reinforced this perception. And similar to the previous situation, resentment over perceived manipulation of the black vote on the part of Mark Townsend added another element to inflame passions among the Reese/Stafford crowd.[14]

Realizing the extent to which local law enforcement was compromised and fearing that it was only a matter of hours until a small incident escalated into a full-scale war in downtown Columbus, District Judge Mumford Kennon wired Governor J. D. Sayers on March 20, 1899: "Trouble brewing out of last week's killing. Peace officers involved. Can you send fifteen or twenty rangers? Pressing."[15]

The governor was quick to respond and ordered not "fifteen or twenty rangers," as requested, but only three rangers to Columbus. Captain Bill McDonald arrived on the March 22 morning train after an overnight trip from Amarillo where Company B Frontier Battalion, which he commanded, was headquartered. Rangers Sanders and Hudson arrived on the evening train that same day.

Captain McDonald's reputation as a fearless and no-nonsense lawman was already well established and preceded him. He had been in many tight spots during his career and appeared undaunted by the two riled and liquored crowds of armed men he encountered. He went to work right away before his reinforcements arrived. Using the courthouse as neutral home base, he summoned representatives of first the Townsend/Burford crowd and then the Reese/Stafford crowd and, using both persuasion and threats, convinced the two groups to disarm and disburse, the Reese faction being the more recalcitrant and difficult. According to McDonald's early biographer, he accomplished this feat single-handedly before his two reinforcements arrived on the evening train, bolstering the "One Man, One Feud" aura that came to be associated with his name.[16]

Eventually, Mark Townsend and Marion Hope were also arrested for the killing of Sam Reese and charged along with Will Clements with manslaughter. Rangers attended the *habeas corpus* hearings to preserve order and all the men were released on bail. To the consternation of the rangers and chagrin of the Reese faction, Will Clements resumed his position as chief deputy sheriff even though he was now under indictment for manslaughter.

In the meantime a palpable tension hung over the community like a noxious cloud. Only the continued presence of the rangers kept a lid on the situation. The rangers numbered between four and six men and effectively took over law enforcement in the county. Reports from the period show that the rangers investigated crimes and made several arrests not connected to the feud.[17]

Later that month, on March 28, someone attempted to shoot Will Clements at his home by firing at him from the darkness of the night through an open window, but the shot missed him and lodged in a door jam.[18] John Goeppinger hinted that he and the Reese boys were behind this attempted assassination. The rangers attempted to arrest Goeppinger but he escaped to Houston and later, to avoid arrest by deputies Gunger Wooldridge and Will Clements, who had travelled there for that purpose, escaped out a back window, hopped a freight train to New Orleans, and then signed up on a boat carrying mules to South Africa during the Boer War (1899–1902). He returned as a revenant two years later to the amazement of friends and family who had not heard a word from him during the two years. His account of his escape and subsequent adventures travelling around the world is quite entertaining. (See Goeppinger Interview #8)

Everyone expected, sooner or later, the fires would reignite. Their fears were shortly realized and the release of Jim Coleman on bond provided the catalyst.

Jim Coleman had faced a *habeas corpus* hearing soon after the assassination of Larkin Hope on the charge of murder. It was customary at the time for the district attorney to hire private attorneys to prosecute cases, and, either by design or accident, Mark Townsend presented the State's case against Coleman, producing much circumstantial evidence to implicate him and arguing vigorously for withholding bail.

Over fifty witnesses were called to testify. Coleman, infuriated at the aggressive approach of the prosecution, made threats against Mark Townsend in open court. Consequently the presiding judge, Mumford Kennon, sided with Mark Townsend and denied bail to Coleman, who spent the next several months languishing in jail.[19] On May 1, 1899, however, District Judge Kennon reversed his decision and agreed to release Jim Coleman on bond.[20] Coleman could not make bond at first, but a week later on April 30, he was released.

Coleman's release is the key to understanding what happened next, for Mark Townsend had not yet learned to fear the sons of Sam Reese who, although seething with hatred, had yet to show their hands. But he clearly feared Jim Coleman, who had sworn revenge in open court for the zeal with which Townsend had prosecuted the case against him in the shooting of Larkin Hope in August 1898 and had been overheard to say in his jail cell that upon release he intended to kill both Sheriff Burford and Mark Townsend.[21] As an experienced trial lawyer, Townsend clearly recognized the sociopathic bent in Coleman's character, which was heightened by addiction to both alcohol and opiates, and his fears were not entirely irrational.

Both sides were spying on one another. Friends of the Burford/Townsend faction informed them that several allies and relatives of Sam Reese from Lavaca County had drifted into town on May 16. Then on May 18 Dick Reese, brother of Sam Reese, arrived on the train from Beaumont. But more ominously, the recently released Coleman had made his way back to Alleyton, across the river from Columbus. They then received information that Dick Reese had gone to Alleyton, presumably to meet with Coleman.

Without definite knowledge, but harboring a strong suspicion, Mark Townsend and Sheriff Burford were convinced that something was afoot in the Reese camp involving Coleman and the Reese men from Lavaca County and decided to act preemptively. Sheriff Burford deputized two other men, Jim Townsend and Step Yates, and then ordered the men to deploy on the east side of the river bridge on the evening of May 17 to intercept Coleman should he attempt to enter the town.

Sheriff Burford subsequently justified his action on the grounds that lately there had been a rash of shooting on the east side of the bridge, disturbing to the night time tranquility of the town, and the deputies had been posted there to arrest the offenders.[22] But this explanation was most certainly a pretext: the real purpose of the deputies was clearly to intercept Jim Coleman should he attempt to enter Columbus.[23]

Once darkness descended on the town, one of the most bizarre incidents connected with the feud occurred. A young woman was taken into custody in the vicinity of the jail, lurking in the shadows. She had dressed herself in men's clothing and blackened her face with charcoal. It was Nuddie Ela (Reese) Lessing,[24] an older married daughter of Sam and Keetie Reese, the wife of Dr. Joe Lessing Jr. She refused to explain her presence or why she was in disguise, but the obvious assumption was that she had been sent out to reconnoiter the whereabouts of the Townsend faction. This turn of events reinforced the suspicion that something was planned for that evening on the part of the Reeses and that Jim Coleman was involved.

Around nine o'clock, a horse-drawn buggy approached the east bridge with two men aboard. It was a dark night. Shortly thereafter, the citizens of Columbus could clearly hear the reports of firearms across the river and could distinguish both shotgun and pistol fire. Seven or eight shots were fired in total. The initial fusillade struck Dick Reese, who fell mortally wounded to the floorboard of a buggy he had borrowed from

Joseph Burttschell. The black driver, Dick Gant, attempted to jump from the hack and flee, but was shot down in a hail of fire and died on the scene, another innocent victim of the feud. With the sudden explosion of gunfire, the terrified horses wheeled and bolted at a dead run in the direction whence they had come. The buggy was found several hours later with Dick Reese still inside. A pistol was also found in the buggy, but it had not been fired.

Once again a call went out for the rangers. This time the quartermaster of the rangers, Captain Lamartine Sieker, answered the call.[25] He arrived by train on May 19.[26] He found a great many armed men, members of both factions, roaming the streets. Four more rangers, including Will Wright and Creed Taylor, joined Sieker the next day.[27] The five rangers set about disarming men who were not legally entitled to carry guns, and urging those who did not live in town to return home. They did not leave, but they did try to remain inconspicuous by staying off the streets. Fearing the worst, Governor Sayers suggested Adjutant General Scurry order Captain McDonald back to Columbus as reinforcement. Scurry issued the order and then took the train to Columbus himself. He arrived May 23 and Captain McDonald and another ranger arrived the following day.

The rangers interviewed a transient couple who had been camped under some live oak trees on the east side of the river and who had witnessed the encounter. Although dark, they identified deputies James Townsend and Step Yates as the shooters, and on the basis of this the rangers arrested and charged the two deputies with murder.

Jim Townsend, although a brother of Sam Reese's wife Keetie, was firmly in the Mark Townsend camp. Sam Reese had defeated Step Yates in his first race for sheriff in 1896, and thus Yates harbored a loser's resentment against the Reese clan. The killing infuriated the Reese family.

They insisted that Dick Reese had come to Columbus as a peacemaker rather than as a conspirator to further violence, and that he believed he could allay the hard feelings arising from the killing of his brother some two months prior by persuading his relatives to discontinue the strife. His widow, likewise, asserted that he had had no intent of doing bodily harm to his brother's enemies. This belief was underscored by the fact that her husband's right arm was paralyzed and that he did not own a firearm. The killing left Dick Reese's widow with seven children, five of whom were dependent on her for support.[28] The killing of the probably innocent Dick Reese and the most certainly innocent Dick Gant made it clear to the citizens of Columbus that a full-scale blood feud was under way.

After the arrival of McDonald, Captain Sieker returned to Austin, but Adjutant General Scurry remained on the scene for a couple of days before departing himself. The rangers took rooms at the Kulow Hotel on the east side of the courthouse square.

While in Columbus, Scurry interviewed District Judge McCormick and County Judge Mansfield about the causes of the troubles and what could be done about it. He was impressed with Judge Mansfield's impartiality and asked him to set down his observations in a formal report that Scurry passed on to the governor.[29] He also met with Sheriff Burford. Scurry had quickly come to the conclusion that Sheriff Burford was part of the problem and he urged him to resign. Scurry, however, did extract a promise from the sheriff to discharge several deputies who were considered highly partisan in exchange for the rangers temporarily taking over local law enforcement. Scurry came away thinking the two had reached an agreement on this score at least.

The task of the rangers, it should be noted, was also complicated by a nasty political squabble among the city fathers of Columbus concerning the city marshal's office. A dispute had developed between Mayor Middlebrook of Columbus and the city council concerning the marshal's office and how to deal with the troubles. In early May Marshal Robert "Bob" Walker, known to be sympathetic toward the Reese party, suddenly resigned his post and moved from Columbus to Yoakum where he opened a pool hall and saloon. Walker's exit caught city authorities by surprise since Walker had been reelected just weeks earlier, besting one Peter B. Martin by a solid majority.

Initially, four aldermen, led by Henry Williams, whose six-year-old son had been wounded in the shoot-out that killed Sam Reese only two months earlier, had voted to leave the marshal's office vacant until the council's next meeting in June. Consequently, the city had no marshal when Dick Reese and Dick Gant were killed. But after the shooting, Mayor Middlebrook decided on his own to hire five "special deputies," a controversial decision since armed deputies were invariably regarded as partisan by one side or the other. The city council disapproved of the mayor's action and declared their "most emphatic and earnest protest against [the mayor's] illegal and unwarranted action in filling the town of Columbus with an unnecessary and useless crowd of special officers that will surely entangle the city in a family feud."[30]

The mayor replied that he had been "solicited by many citizens to have some special police appointed to protect the law-abiding and innocent citizens of Columbus from the violence of any opposing parties who should try to run riot over our city." He insisted, moreover, that, "I am and have been non-partisan in the feuds that exist in our city," and said the same of his new special policemen. The dispute was not resolved until July 3, when the mayor and the council agreed on a curfew and settled on one special deputy, the aforementioned Peter Martin, to fill the post.

Despite these problems the rangers had succeeded on defusing the situation in the immediate aftermath of the killings, but on June 6, 1899, Governor Sayers felt obliged to order Captain McDonald away from Columbus to Athens, Texas, where another feud was brewing. And with his departure matters heated up once again. The two rangers who remained, privates Wright and Taylor, felt overwhelmed. On June 5, Ranger Wright arrested Walter Reese, the son of the dead sheriff, "for using abusive language." Two days later Wright and Sheriff Burford were in the countryside investigating cattle thefts when one of the Reese faction fired a pistol inside Brunson's saloon in Columbus. According to Ranger Wright's official report, "a riot was almost precipitated" in town because of the shot. Cartridges from the shotgun confiscated from Walter Reese had initials of Sheriff Burford and Mark Townsend etched on them.[31] Private Wright requested more rangers: "There are more violations of the law in this county than any other in the state I believe ... the Sheriff has turned off his deputies and relies on Taylor and myself to do all his work ... I think there ought to be two more here all the time."[32]

Both factions were moving toward a showdown. Numerous men of the Reese faction, many of them from Lavaca County, were in Columbus or on their way there. On June 10 Wright and Taylor arrested five men of the Townsend faction—Mark Townsend, Jim Townsend, Marion Hope, Jim Clements, and Step Yates—for carrying pistols. The next day, with Taylor too ill to help and two dozen sympathizers gathered at the Reese home, Wright wired once again with an urgent plea for more rangers. On June 12 Adjutant General Scurry obliged the request with two more rangers whom he personally accompanied to Columbus.[33]

Scurry was furious to find Deputy Clements still present on the streets of Columbus and still carrying a weapon.

His presence, he reported, "is like waving the red flag to the Reeses."[34] When he confronted Sheriff Burford, the sheriff said that they must have misunderstood each other; that it was his understanding that Clements was only to be relieved from active duty and that, moreover, "even if Clements were discharged and arrested forty times a day for carrying a concealed weapon, it would avail nothing, as it was well-known in Columbus that Clements life had been threatened."[35]

Together Scurry and McDonald adopted the strategy of attempting to persuade, cajole, and threaten the principal trouble makers and lightning rods to remove themselves (if only temporarily) from Columbus until things could cool down. Scurry had been unsuccessful in regard to Will Clements, but Mark Townsend did agree to leave for a while. He hoped to also get agitators from the Reese side to leave.

Scurry had gotten to know Pee Dee Reese, who had appeared in Columbus with a group of five armed men from Lavaca County soon after the shooting of his brother Dick Reese.[36] He appeared to be a reasonable and levelheaded man. He promised to get all his men and leave town the next day. Scurry then had one of his men stay at Pee Dee's side as a body guard. But when the following day arrived, only Pee Dee and one other Reese man had left. Pee Dee had told the ranger that as soon as he had convinced his men to leave, Sam Reese's widow Keetie did all in her power to inflame them and prevail on them to stay.[37] From the way Pee Dee comported himself to the ranger, it was clear that he made several attempts to influence his men in the right direction, only to have Keetie Reese undercut his efforts.[38]

Scurry then returned to the house of Sam Reese to announce to those who stayed behind that if they wanted a fight, they would be disappointed because the rangers had no intention of allowing them to shed blood. Scurry told all of the Reese party that unless they lived in Columbus, they absolutely must leave by the next day, but when the next day arrived no one had departed. Scurry went to talk to the men once more. A spokesman for the Reese bunch explained to Scurry that they intended to leave but were awaiting the arrival of Walter Reese, who was stranded on the other side of the Colorado River due to high water. As soon as he arrived they all intended to go back to Hallettsville together. The leader told Scurry that the water level would fall within eighteen hours.[39]

Scurry was certainly glad to hear that Walter Reese was leaving Columbus for a few days. Young and seething with indignation, Walter was a thorn in everybody's side. The adjutant general had asked Walter to leave before but he had refused. Scurry believed that the young man was an impulsive hotspur who had done much to aggravate the situation. Scurry told the Reese men who were supposedly waiting on Walter that they had until 9:00 a.m. on Thursday (the next day) to leave, else he would arrest them all and charge them with "unlawful assembly." He added that if they returned in the future, a ranger would not allow them to come armed. If a search turned up a gun or guns, the ranger would arrest them on the spot.[40]

Scurry's stay in Columbus had offered him insight into the troubles. It appeared to him that Keetie Reese was "egging on" those loyal to the Reese family. Other sources corroborate his observation. In a later interview, Allie Wetteroth, one of Keetie's friends, related that "Mrs. Reese lost her mind for a while after her husband's death."[41] She also said that forever after, Keetie had a gun in her purse whenever she left home and "would have gladly killed" anyone who irritated her. At home that gun was always handy, and at night Keetie put her gun under her pillow when she was ready for bed.

In his report to Governor Sayers, Scurry wrote that he had learned that she planned to move away. Talk was that she would move to Yoakum, Hallettsville, or San Antonio. Scurry noted, "if she does [move], I think it will about end the trouble." To inform the governor of the problems she posed, Scurry illustrated his point with an anecdote from Ranger Wright whom she had pulled aside on one occasion and taken to her bedroom. She showed him pictures of Sam Reese and extolled his many virtues, including his honor and his courage. She then removed a sheet from two chairs setting close to each other to unveil a macabre site. The bloody clothes that her husband wore the day of his death were spread out on the first chair. On the other chair was the bloodstained shirt of Dick Reese. She told Wright that nothing would satisfy her "but the heart of Mark Townsend."[42]

Scurry departed after two weeks, but Rangers Wright and Taylor remained behind. Once again, trouble was averted. But the atmosphere remained tense. On June 22, the *Colorado Citizen*, only half in jest, suggested "to the young ladies of the city and county that they relegate to the rear their lawn tennis, croquet and other amusements for a time, and form a six-shooter club, to meet and practice two or three times a week," for in Columbus, "every lady should know how to shoot accurately and have a pistol in her room."[43]

Things quieted down markedly with the departure of Walter Reese and his armed supporters from Lavaca County, but trouble loomed on the horizon. The fall term of district court was scheduled to convene in Columbus in September 1899 and the rangers feared that this could become a catalyst for further private justice. Three important cases were scheduled for trial involving the feud: the case against Jim Coleman for the murder of Larkin Hope, the manslaughter charges against Will Clements, Mark Townsend, and Larkin Hope for the death of Sam Reese, and the murder charges against James Townsend and Stephen Yates for the deaths of Dick Reese and Dick Gant. The cases were sure to bring throngs of partisan spectators and witnesses to town and the potential for bloodshed was great. In consideration of the threat, Scurry ordered Ranger Captain John A. Brooks and a detachment of six men to Columbus to augment Rangers Wright and Taylor who were already there.[44]

When court convened, Brooks had a total force of eight rangers. The captain posted men at all entrances into the district courtroom. Then, just before the court convened, they searched everyone entering the court, disarming anyone who had a weapon, and there were several who did. Due to the large law enforcement presence, the proceedings went off without incident. At least one news editor believed that the war between the Townsend party and the Reese party was finished and that the killings were at an end: "The two factions were about evenly represented among the witnesses and persons leaving [Columbus and Weimar] for the trial. It is not generally believed that there will be any further trouble. Both sides say they are willing to submit their grievances to the courts."[45] Another newsman expressed the thoughts of many: "A legal battle is expected, as the attorneys on both sides are bent on stubbornly contesting every inch of ground for their respective clients."[46]

The legal proceedings were short-lived. In quick succession, District Judge Mumford Kennon threw out the manslaughter indictments against Mark Townsend, Marion Hope, and Will Clements, accepting their plea of self-defense.[47]

The court next addressed the case of Jim Townsend for the murder of Dick Reese and Dick Gant. His codefendant Yates had escaped the indignity of a trial by conveniently dying of natural causes just as court convened. In his last days, Sheriff Burford and his family took Yates in and cared for him as best they could. He had suffered health problems for some time and succumbed quickly to a fever after two days in bed. The lawyers for Jim Townsend asked for and received a change of venue to Bastrop County and the date of the trial was set for January 1900.

Jim Coleman viewed these happenings from his jail cell. For reasons not entirely clear, his bail had been revoked and he was remanded back to jail shortly after his release in May. When his case came to trial, he pleaded not guilty and his defense attorneys requested a change of venue. On September 25, 1899, the judge granted the change and transferred Coleman's case to Fort Bend County. He was granted bail once again and set free.

1899 had been a bad year for Columbus and Colorado County. The feud had led to several innocent deaths and left the county in an almost continual state of uproar and excitement for at least six months. Partisanship on the part of both the city and county authorities had undercut their effectiveness and exacerbated tensions. The continuous turmoil had also exerted a depressing effect on the business climate of the town. The accidental death of the German farmer Boehme had led to a boycott of the town by many of the German farmers who lived in the northern and eastern parts of the county with serious consequences for many of the businesses in town. The town gained an unwelcome reputation as "Hell's Half Acre" and passengers on trains often ducked their heads while passing through.[48]

There was one bright spot at least: the ranger service acquitted itself with a degree of impartiality and competence and earned the approbation of all parties and pointed the way for a new ranger ethos based on a higher degree of professionalism. Over a period of eight years the rangers would spend more manpower attempting to keep a lid on the Colorado County feud than on any other comparable trouble spot in Texas, before or since. All four of the iconic "Great Captains," John Abijah Brooks, John R. Hughes, William J. McDonald, and John H. Rogers, as well as the Quarter Master and

Commandant Captain, Lamartine Pemberton Sieker, and Texas Adjutant General, Thomas Scurry, took an active hand and appeared on the scene at one time or another. This happened in no other situation in Texas.

It also was a poignant and ironic development for Columbus and Colorado County, since the "Rangers" of Austin's Colony, organized in present Columbus in 1823, were the earliest recorded force of this type raised in Texas and served as a model for the later formation of the Texas Rangers. The force was organized then to protect the settlers from Indian depredations; this time, the rangers arrived to protect the citizens from themselves.

COLORADO COUNTY

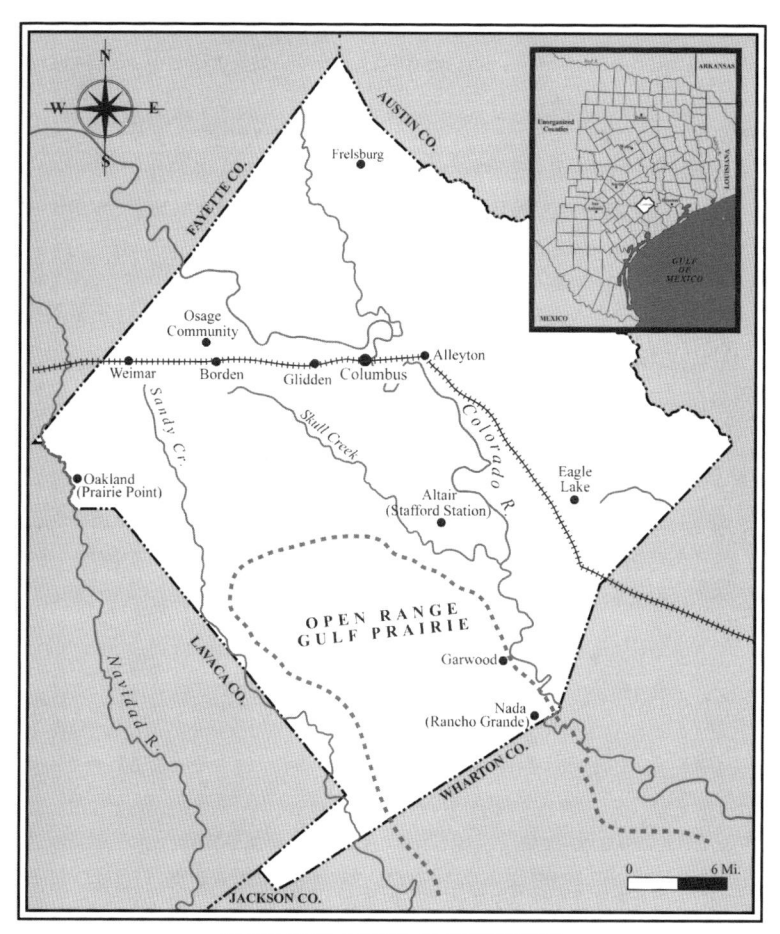

Colorado County map, ca 1875. *Courtesy Alex Mendoza.*

Antebellum Plantation House (Tait House) Columbus. *Courtesy Nesbitt Memorial Library Archives.*

Black women Colorado County, ca. 1900. *Courtesy Nesbitt Memorial Library Archives.*

Colorado County cowboys on the Prairie, ca. 1900. *Courtesy Nesbitt Memorial Library Archives.*

Wegenhoft brothers, Colorado County cowmen, ca. 1900. *Courtesy Nesbitt Memorial Library Archives.*

Asa Townsend. *Courtesy Nesbitt Memorial Library Archives.*

Rebecca Townsend, wife of Asa Townsend. *Courtesy Nesbitt Memorial Library Archives.*

Bob Stafford as a young man. *Courtesy Nesbitt Memorial Library Archives.*

Bob Stafford bank and residence, Columbus, Texas. *Courtesy Nesbitt Memorial Library Archives.*

John Stafford residence, three miles south of Columbus. *Courtesy Nesbitt Memorial Library Archives.*

Stafford meat packing plant, Columbus, Texas. *Courtesy Nesbitt Memorial Library Archives.*

Colorado County Courthouse, ca. 1895. *Courtesy Nesbitt Memorial Library Archives.*

Sheriff J. Light Townsend, ca. 1894. *Courtesy Nesbitt Memorial Library Archives.*

Marcus Townsend. *Courtesy Nesbitt Memorial Library Archives.*

Bob Stafford at the time of his death. *Drawing by the author*.

John Stafford. *Courtesy Nesbitt Memorial Library Archives.*

Larkin Hope, City Marshal. *Courtesy Nesbitt Memorial Library Archives.*

Sheriff Sam H. Reese (on the right) and Deputy Kollmann, ca. 1896. *Courtesy Nesbitt Memorial Library Archives.*

Judge Mansfield (in white suit) and Colorado County Commissioner's Court, ca. 1896. Sam Reese is third from left. *Courtesy Nesbitt Memorial Library Archives.*

Assassination of Larkin Hope, 1898. *Drawing by the author.*

The death of ex-Sheriff Reese, 1899. *Drawing by the author.*

Walter Reese. *Courtesy Nesbitt Memorial Library Archives.*

Keron Blanche "Keetie" Reese. *Courtesy Nesbitt Memorial Library Archives.*

Herbert "Hub" Reese. *Courtesy Nesbitt Memorial Library Archives.*

Lillian Reese. *Courtesy Nesbitt Memorial Library Archives.*

Walter Reese (on the right) and Lavaca County supporters. *Courtesy Nesbitt Memorial Library Archives.*

Marcus "Mark" Harvey Townsend (later picture). *Courtesy Nesbitt Memorial Library Archives.*

Annie Euphemie (Burford) Townsend, wife of Marcus Townsend. *Courtesy Nesbitt Memorial Library Archives*.

Marcus Townsend Home Columbus. *Courtesy Nesbitt Memorial Library Archives.*

Sheriff W. T. Burford. *Courtesy Nesbitt Memorial Library Archives.*

Arthur Burford, son of Sheriff Burford. Arthur was killed in the shoot-out at Bastrop. *Courtesy Nesbitt Memorial Library Archives.*

Jim Coleman (on the left) and Walter Reese (on the right), Bastrop 1900.
Courtesy Nesbitt Memorial Library Archives.

Walter Reese (in center without a weapon) and Texas Rangers, Bastrop 1900. *Courtesy Nesbitt Memorial Library Archives.*

MASS MEETING

Deploring the existing conditions in Columbus, it is desired and earnestly urged that

Every Good Citizen

Of this city assemble in the

Courthouse

At 9 o'clock in the morning

THURSDAY, JULY 19

Then and there to discuss

Ways and Means

For the betterment and relief of the

DEPRESSION!

Which has settled upon all the interests of all our people. Therefore, all citizens interested in the good and welfare of the town are not only warmly asked to attend, but they will be EXPECTED to be present.

MANY CITIZENS

Call for Mass Meeting of Citizens of Columbus 1906. *Courtesy Nesbitt Memorial Library Archives.*

Newspaper drawing 1907 Marion Hope trial. *From San Antonio Light.*

Captain John Reynolds Hughes, Texas Ranger. *Courtesy Texas Ranger Hall of Fame and Museum, Waco, TX.*

Captain John H. Rogers, Texas Ranger. *Courtesy Texas Ranger Hall of Fame and Museum, Waco, TX.*

Captain James Abijah Brooks, Texas Ranger. *Courtesy Texas Ranger Hall of Fame and Museum, Waco, TX.*

Captain Bill McDonald, Texas Ranger. *Courtesy Texas Ranger Hall of Fame and Museum, Waco, TX.*

Captain Leander H. McNelly, Texas Ranger. *Courtesy Texas Ranger Hall of Fame and Museum, Waco, TX.*

Captain Lamartine P. Seiker, Texas Ranger. *Courtesy Texas Ranger Hall of Fame and Museum, Waco, TX.*

Gathering of former Stafford men, ca. 1911 (probably for the Stelzig trial in Bay City); Ike Pryor on the far left. *Courtesy Nesbitt Memorial Library Archives.*

John Goeppinger (seated, center) at the time of his retirement from the Southern Pacific switching yard at Glidden, ca. 1954. *Courtesy Nesbitt Memorial Library Archives.*

HERE RESTS
IKE TOWELL
AN INFIDEL WHO HAD
NO HOPE OF HEAVEN
NOR FEAR OF HELL
WAS FREE OF SUPERSTITION
TO DO RIGHT AND LOVE
JUSTICE WAS HIS RELIGION.

Ike Towell's tombstone, Odd Fellows Cemetery, Columbus, Texas. *Courtesy Nesbitt Memorial Library Archives.*

CHAPTER SIX

The Terrible Affray at Bastrop and the Shoot-out at Rosenberg

As the new century dawned, Columbus grew lively with talk of the approaching trial of Jim Townsend, set to begin in the Bastrop County District Court on Monday, January 15, 1900. On January 11, a headline in the Columbus newspaper asked rhetorically, "Are you going to Bastrop?" Scores answered in the affirmative for, reportedly, about 300 people made the trip, necessitating a special train from Columbus on the Sunday before the trial.[1] Among the passengers were the defendant, Jim Townsend, and three of his sisters, Keetie Reese, Jennie Brown, and Molly Dudley, all three of whom were scheduled to testify against their brother as witnesses for the prosecution. The rangers took pains to seat the two factions in separate cars.[2]

Just as with the 1899 fall term of district court in Columbus, the people of Colorado County anticipated the coming trial of Jim Townsend in Bastrop with a mixture of excitement and trepidation. In the fall, the three cases associated with the feud—the case against Jim Coleman for the murder of Larkin Hope; the case against Mark Townsend, Marion Hope, and Will Clements for the death of Sam Reese; and the case against Jim Townsend and Step Yates for the murder of Dick Reese—had generated a threefold potential for violence. But in the end, it had been anti-climactic; District Judge Kennon had disposed of the cases in quick order, either through change of venue or dismissal, while the rangers had showed up in force and by all accounts had acted to keep the peace in a firm but impartial manner.[3]

In consequence, although the excitement level remained high for the Bastrop trial, the fear of violence had lessened. Similar to Columbus the previous fall, the rangers would keep a lid on things, while the removal to Bastrop, a neutral ground, would diminish the potential for large numbers of armed partisans to congregate unnoticed.

Captain Brooks travelled to Bastrop ahead of time in order to work out a coordinated plan with District Judge Edward R. Sinks, Bastrop County Sheriff George W. Davis, and Bastrop City Marshal Julius F. Nash for keeping the peace.[4] On January 12 they decided "that all parties would be disarmed and searched on the streets and at the court house during the trial."[5] Interestingly, they decided to essentially exclude Colorado County lawmen from any role in the peacekeeping, reflecting their belief that the sheriff and his deputies were too compromised.

When the train arrived, Davis and Brooks met with both factions at the depot and notified them that they would be disarmed and escorted to their hotels; all seemed satisfied with the plan.[6] There was, as it turned out, a fatal flaw in their strategy: the rangers permitted those who placed firearms in their luggage or otherwise managed to secret them to Bastrop to deposit them at the several hotels and boarding houses where they had taken rooms and where they could be easily retrieved.

In the rangers' defense, however, the 1871 gun law that was still the law of the land forbade private citizens from carrying firearms (or any other weapons) in public, but permitted them to own and keep weapons in their homes (and, by extension, in their hotel rooms). It also permitted them to carry firearms in their baggage while travelling.[7] Although Governor Sayers had ordered the rangers to

Bastrop, he had not declared martial law or issued any proclamations to suspend the normal workings of law; the rangers, therefore, could only act within the parameters of the laws that were on the books.

The morning of the trial the courtroom was packed. Local law enforcement officers, including Sheriff Davis, Marshal Nash, and four Texas Rangers patrolled the courthouse and the town according to plan and felt confident a show of force would prevent trouble. They saw to it that no one with arms entered the courthouse, including Sheriff Burford and his deputies from Columbus.

When Judge Sinks convened his court, the opposing lawyers asked that the trial be postponed until one o'clock that afternoon so that they would have time to interview at least some of the more than one hundred persons who were on hand to testify. Later that morning, the lawyers asked that the trial be postponed until July. With so many witnesses present and so much law enforcement authority in place, Judge Sinks must have been reluctant; nevertheless, he set a new trial date of July 11, 1900. To ensure that the witnesses would return, the court placed them under bond. There were fifty-six witnesses for the state and seventy-seven witnesses for the defense, all of whom agreed to pay $200 if they did not show up on the new trial date.

The day of court seemed to pass without incident. The presiding judge accepted a motion for continuance and dismissed court at four-thirty. Many people from both factions had indicated a willingness to depart for home on the evening train from Bastrop while others decided to spend the night. Rangers accompanied the throngs of spectators and witnesses as they made their way to the depot. Arthur Burford, younger son of Sheriff Burford, was in fine spirits as he left the courthouse in Bastrop on this crisp and clear January day. He had come both as observer and character witness for the defense. Young Burford exited the courthouse in the company of his cousins, Will Clements and Howard Townsend—both deputy sheriffs of Colorado County and both considered highly partisan on the side of Mark Townsend. Howard Townsend was the son of former sheriff Light Townsend.

Arthur Burford, on the other hand, was entirely free of any involvement. He was just twenty-three years old, but seemed poised for a productive and successful life. He had graduated from the Coronal Institute in San Marcos in 1897 and from the law school at the University of Texas in Austin two years later. He was engaged to be married[8] and had taken a job with the leading law firm in Columbus, Foard, Thompson & Townsend, the latter being his uncle, Mark Townsend.[9]

The night before the trial, young Burford penned a letter on the stationery of The Midland Hotel at Bastrop to his anxious mother, who had remained in Columbus:

Bastrop, Texas, Jan 14th 1900

Mrs. W. T. Burford

Dear Mama,

We arrived here this evening without the least inclination on the part of any one to raise a fuss. Everone [sic] has kept perfectly quiet and have shown not the least sign of fussing. We all have places to sleep and had a good square meal for supper, which was certainly relished, as we were very hungry. Captain Brooks and his force of Rangers are on hand and will keep everybody quiet ... Don't be in the least uneasy about any of us. Love to all,

Your Son,
Arthur.[10]

Arthur Burford could not have been more wrong; he was about to become the next victim of private justice, Colorado County style transplanted to a neighboring county, even as the nineteenth century rolled over into the twentieth.

As they emerged from the courthouse, a Texas Ranger frisked all three men to ensure that they carried no weapons just as another ranger had checked them before they had entered hours earlier. Pleased with the continuance, which put the trial on the path to eventual dismissal, and confident that, just as in Columbus six months previous, the rangers were in firm control of the situation, the three cousins strolled leisurely back to their lodging at the Midland Hotel, Burford with his hands in his pockets. Their path would take them past the Golden Rule Saloon, a couple of blocks from the courthouse.

As they approached the saloon, tragedy beckoned. Unaware that twenty-one-year-old Walter Reese, who had preceded them from the courthouse, was present in the saloon with a large party of his relatives and friends, the three continued to amble down the street oblivious to the danger that awaited them. Although Walter Reese had been called as a witness, most of his accomplices had chosen not to attend the court proceedings and, instead, had taken up positions in the saloon below their rooms where they had a clear view of the comings and goings of the courthouse. They also were armed with handguns, shotguns, and rifles.[11] Disdainful of the legal proceedings, liquored up, and intent on private justice, they were primed for a crime of opportunity, which the three unarmed men approaching them now provided.[12]

The Reese party spotted the three men at about 4:40 p.m. while they were still some distance from the Midland. Their prime target was most certainly Will Clements, whom they regarded as one of the co-murderers of Sam Reese and whose haughtiness and taunting behavior had inflamed their passions on several occasions. When the trio approached within pistol range, shots exploded from the saloon. In a split second, the three defenseless men encountered a virtual fusillade erupting from the establishment. First, the guns reported twice, followed by a number of simultaneous volleys, and that followed by the noise of at least three more weapons. A lethal shot hit young Burford in the head near his right eyebrow and slammed into his brain. The force of the impact also broke his neck. He collapsed where he stood and died instantly.[13]

Townsend and Clements ducked and jumped as best they could while sundry bullets whizzed around them. Realizing their targets were unarmed, several shooters exited the saloon to the sidewalk and then onto the street to get closer shots with their pistols and rifles. Townsend and Clements took to their heels as fast as they could run with several of the shooters in pursuit. Townsend escaped unscathed, but Clements was hit twice, the first bullet striking him in the right shoulder before lodging at the edge of the shoulder blade. The second round struck him at the right side of his back and passed through his liver, slicing off about one-third of it, before emerging from the bottom of his belly.[14]

Amazingly, Clements continued to run even though he had to keep both hands at the exit wound to check his intestines from spilling out. Still, filled with adrenalin and driven by the primal urge to survive, the man escaped by leaving the street, running down a side alley, ducking through the side door of a saddle shop, entering a back alley, and climbing over a solid wood fence, a move that hid him from any pursuers. Somehow he managed to scale the fence while keeping his intestines inside. Finally, Clements picked himself up and ran through the local opera house before reaching the Exchange Hotel where some staff members took him to the nearby home of one Sutton Brown, whose family took him in and put him in a bed.

They immediately summoned a physician, H. P. Luckett, who arrived quickly and began tending Clements's wounds. Those trying to help Clements were unanimous in their judgment: the man would not live through the night.[15] But somehow he did survive the night, defying the odds and eventually making a complete recovery.

The third man, Howard Townsend, miraculously escaped untouched. He made his way back to the Midland Hotel where he retrieved his weapon, a .38 caliber pistol, and headed back for the Golden Rule Saloon, determined on challenging the Reese men who had ambushed him and his cousins. It was a fool's errand that would have led most certainly to his death, but his blood was up and he was intent on revenge. Luckily, a Texas Ranger intercepted Townsend and arrested him for carrying a weapon before he could carry through on his suicidal mission.[16]

When the shooting commenced, Ranger Winfred Bates blocked the only courthouse door that was not locked and prevented several members of the Townsend party, including Sheriff Burford, from leaving and starting a bloody war on the streets of Bastrop. Ranger Will Scurry was patrolling near the Golden Rule when the shooting broke out. He immediately entered the saloon intent on arresting the multiple malefactors. But upon his entrance, at least a dozen guns covered him as Walter Reese calmly informed him to get out if he wanted to live. Scurry prudently retreated, but positioned himself close by where he could observe the saloon and its surroundings while awaiting reinforcements. The Reese party then left the saloon and (for reasons unknown) congregated at the Hodges Barber Shop nearby. Scurry followed without challenging them.[17]

Captain Brooks and City Marshal Nash were returning from the depot when they heard the shots. They spurred their horses and arrived at the scene quickly, "before the echo of the pistol shots died out," as the local newspaper put it.[18] After a tense but brief standoff, the three disarmed and arrested Walter Reese. They then returned to the saloon with other rangers and local officers, searching every man, room, and piece of luggage there, confiscating all weapons and ammunition. They arrested at least ten more men: Hub Reese, Jim Coleman, Tom Daniels, Les Reese, Buster Reese, Pee Dee Reese, Fleming Reese, August Burttschell, and Henry Burttschell. Most, according to the newspaper reports, were in an inebriated state, including their leader, Walter Reese. Considering that the circumstances now warranted it, they combed the town, taking up the weapons and ammunition they had allowed the parties to store at their hotels and boarding houses. Before they were done, they had confiscated nearly one hundred guns and believed that they had completely disarmed both factions.[19]

Rumors of the shooting reached Columbus by telephone almost immediately. A crowd gathered at the telephone office, prompting the operator to lock the doors. However, some people were so eager for the news that they scaled a telephone pole and went in through a window. Finally, the operator confirmed that the murder had occurred and offered a few details. Dr. R. H. Harrison, the highly esteemed head physician at the Southern Pacific Hospital at Glidden, had just gotten back from Bastrop. He immediately returned to care for Will Clements. Clements's wife and children also went to Bastrop.

Clements, conscious and able to speak, named Walter Reese, Jim Coleman, Tom Daniels,[20] and Les Reese[21] as the shooters. Judge Sinks called the grand jury back into session on Thursday. Six more Texas Rangers came to town, bringing the number to twelve in the total. The grand jury quickly issued two indictments for each of the four accused men, one for murder and one for assault with intent to commit murder.

That Friday, January 19, the court set the murder trials to begin on the following Monday. However, they were again delayed for a couple of more days.

On January 20, Captain Brooks and Sheriff Davis went to Austin to consult with the governor, Joseph D. Sayers, and the adjutant general, Thomas Scurry. Following the meeting, even more rangers were sent to Bastrop, bringing the total to "about twenty," according to Scurry, who went to Bastrop himself. The list now included Captains Brooks, McDonald, and Rogers. Scurry, citing a statement by Governor Sayers "that further trouble must be avoided at any cost," declared, "Strict orders are given [to the rangers in Bastrop] that any person making any demonstration such as drawing a pistol for the purpose of shooting shall be riddled with bullets." [22] The governor was serious.

Once again a special train was commissioned to take the witnesses from Columbus to Bastrop, this time numbering about 150. The train left Columbus at seven o'clock on the evening of Tuesday, January 23. Detachments of rangers under Rogers and Brooks were sent to the railroad depots at La Grange and West Point respectively, where they met the trains carrying witnesses and other people from Columbus and Yoakum to Bastrop. As the trains proceeded to Bastrop, the rangers searched the passengers and their luggage, confiscating weapons. At Bastrop, they accompanied the witnesses and others to their hotels, and remained on guard around the hotels day and night. McDonald checked all the packages coming into Bastrop and seized three pistols and some ammunition.

The court waited two days to once again postpone the trials, this time setting them for July 11. The four accused murderers remained in jail until at least February 15, when they were allowed bail: Walter Reese and Jim Coleman at $5,000 apiece, and Tom Daniels and Les Reese at $3,000.

All had friends present who agreed to put up the money. Clements, who was ambulatory by February 6, attended the bail hearings, though he was described as "somewhat thin and pale."[23] Only one entrance to the courthouse was kept open, and police officers searched every person who entered the building and the courtroom. Rangers also escorted some of the people who attended the hearings from the courthouse to their rooms. Afterwards, everyone went home. There was no further trouble.[24]

On the day he was killed, Arthur Burford's body was taken to a Bastrop undertaker, who prepared it for shipment to Weimar. The next morning, his father and friends loaded his body onto a train. He was buried among his ancestors at the small rural Osage Cemetery, northeast of Weimar, that same evening. A very large crowd of onlookers attended the ceremony. In its next edition, the *Weimar Mercury* called him "one of the most noble, upright men we ever knew" and declared that his killers were "cowardly fanatics whose very existence is a blot on civilization."[25] His mother received his last letter only after she had learned of his death.

None of the men indicted for the murder of Arthur Burford ever went to trial. Neither did Jim Townsend. The two murder cases against him, and the cases against Walter Reese, Jim Coleman, Tom Daniels, and Les Reese, were all eventually dismissed by the district court in San Antonio on November 4, 1904. As ridiculous as it might sound, one of the defense attorneys, J. M. Mathis, apparently had the last word. He argued that Burford's death was an accident because the shooter was aiming at Clements and his bullet hit the young attorney in the head by mistake, as if this were somehow exculpatory. He claimed, moreover, that the shooter's inebriated state should be considered a mitigating factor since his condition likely made aiming his gun a major problem.[26]

The case against Coleman for the murder of Larkin Hope also disappeared. It was scheduled for trial in Richmond, the county seat of Fort Bend County, on March 12, 1900, just two months after the shootings at the trial in Bastrop. Accordingly, a force of Texas Rangers arrived in Richmond to keep the peace.[27] Again, however, no trial occurred. Instead, the judge ordered the case transferred to the 37th Judicial District in Bexar County. A month later, he revoked the transfer order. The case lay dormant for another year. Then, on April 15, 1901, the judge again ordered it transferred to Bexar County, setting the scene for another chapter of private justice.[28]

The various judicial proceedings, however, kept the rangers very busy. They felt it necessary to keep a presence at all the venues, including both Bastrop and Richmond. They also maintained a more or less continuous presence in Columbus until the middle of March 1900.

Since the killing of Larkin Hope in 1898, the pendulum of public opinion had swung back and forth. Clearly no member of the Stafford family had any part in the assassination of Larkin Hope, but former friends and associates of the Staffords—a sizeable number of prominent citizens—openly applauded his death and some may even have privately encouraged it, for Larkin and his brother had gunned down Bob and John Stafford in cold blood, and he who lives by the sword dies by the sword. Thus the murder did not bring about general condemnation, though many suspected (correctly) that one or more of the Reese family had been involved. The killing of first Sam and then Dick Reese, on the other hand, definitely shifted sentiment in favor of the Reese family. But such good will as the family enjoyed largely evaporated with the murder of Arthur Burford and the cowardly manner in which it was carried out.

The shootings in Bastrop finally motivated the city government in Columbus to fill the post of city marshal. On January 22, 1900, the council approved Mayor Williams's appointment of Gunger Wooldridge, a friend of the Townsends, as marshal. It was a sign that whatever sympathy the city council might have had for the Reese faction had evaporated.

The shooting at Bastrop created a sensation, generating more press coverage than any other episode since the deaths of the Stafford brothers, ten years previous. Several out of state newspapers picked up on the story[29] while every major newspaper in the state felt obliged to devote front page attention, often announced in sensational headlines, such as: "A BLOODY TRAGEDY ENACTED/OUTBURST OF AN OLD FEUD,"[30] or again, "COLORADO COUNTY FEUD BROKEN OUT."[31] The leading role played by the rangers as well as the direct involvement of the adjutant general and governor definitely added to the high dramatic contour of the story.

Adding to the poignancy of the death of Arthur Burford, On January 23, 1900, eight days after he was killed in Bastrop, his sister-in-law, Jessie Burford, delivered a son. The newborn was given the name Arthur Lee Burford, in honor of his recently buried uncle.[32]

The affray also became a cause for reflection by several editors across the state. The *Weimar Mercury* called the many postponements and continuances, "Another black eye for justice!"[33] On February 10 the *Mercury* reprinted an article from the *Beeville Bee*, which hit the mark: "It is safe to say," the editor opined, "continued postponements can be had until an acquittal can be secured. It is a deplorable fact that under the maladministration of justice in Texas no man of prominence with money and friends can be convicted."[34]

It was clear that the new century had not brought about a revised and more civilized sensibility concerning private justice.

Old attitudes of family honor and extralegal action, forged over many decades of frontier and Reconstruction violence, had survived the turn of the century intact, leading, once again, to tragic consequences for an innocent bystander.

The Reese family remained unrepentant and unapologetic. In *Flaming Feuds of Colorado County* Walter and Lillian Reese devote a mere six pages to the Bastrop shooting and offer an account of the shooting that conflicts in every particular with the sworn testimony of several eyewitnesses. Accordingly, Walter Reese maintains that he stepped outside of the saloon to offer Will Clements a fair chance to pull his pistol, for he intended to shoot him for publicly insulting his mother. Clements, by this version, then saved himself by "throwing" young Burford in front of himself to save his own scalp, whereupon he commenced running "like a scared rabbit." In a subsequent paragraph, the book emphasizes that Arthur Burford had been forewarned not to associate with Will Clements, as if this somehow mitigated the circumstances of his death. The brother and sister then devote the remainder of the chapter to cataloging the insults that both his mother and aunt, Mrs. Joe Lessing, had endured at the hands of the Mark Townsend faction.

The passage shows clearly the intense humiliation the Reese family had felt as a result of being banished from the fold by Mark Townsend. One gets the sense that the brothers and cousins of Sam and Dick Reese who were also in the Golden Rule Saloon were looking only to avenge the deaths of their brothers and uncles, but for Walter Reese it was more than that. It was a question of Townsend family pride, turned inside out. Will Clements, through his taunts and insults, had rubbed salt into the wound, and so was clearly marked for revenge. But the three cousins walking down the street, also relatives of Walter Reese, represented the branch of the Townsends to which the Reese family no longer belonged;

for Walter Reese they had also become the enemy. Myopic hatred of this intensity was bound to generate another episode in the feud, and it was not long in coming.

Reacting to the growing atmosphere of hostility in Columbus, Keetie Reese, son Herbert, and daughters, Sadie and Lillie, moved away from town on January 23, 1900, while her older son Walter still awaited a bond hearing in the Bastrop County jail. One report stated that they moved to Smithville, another that they intended to open a hotel in Victoria.[35] If they went to either place, they did not remain long. Before the summer, they had settled in Rosenberg, in Fort Bend County, but they retained possession of their home and farm in Colorado County.

Soon after the relocation to Rosenberg, Walter, still under indictment for murder and attempted murder but now out on bond, joined his mother and siblings, and (unbelievably) was hired on as a deputy constable. Even more astonishingly, Jim Coleman, also under a double indictment for murder, soon joined Reese as a deputy sheriff of Fort Bend County. Their new neighbors would soon come to regret their presence.[36]

About six o'clock on the evening of July 31, 1900, almost six months to the day after the events in Bastrop, Deputy Walter Reese and his friend Jim Coleman hurried to the Rosenberg railroad depot of the Southern Pacific in time to greet the eastbound passenger train from Columbus. Both men were armed with Winchester rifles and pistols. Rosenberg, a relatively young town, had sprung up on the Katy prairie in the 1890s just to the west of Richmond, the county seat of Fort Bend County, at a junction of three railroad lines. All passenger trains from the west, including Columbus, passed through Rosenberg on their way to Houston and points east, and most were obliged to make a stop. On board the train were five men from Colorado County, including Will Clements and Mark Townsend. Clements, only recently recovered from his wounds in Bastrop, had resumed his duties as deputy sheriff. With Clements and Townsend were Clements's older brother, Jim, newly appointed Columbus City Marshal Gunger Wooldridge, and Frank "Red" Burford. Will Clements had been the object of the attack in Bastrop that had left Arthur Burford an innocent victim. But Walter Reese had also sworn vengeance on Mark Townsend, whom he held responsible above all for the death of his father.[37] At least two of the Townsend men on the train were armed.

Frank Burford was from Belton, but had undertaken the study of law and had been living in Columbus with Mark Townsend. He was a first cousin of Townsend's wife, Annie, and the nephew of Colorado County's sheriff, Will Burford. He was inclined to violence. Only two years before, on August 19, 1898, while serving as a private in the First Texas Cavalry at Brownsville, he had stabbed and killed another private in his unit, Dan McCarty. After moving to Columbus, he certainly became known to Reese and Coleman. Still, except for his relationship to Mark Townsend and Sheriff Burford, he had no reason to be involved.[38]

As the train pulled into the station, Gunger Wooldridge spied Reese and Coleman from his window seat, rifles in hand, approaching along the platform, and turned to warn Will Clements. Their presence, as several witnesses who were in the passenger car later testified, was not unexpected. The marshal urged Clements to hide whereupon he positioned himself at the end of the car and out of view of Reese and Coleman. Coleman stepped into another car, took a quick look around, then exited back onto the platform and rejoined Reese. Together they moved down the length of the train, peering into the windows of the cars one by one and questioning the porters. When Coleman spotted someone from the Townsend group sitting in the train, he raised his Winchester as if to fire through the window. Suddenly, gunfire erupted from both sides. Several shots from Reese and Coleman shattered the windows of the train and set the fifteen or so passengers inside scurrying for cover while those on the platform scattered "like quail," as one witness put it, over the wet and boggy prairie in all directions away from the station. Clements emerged from the car's doorway, six-shooter drawn, to confront Reese. Each fired at the other more or less simultaneously, Reese with his Winchester and Clements with his six-shooter. Reese, hit in the hip, went down. Burford, apparently armed with a shotgun, also opened up from the train and some of the shot also struck Reese. Coleman was hit three times, once in each arm and once in the back. The last wound was very severe and thought to be fatal. During the brief but intense exchange of gunfire, between fifteen and twenty shots were fired.[39]

The train had started moving even as the shooting commenced, and it was soon well down the track toward Houston, ending the fight. The telegraph operator in Rosenberg wired ahead and when the train arrived in Houston, the two shooters, Frank Burford and Will Clements, were arrested for the wounding of Coleman and Reese. The others in the party, including Mark Townsend, were not implicated and took rooms at the Capitol Hotel. The two men in custody were taken back to Fort Bend County the next day, where both were released on $250 bail.[40] Curiously, neither Coleman nor Reese faced charges.

Once again headlines across the state announced the shoot-out in lurid terms.[41] The *Houston Post* sent a reporter to interview members of the Townsend party: those in jail and those at the hotel. Both declined to discuss the events leading up to the shooting, but Gunger Wooldridge gave a detailed account of the actual shoot-out as it had unfolded. A passenger who witnessed the affray, whom the *Post* article quoted at length, corroborated his account. All the other papers that covered the event, including the *Weimar Mercury*, clipped the *Post* article verbatim.

The reader, therefore, is left with a fairly accurate account of how the shoot-out unfolded, but is left with many questions concerning the lead-up. Why were five men led by Mark Townsend, at least two of them armed, on a train heading for Houston? How did Walter Reese and Jim Coleman know that the Townsend party would be on board the train?

Walter Reese, apparently unhappy with the *Post* coverage, wrote a long letter to the editor the day after the shooting giving his version of events.[42] The Reese account, repeated in *Flaming Feuds of Colorado County*, offered a more or less accurate account of the shooting, with the exception that he most certainly exaggerated the number of shots fired (thirty to forty). The assertion that he and Clements had approached the train, armed with rifles and six-shooters, merely to retrieve his brother Hub Reese's hand luggage is also not credible.

Drawing from all the sources and accounts, the most plausible explanation is as follows: during this period of time Mark Townsend was involved in several large land deals, including the development and sale of large tracts of land in the Panhandle of Texas. These dealings required much travel, often reported in the papers of the period, which probably explain his conspicuous absence from the Bastrop trials.

Knowing that Walter Reese and Jim Coleman had moved to Rosenberg and that both had become law officers and thus legally permitted to carry guns, Mark Townsend was wary to travel through Rosenberg without body guards, which the local sheriff's office and city government conveniently supplied. By chance, Walter's younger brother Hub Reese, who was only nineteen years of age, happened to board the same train. Discovering this, the Townsend party began to harass and bully the younger Reese, who had a delicate, almost effeminate build, at which time he removed himself and took a seat in the coach reserved for blacks. He got off the train at the first opportunity (Eagle Lake) and called ahead by telephone to his brother in Rosenberg to report the incident and inform Walter that both Mark Townsend and Will Clements were on board. In the meantime, the Townsend group must have anticipated that the younger Reese would make the call, and thus were prepared for Reese and Coleman when the train pulled into the station. It is highly unlikely that the Townsend party had actually travelled to Rosenberg to seek out a fight with Walter Reese and Jim Coleman. Had this been their intention, all in the party, including Mark Townsend, would assuredly have armed themselves, and not just Burford and Clements.

Nonetheless, Will Clements, at least, must have been happy with the outcome, for he (with the help of Frank Burford) had managed to best his adversaries in a more or less fair shoot-out of two against two, a sweet measure of revenge on behalf of the whole Mark Townsend faction for the Bastrop ambush.

Once again Dr. Harrison from Columbus took the first available train to Rosenberg to minister to both Walter Reese and Jim Coleman's wounds. His competence was obviously appreciated by both factions. Walter Reese's wounds proved to be serious, but not life threatening. Coleman's wounds, on the other hand, were at first thought to be fatal. His brother, Tom Coleman, and two sisters, Lizzie and Rosa Coleman, rushed to Rosenberg to be at his bedside but, similar to Will Clements, he eventually made a full recovery.[43]

The shoot-out also became another cause for reflection on the part of the editor of the *Weimar Mercury*. Under the heading "Chronic Gun Toters" the editor lamented, "Feuds there will be to the end of time, but civilized society cannot maintain its influence and tolerate feudists going into public places and shooting down one another if they can and innocent bystander if these happen to be in the way."[44] In a later edition, the same editor referred to an article in the *Memphis Commercial Appeal*, which had referenced the Rosenberg affair and pointed out that Texas had a murder rate double that of any other state. The editor took issue with the tone of the article but conceded that, "this statement, however, should set Texas people to thinking seriously over this homicidal matter. It is giving our state a very black name abroad, and should be frowned upon and discouraged in every way possible."[45]

1900 was not a good year for the Reese family. The events at Bastrop had been disastrous in terms of public opinion, and then there was the sheer expense of all the legal proceedings. The outcome of the Rosenberg shoot-out only made matters worse. Although neither Walter Reese nor Jim Coleman faced charges as a result of the affray, they both had to seek other employment. Walter Reese, who had never really taken up a profession, though he was in his mid-twenties, moved to Shiner, closer to Reese relatives in Lavaca County, where he took a position briefly as a clerk in a store, the first of many odd jobs and half-hearted business ventures he would pursue, punctuated by occasional stints as a lawman.

From this point, the feud went into a six-year hibernation only to reemerge with a vengeance in 1906. In the meantime, the constellation of political and social forces that had kept the Townsend faction in control of the sheriff's office in Colorado County for the past twenty-five years had changed dramatically, the focus of the next chapter.

CHAPTER SEVEN

The Interim

The events of 1899 and 1900 had left Mark Townsend and his allies firmly in control of law enforcement in Colorado County. The Reese attempt to challenge Townsend by both legal and extralegal means had failed miserably, and even led Keetie, the widow of Sam Reese and the matriarch of the family, to pack up and move away from Colorado County. The Reese family had been expelled, literally and figuratively, from the circle of power and influence built up and maintained over the years by Mark and Light Townsend with the help of the black vote. But events larger than an internal dynastic row portended the end of Townsend dominance.

Will Burford ran for reelection in 1900,[1] but drew a strong opponent in W. E. "Dick" Bridge, a fifty-year-old resident of Columbus. Burford had been overheard to say that the sheriff's office had brought him nothing but heartache and pain and had been a financial burden on his family. During the election he felt it necessary to write a letter to the editor of the *Citizen* countering these rumors.[2] Sympathy existed for Burford over the loss of his son, but there was also an undertow of resentment. Burford represented a power structure that many in the white community had long resented and now considered a relic of the past. On Election Day, Burford lost Columbus, but garnered comfortable majorities in Eagle Lake and Weimar. Burford won with 54 percent of the vote, but this was closer than anticipated.³ Once again, the black vote reduced the margin of his loss in Columbus and carried the day in Eagle Lake, while hometown sentiment bolstered his tally in Weimar.

Meanwhile, the influence of the Republican Party had waned over the years both statewide and at the county level. On June 5, 1900, the county's Republican Party held its convention in Columbus, nominated no one, and accomplished little. In a meeting described by the *Weimar Mercury* as "an exceeding tame affair," the party agreed to support all of the county's existing office holders (all Democrats or Independents).

The situation for black people had also eroded steadily since the conservative wing of the Democratic Party had ousted Governor Davis and the Reconstruction party in 1875. The Texas Legislature passed the first "Jim Crow" ordinances in 1891 and the law was made more and more restrictive in subsequent years. Columbus City Marshal Ike Towell took it upon himself to enforce segregation at the Columbus train station as early as 1887 and prior to the passage of the state law. (See Goeppinger Interview #3) These ordinances became ever more restrictive as they spread across the South so that by 1900, a rigid system of so-called "separate but equal" regulations governed what black people could and could not do whenever they were in public places. Law officers enforced the rules, but when blacks overstepped the line, there was also the threat of mob violence and terroristic action on the part of the Ku Klux Klan and similar organizations dedicated to white supremacy.⁴

For die-hard ex-Confederates and conservatives, who had made it their mission to deconstruct all laws and initiatives from the Reconstruction Era that sought to put blacks on an equal footing with whites, this was not enough. Black people still had the right to vote, and this became the focus of their final assault. Neighboring Fort Bend, Matagorda, and Wharton counties had shown the way with the organization of a White Man's Union and the introduction of the first White Man's primaries in the state in 1898.[5] The idea for an exclusionary primary, however, had gained support among a wider swath of the white electorate in Colorado County than out-and-out avowed racists. This was because the proposal was packaged and promoted in the first instance as a "reform" measure to purge the system of corruption, which many agreed had gotten out of hand and had been particularly egregious in the previous two election cycles.

Since being granted the right to vote, black voters had naturally preferred Republican candidates so long as the party was still viable, especially on the state and national slates. At the county level, however, they often exhibited more flexibility, preferring to vote for the man rather than the party. Thus all but the extreme conservative faction had felt obliged to court the black vote to one degree or another, and this often led to excesses. The most common practice was to throw free barbeques, at which time the candidates would introduce themselves and make their appeal. But there was undeniably much out-and-out bribery as well, a practice universally known as the "boodle." It should be made clear that there is little evidence that the black electorate as a whole could ever be persuaded (or bribed) to vote against their fundamental self-interests. Still, there was undeniably widespread discontent about the situation among the white electorate, even among those who were inclined to be sympathetic to black people.

On June 7, 1902, local Democrats held their convention at the Stafford Opera House, and changed the face of politics in the county for years to come. Hundreds attended in what was described as the "most harmonious" convocation in decades.[6] After agreeing to support certain candidates at the state and district level, the Democrats decided not to nominate any candidates for county or precinct offices. Instead, as declared, "we believe it to be for the best interests of Colorado County that the white voters of the county irrespective of party should control its politics and policies."[7]

They set the White Man's primary election for July 19, 1902, and declared that "only white citizens of said county, qualified under the constitution and laws of Texas to vote shall participate."[8] They made each candidate who entered the primary swear that if he lost, he would not seek by other means any county office in the November general election. The meeting closed with acknowledgement of the new White Man's Party chairman, and a lusty singing of "For He's a Jolly Good Fellow."

An 1898 example from neighboring Wharton County underscored that anyone who decided to go against the new system did so at his own peril. An area newspaper reported: "Hope Adams, independent candidate for sheriff, was shot and killed this afternoon. The death of Adams was the result of a street fight growing out of political difficulties."[9] The episode served to reinforce the perception that those who were determined to exclude the black population from local elections were deadly serious.

The date set for the primaries was Saturday, July 19, 1902. Burford and Bridge again ran for sheriff. Two other candidates joined them: Henry S. Williams, the mayor of Columbus and the man whose young son had been seriously wounded by a stray bullet at the killing of Sam Reese in 1899, and William R. Kinard, the city marshal of Eagle Lake. With black voters effectively disenfranchised, only two-thirds as many people voted in the primary on July 19 as had voted in the general election in 1900. Blacks constituted 43 percent of the county's population in 1900. Black exclusion from the White Man's Primary accounts for the extreme reduction in voter turnout. Only two candidates lost their bids for reelection, but one of those was Sheriff Burford. Bridge won by 275 votes, with a count of 1,097 to Burford's 822. Bridge got only 500 fewer votes than he had two years earlier; Burford more than 1000. The sheriff, predictably, lost considerable support in Eagle Lake and Columbus, both towns with large black populations. Kinard siphoned off 174 votes in that city, but, whereas Burford had gotten 423 votes there in 1900, he got only 31 in 1902. Thus, though it would not be official until the general election in November, Burford became a lame duck sheriff.[10]

The Reese brothers, Walter and Hub, campaigned actively for Dick Bridge during this election cycle. Bridge, however, was not a party to either faction so the Reese involvement in the campaign appears to have been more a gesture against Sheriff Burford than a mark of active support for Bridge. In *Flaming Feuds of Colorado County*, Lillian Reese devotes several pages to the campaign and inserts two anti-Burford poems composed by Walter Reese, who fancied himself quite an orator. The poems are of dubious literary worth, but they do throw some light on an interesting dynamic to the elections in both 1900 and 1902. The accidental killing of the German farmer Boehme during the street fight in 1899 where Sam Reese was killed had deeply alienated the German community and the Reeses attempted to exploit this backlash for political gain.

It was while serving as a lame duck that Burford encountered his most difficult case. In early October 1902, a mob led by over a hundred men from Eagle Lake broke into the Columbus jail and forcibly removed a young black man, Davis "Utt" Duncan, who had been accused of the rape of a white woman in Eagle Lake. The mob took him to the grove north of town and lynched him.[11] Burford left the sheriff's office with the stain of a lynching on his record, but in truth both he and his wife Martha, who had bravely confronted the mob in the absence of the sheriff, had done all in their power to prevent the mob action. In this case, at least, he had stood firm against the exercise of private justice.

This episode, unfortunately, was not the only incident of mob violence during the period directed against blacks in the county. At least two other lynchings occurred in Colorado County, both in Weimar.[12]

After losing his bid for reelection as sheriff in 1902, Will Burford retired to his Columbus home. He placed his name on the ballot again in 1904, but once again lost. He died in Columbus November 3, 1908, ten years to the day after he had first been elected sheriff. He had been in poor health for several months, though he was only fifty-eight years old. His wife, Martha, who had stood up to the lynch mob at the jail in 1902, lived on until December 9, 1929, when she died at the age of seventy-three.[13]

The loss of the sheriff's office in 1902 marked the end of Townsend dominance of county politics. Mark Townsend had won the feud (so it seemed), but his machine had lost the election, which had immediate personal ramifications concerning his own security. The episode in Rosenberg, where both a deputy sheriff and a city marshal had accompanied him on a business trip, exemplified this habit of using local lawmen as private body guards, which, from the standpoint of Townsend, had worked to perfection on this particular occasion. His men probably saved his life in the shoot-out, but they also bore the brunt of the legal fall-out, mild as it was, which Townsend avoided. The city council of Columbus abolishing the city marshal's office on January 5, 1903 was also a further setback for Townsend.[14]

After the election of 1902 the feud parted ways with its ostensible cause, namely control of the sheriff's office, and simply continued from its own momentum. Such a dynamic usually provides the essential ingredient of a *bona fide* feud: henceforth a primal, preemptive fear and/or an exaggerated sense of family honor, which demanded revenge for past grievances, provided the sole drivers for continued bloodshed.

With the defeat of Sheriff Burford and the demise of the Townsend machine, Mark Townsend and his close allies, Will Clements, Jim Townsend, and Marion Hope, now felt vulnerable and exposed, and over the next few years all departed Columbus for other places. Walter and Hub Reese still had supporters in Columbus, principally among former friends and associates of the Stafford brothers, men who still harbored an intense hatred for Mark Townsend and his allies. The Townsend faction, however, could no longer count on law enforcement to shield them from their enemies. Several incidents from the period underscored this reality.

John Goeppinger has left an account of one such episode. According to this, Goeppinger, at the behest of a group of men friendly to Reese and the Staffords, bushwhacked and killed a black foreman who worked at the Townsend farm southwest of town simply because he was a Townsend man. (See Goeppinger interview #6) The incident never made the headlines, and there is no record of charges being filed.

In the spring of 1905, another incident in Houston had emphasized that the feud had merely gone underground and that the old feelings were still alive. Frank *"Red"* Burford, the nephew of Townsend and a participant in the Rosenberg shoot-out, faced charges of unlawfully carrying a pistol in Houston. Sam B. Bates, a former ranger who had been stationed in Columbus and present in Bastrop during the affray there, had resigned from the rangers to become a deputy constable in Houston. Familiar with all the parties involved, he noticed members of both factions were in town. Desirous of avoiding trouble, he took the precaution of arresting Burford at the Rice Hotel.[15] In the course of his trial before the justice of the peace for illegally carrying a pistol, Burford took the stand in his own defense and rehashed the whole story of the feud in great detail.[16] Burford testified, "that he stood in imminent danger of Walter Reese of this city," who formerly resided in Colorado County. He testified further that Reese had "made many threats against his life that had been communicated to him." He had come to Houston on business, had seen Reese, and armed himself for protection.[17] Nonetheless, Burford was found guilty and fined twenty-five dollars.

It was too much for Mark Townsend. At the end of 1905 he also closed down his Columbus residence, withdrew from active involvement in the local law firm, and moved with his family to San Antonio, where he felt removed from the feud and its lingering legacy. But, as will be seen in the next chapter, the feud was long from being over and was destined to follow him.

CHAPTER EIGHT

The 1906 Skating Rink Shoot-out

By 1906 the shootings at Bastrop and Rosenberg had receded into the past. The Townsend political machine that had controlled law enforcement in the county for decades was a relic of a bygone era. Mark Townsend now resided in San Antonio where he presided over his far-flung business empire and also served as the lead attorney for the Southern Pacific Railroad in Texas. The rapidly expanding rice industry, which Mark Townsend and Will Burford had helped to pioneer with the establishment of the Red Bluff Irrigation Company and the town of Garwood in 1901, attracted Will Clements to Wharton County where his brother Jim Clements had established a large and successful rice farm at Lane City. Jim Townsend also made the move with his family to the area. For the time being Marion Hope remained. He opened up a saloon in the railroad community of Glidden a mile west of Columbus, but later testified that he lived in constant fear of his life from the Reese boys and from Jim Coleman.[1]

Keetie Reese still made her home at Rosenberg while Walter Reese had taken a job as a sergeant with the McCain Detective Agency in Houston.[2] Lillian Reese, the youngest of the Reese siblings, had moved to Austin where she established a music school, the Austin Conservatory.[3] Matters had quieted down to the point that Walter and Hub now felt comfortable to return to Columbus from time to time where they still had a house, loyal friends, and a farm to manage.

When the brothers showed up in the summer of 1906, however, it left many in the city uneasy. Although Marion Hope had exchanged his grocery story business in downtown Columbus for a saloon in Glidden, he alone among the former Townsend faction remained and was still very much in evidence. He also harbored a deep resentment against the Reese brothers for the assassination of his brother Larkin in 1898. The Reese brothers, on the other hand, remained convinced that Hope was one of the co-assassins of their father in 1899. Trouble between them was not unexpected for it seemed inevitable that their paths should cross.[4]

An altercation was not long in coming. For the summer season the upper floor of the Stafford Opera House had been converted into a skating rink, a popular venue for young and old alike to see and be seen. On Saturday morning, July 5, 1906, Hub Reese entered the rink around 10:30 and, according to John Goeppinger, strapped on a pair of roller shoes and joined the flow of the reveling crowd. As he passed by one end of the bleachers, Marion Hope stuck the lit end of a cigar in his face and cursed him. The provocation resulted in a fracas in which Reese was choked, pushed in a corner, and slapped in the face.[5]

After the altercation, four men dispersed in different directions, each intent on arming himself for the coming confrontation, which appeared inevitable. Hub Reese, smarting from his abuse and humiliation, hurried home, which was only a block and a half away, and returned with his brother Walter, one armed with a rifle, the other with a shotgun. Marion Hope exited the rink and went up Milam Street to the Franz saloon, which was in the middle of the block and opposite the courthouse. He had stashed a shotgun and pistol in the establishment for just such a contingency. Hiram Clements, younger brother of Will Clements, had also been present at the altercation and hurried to the law offices of Townsend, Foard, and Thompson, located on the north side of the square, where he secured a Winchester rifle. Dr. Joe Lessing, Jr., the brother-in-law of Hub Reese and half-brother of Marion Hope, hastened to his office on the second floor of the building on the corner of Milam and Walnut streets where he also kept a weapon.

In the meantime, Marion Hope, now armed with a shotgun and a pistol, found a place of concealment at the Zumwalt drugstore, the next to the last building at the corner of Milam and Walnut streets. According to one detailed account, Walter and Hub went across the courthouse square to the Stafford Opera House only to learn that Hope had departed. The brothers then proceeded up Milam Street checking each building in turn. As they neared the Franz Saloon, Hope jumped out from his place of concealment at the drugstore and unloaded on the two with his double-barreled shotgun. The brothers went down, wounded in the arms and legs, but still able to return fire.

A general discharge of firearms from several points then ensued, in the course of which bullets flew indiscriminately in all directions. Witnesses testified that about twelve shots were fired. A fine mule that had the misfortune to be in the way of one stray bullet fell dead while numerous windows, awnings, and door facings suffered damage as well. The battle could be heard throughout the town sending throngs into the streets in stunned amazement. Sheriff W. E. Bridge was absent from the city for the day. Constable John Hester, being the only peace officer available, rushed to the scene and with the aid of several citizens formed an armed cordon around the Reese brothers.[6] They then escorted them to their home. They also secured Marion Hope at the drugstore where he had taken up position.[7]

When the smoke finally cleared and the parties separated, it was discovered that Hiram Clements of the opposing side also had been severely wounded. Clements, armed with a Winchester, had emerged from the post office next to the law office when the shooting commenced. It appeared as if he were fired on from behind, which would have made it improbable that the Reese boys could have been responsible since they were to the south of Hope and Clements. Two bullets had struck him, both passing clear through his upper torso. His weapon appeared never to have been fired. He staggered back to the steps of the law office, collapsed, and was dragged inside. He clung to life throughout the day and night but succumbed to his wounds around 1:30 on Sunday morning.

Just who had fired the shots that killed Clements remained something of a mystery until sometime later. Suspicion quickly fell on the dentist, Dr. Joseph Franklin Lessing, Jr. From his second story office window he had a clear field of view at the action below. He also had a motive for firing the fatal shots.

Dr. Lessing, although a half-brother of Marion Hope, had married Nuddie Ela Reese, one of the daughters of Sam Reese, his own second cousin, and become an ardent supporter of the Reese side. The battle, as it turned out, took place exclusively among the grandchildren of Asa and Spencer Townsend: Hiram Clements and the Reese brothers descending from the Spencer line; Marion Hope and Dr. Lessing from the Asa line.[8]

Hiram Clements was just twenty-four years old, married with a baby girl, and worked for the Southern Pacific in Glidden. The newspaper described him as, "an energetic, hustling young man, of sober habits, and popular among his friends and associates, who deeply and sincerely deplore his tragic death."[9] Up to this point, he had had no connection to the feud, other than the fact that he was the younger brother of Will Clements.[10]

When Sheriff Bridge returned to Columbus the following day he arrested all the parties involved and placed them in the county jail.[11] Curiously, the rifle Lessing had allegedly used could never be located, so the charge against him remained circumstantial and was eventually dropped. Many years later, as related by John Goeppinger, the tree in front of the upstairs window of Dr. Lessing was cut down. The long-missing Winchester was found inside, now rusted and unserviceable. Lessing had apparently disposed of it hastily in a hollow in the tree where it remained unknown and forgotten for many years, finally to emerge and corroborate the suspicion that Lessing had indeed fired the shots that killed Hiram Clements. (see Goeppinger interview #7.)

After their release on bond July 14, the *Weimar Mercury* reported that Herbert Reese had since been seen about town and at the courthouse in the company of friends.[12] The younger Reese, often the victim of bullying and the brunt of jokes because of his delicate frame and musical inclinations, had, if nothing else, showed pluck in confronting his tormentors at the side of his brother in the shoot-out. The same issue, however, also reported that Dr. Lessing's mother was said to be beside herself with grief as Marion Hope and Dr. Lessing, both her sons, had most likely traded shots in the affray.[13]

Once again, armed parties began arriving by train. The three brothers of Hiram Clements—Will, Jim, and Fulton—took up temporary residence in the Townsend law office next to the post office. David Larkin Hope, the son of the slain Larkin Hope, joined them. He had recently married Alice Clements, younger sister of the Clements brothers, continuing the tradition of marrying within the family.[14] The Reese boys, in the meantime, had chosen to stay at the farm east of town.

The shoot-out provoked an immediate outpouring of disgust and outrage among the preponderance of citizens in the community. Many had hoped that the dormant feud was a thing of the past—a feud that had depressed business and given the community a black eye for many years. Enough was enough; the situation required dramatic action.

On July 19, the citizens called for a mass meeting at the courthouse.[15] The assembled citizens elected J. W. Towell chairman and appointed a committee to visit the feudists and, if possible, arrange a truce.[16] Once again the call went out for the rangers from Sheriff Bridge and Judge Kennon. As the local paper pointed out, the presence of rangers always had a calming effect when the potential for further violence was there.

This time Ranger Captain John R. Hughes answered the call with privates Tom Ross, H. A. Carnes, and J. C. White.[17] The rangers arrived July 18, 1906. In his first communication to the adjutant general, Captain Hughes reported "that the Clements party have left town temporarily. The people were very uneasy yesterday as some of both sides were in town and the Clements boys were housed up in a law office."[18] Governor Lanham also sent word that he had agreed to post a ranger indefinitely at Columbus. Accordingly, Ranger White remained in Columbus after Captain Hughes and the other rangers departed in September. The *Weimar Mercury* reported that he was "affable and well liked."[19]

The first meeting presented certain demands to city government, but these requests were not satisfactorily addressed. The foot-dragging on the part of city officials called to mind the unfortunate political squabbles of the past that had hamstrung city government and, in the minds of many, contributed to the culture of gun violence in the town. The practice of deputizing partisan individuals, who would then be able to legally carry pistols, was especially egregious in the past. This time the situation had changed: the city refused to reestablish the office of city marshal, which had been done away with in 1903.

On July 24, therefore, Chairman Towell called another mass meeting for the purpose of solving the impasse by disincorporation. If city government would not cooperate it would be disbanded entirely, a dramatic, almost histrionic measure, but one which showed how fed up the citizens had become with the feud.[20] The resolution to do so passed unanimously; a petition was handed over to the county judge who ordered an election. "Chairman Towell," the *Weimar Mercury* reported, "is not leaving a stone unturned to prevent further trouble upon our streets."[21]

Commissioner's Court ordered an election and on August 8, 1906, the City of Columbus held a referendum, resulting in a vote of ninety-nine for and thirty-five against abolishment of city government.[22] The measure carried easily, and the county duly petitioned the state to dissolve the city's charter, which was granted. The county government then assumed administrative and law enforcement responsibilities for the city, and this situation endured for twelve years until the city finally reincorporated.

The frantic measure raised eyebrows across the state. The *San Antonio Light*, to take one example, responded with the headline: "COLORADO COUNTY DISGRACED."[23]

The grand jury convened in September and, once again, no-billed all the participants in the street fight. The action was emblematic of the almost schizophrenic reflex within the community to the shoot-out: on the one hand, the citizens were willing to do away with city government, but, on the other hand, they refused to hold anyone accountable before a court of law.

The shoot-out on the courthouse square in 1906 was the last major episode of the feud to take place in Colorado County,[24] but it was not, unfortunately, the last chapter in the feud. The next episode of private justice would follow Mark Townsend to San Antonio where he had moved in 1905.

CHAPTER NINE

The Assassination of Jim Coleman

After the big shoot-out on the streets of Columbus in the summer of 1906, Marion Hope traded the saloon business in Glidden for another saloon in Lane City in Wharton County where Jim and Will Clements as well as Jim Townsend now lived. The area to the south, it seems, had become a safe enclave for former supporters of Mark Townsend. After the death of his first wife, Hope had remarried and, in a familiar replay, once again chose to wed within the family, this time to a second cousin, the daughter of Jim Townsend. It appeared as if the intensity of the family conflict had somehow reinforced this old habit on both sides of the conflict.

With most of the confederates of Mark Townsend now residing in Wharton and Matagorda counties, the Reese family felt comfortable in taking up full-time residence in Columbus for a while. Lillian Reese had already made the move in 1906 while her mother soon followed suit. In June 1907 Hub Reese married Ivy Ilse at the First Baptist Church in Houston. The bride was the daughter of a prominent Columbus businessman. Only a small crowd of relatives and close friends attended the ceremony. There is no clear reason why the wedding was conducted in Houston rather than in Columbus, where both the bride and groom lived. Perhaps the family feared one of their enemies might disrupt the ceremony. In any case, Hub and Iva Reese returned to Columbus to start their married lives. Later that year in November, Walter Reese returned to Columbus and purchased a brick livery stable, formerly the possession of Thomas Bouldin.[1]

For Will Clements, the habit of violence and extra-legality was hard to put aside and found fresh expression in his new home at Lane City. In 1907 two incidents involving Will Clements's wife led to two deaths: one a white man, the other a black man. On April 12 Clements shot and killed a young white man by the name of Sam Grace in Matagorda County. According to the newspaper reports of the incident, Grace, who lived on a neighboring farm, had insulted his wife.[2] An examining trial took place April 17.[3] Marion Hope and his nephew David Hope made the trip to Wharton to attend the hearing.[4] Family and friends helped to raise $5,000 for Will's release when he was granted bail. But, like a broken record, once again a case of private justice died on a technicality and never came to trial.

In December of the same year, Will Clements unexpectedly returned to his house and heard screams in the back yard. He rushed through the house to find a black man attempting to assault his wife. Seeing Clements, the assailant released his grip and made his escape, leaving the wife unharmed. Clements quickly got up a posse of friends and neighbors and succeeded in capturing the man, whom they then lynched without making any attempt to involve the authorities. He faced no legal charges for the action. The paper remarked that it was the first episode of this nature in recent memory.

After recovering from his wounds at Rosenberg, Jim Coleman continued to drift around, never really taking up a serious profession and becoming, by the Reese family's own admission, ever more addicted to opiates and strong drink.[5]

The final change of venue for the murder of Larkin Hope brought Jim Coleman to San Antonio for the winter term of district court in 1906/1907, where the local district attorney refused to try the case due to lack of evidence. Coleman, however, stayed in the city after the legal procedures were behind him, but it did not take him long to run afoul of the local police in a case that put him in the headlines. A San Antonio constable, Charles Stevens, arrested Coleman for illegally carrying a pistol. Coleman's defense was that his possession was legal because none other than the mayor of the city had deputized him as part of a posse that was searching for one "Bub" Williams, a man wanted for assaulting a policeman and stealing his gun. The case went this way and that and took on farcical proportions, but eventually Coleman was found innocent.[6]

Naturally Mark Townsend took note of Coleman's presence in the city, and it is safe to assume it made him very uneasy. However disconcerting the feud had grown to be, Mark Townsend probably clearly comprehended what had motivated and stirred his Reese kinsman to seek revenge for the humiliations his family had suffered, for they both drew inspiration from an extreme code of family honor that condoned private justice, a code they both shared and understood. Had the shoe been on the other foot, Mark Townsend may well have acted as the Reese brothers had. Jim Coleman was different. Where his homicidal tendencies sprang from was less fathomable, and, hence, more frightening. No immediate stake in Townsend family honor had spurred him to murder Larkin Hope, to take part in the Bastrop killing, or to join Walter Reese on the train platform in Rosenberg. Rather, in the course of events, he had simply developed a bottomless hatred for Mark Townsend, and he was a killer.

This observation is the key to what happened next. Now seemingly a full-time resident of San Antonio, Coleman supported himself by taking on odd detective jobs and was engaged that spring in trying to recover a lost ring for a young San Antonio socialite, Edna Neuman. Mark Townsend, in the meantime, hired a couple of former city detectives, Frank Maibaum and George Shoaf, to keep tabs on Coleman and ascertain his intentions. He also hired J. W. Kincheloe,[7] a former lawman from Wharton County, whom John Goeppinger described as "badder than hell," to be his private bodyguard. (See Goeppinger Interview #12) He also sent word to Marion Hope that he could also use his services as a bodyguard. Hope responded by moving temporarily to San Antonio and taking a room at a boarding house the first part of May 1907. As part of their job, the private detectives Shoaf and Maibaum befriended Coleman and became parties, perhaps unwittingly, to a premeditated and orchestrated assassination; Mark Townsend, it seems, had decided to strike preemptively.

Coleman may have suspected Shoaf and Maibaum were playing a double game with him, but, if he did, he kept it to himself until the day of his death. On May 17, 1907, Will Clements, still under indictment for the murder of Sam Grace but free on bail, also arrived on the evening train from Lane City where he still made his home, presumably to reinforce Hope and Kincheloe. On the evening of May 18, 1907, Hope and Clements took a stroll downtown, where they joined up with Kincheloe. Hope was illegally armed with a concealed pistol but apparently Clements was not. Together the three then walked down West Houston Street to the Silver King Saloon. They entered the side door of the saloon and headed toward a back room where they rendezvoused with one of the detectives hired by Townsend, George Shoaf. Shoaf took his leave first and then, after a brief wait, the trio departed the Silver King and headed for the Iron Front Saloon, located only a couple of blocks away at the intersection of St. Mary Street and East Houston Street. They entered the front of the establishment and walked straight to a back room where Jim Coleman was seated with his back toward the door. He was engaged in a conversation with both Shoaf and Maibaum. Without speaking a word, Hope (and others) pulled their pistols and began firing, striking Coleman six times.

After Coleman fell to the floor, Hope, Kincheloe, and Clements quickly departed out a side door onto St. Mary's Street. Shoaf followed them. Other people inside the saloon ran into the back room. The bartender telephoned the police, then went into the back room and found Coleman on the floor. Maibaum remained and began ministering to Coleman. When Shoaf caught up with the men at the corner, Hope declared that he wanted to surrender himself to the authorities. Shoaf took his pistol and walked him toward City Hall. Officials there contacted a local constable, Charles Stevens, who took Hope to the county jail. Ironically, Stevens was the officer who had once arrested Coleman for illegally carrying a pistol. Two other police officers responded to the bartender's call. They found Coleman, mortally wounded but not yet dead and lying on the floor with Maibaum holding his head.

One of the officers asked Coleman who had done the shooting, and Coleman replied, taking a long pause between each name, "Maibaum, Marion Hope, Kincheloe." The other officer asked Coleman why he had been shot, and he enigmatically replied that Shoaf knew the reason, thus confirming that he suspected the men were all party to the assassination.

As he lay dying, Coleman slowly pulled a small black leather pouch out of his pocket and held it in his hand, but never opened it. He died in the saloon about eleven o'clock, some forty minutes after he was shot. When the pouch was opened, it was found to contain a syringe, which Coleman had habitually used to inject himself with morphine, likely a legacy of his severe bullet wounds from nearly seven years before.[8]

The police recovered ten bullets from the scene in all. One was said to have dropped out of the leather pouch. Five of the bullets were .38s, and five .45s. As at least two guns had obviously been used, the district attorney deduced that there had been two or more shooters. He ordered the arrest of the two other men known to have been in the room, Maibaum and Shoaf.

Officers found them in the back room of the Iron Front Saloon, discussing the shooting with Hope's attorney, none other than Mark Townsend. Both men were immediately placed in custody, to their surprise and indignation. They explained that two calibers of bullets had been used because Hope had had two pistols. But Hope strongly denied it, declaring that the only gun he had had was the .38, which he surrendered to Shoaf the night of the shooting. Shoaf also could not explain the several rounds of ammunition he had in his pockets. Still Shoaf insisted, "I don't know what he did with that other gun. He may have given it to some of the men outside or he may—I don't know what became of it." He went on to declare that he had risen from the table to shake hands with Kincheloe, and that he was facing away from Coleman when the shooting took place. He also stated that he only knew Hope "casually" and that he and Coleman "were good friends." If he had wanted to kill Coleman, he asserted, he had had plenty of opportunities to do so.[9]

Hope, questioned about the shooting, left no doubt why he shot Coleman: "He killed my brother, and ever since he killed my brother he has been saying he was going to kill me. I didn't want any trouble. He laid for my brother and shot him with a shotgun when he wasn't looking." He reiterated that their confrontation had been accidental, saying "I was walking along the street with some friends and we just happened to drop in to get a drink. We strolled back there and I saw Coleman. He made a dive for his hip pocket.

I knew what that meant. He never was known to be without a gun. So I pulled my gun and fired."[10]

On May 25 Bexar County Justice of the Peace Joseph Umscheid ended his inquest, concluding that Coleman had been murdered by "Marion Hope and some other person or persons to me unknown."[11] Meanwhile, a rumor began circulating, fostered by Hope's defense attorneys, that Coleman's watch fob was engraved with the initials of the men he had killed.[12]

On May 27 a grand jury convened and began hearing evidence in the case. Many potential witnesses were reluctant to testify, having heard that the killing was part of a feud in which numerous men had been killed. Finally, on June 5, the grand jury indicted Hope, Maibaum, Shoaf, Kincheloe, and Clements for the murder, confirming the suspicion that all the men were part of a plot to kill Coleman.

The same day, Hope was released on $10,000 bail and the others on $5,000 each. Mark Townsend represented Hope and signed as a surety to the bail along with former sheriff, W. T. Burford, who had travelled to San Antonio for the proceeding.[13]

Some observers of the doings in San Antonio realized that the old feud, seemingly dead, had flared again. The editor of the *Weimar Mercury* pointed out that five of the parties involved in the latest violent encounter, including Mark Townsend, had been involved in the old feud. Continuing, the editor said that apparently the blazing feud had just shifted locations. The men who moved to San Antonio to escape the feud had actually brought the feud to San Antonio because their hate came with them.

Meanwhile, the *San Antonio Light* ran a special article that helped put the feud in perspective. The troubles in Columbus, the paper said, were caused by "one of those old family feuds" which broke out anew when one party sees the perfect time to renew the struggle. More bloodshed results, and retaliation comes that leads to yet more mayhem. Continuing, the editor said that lax law enforcement allowed the Colorado County feud to take a life of its own as it took "the bridle in its teeth and ran away with its rider." These things "disgrace a state." The editor concluded, "Colorado County can take care of these feudists if given a chance [and] if authorities would actually enforce the law."[14]

By securing indictments against all five men who had been in the back room of the Iron Front Saloon when Coleman was shot, that is, against all five eyewitnesses, the district attorney effectively sabotaged his case. Nobody was left to testify. As a consequence, none of the five, not even Hope, who admitted to the shooting, would ever be convicted. In fact, none of the five would even be brought to trial. On December 23, 1907, the district court in San Antonio set the trials of Hope, Maibaum, Shoaf, Kincheloe, and Clements to begin in less than a month. However, on January 21, 1908, all the cases were postponed. They were not mentioned again for nearly three years. Finally, on November 3, 1910, all five cases were dismissed. One of the five men, Maibaum, however, had already been sent to prison. On October 26, 1909, he had been convicted of the November 5, 1907, robbery of the often-robbed Alamo Bar in San Antonio, and handed a three-year sentence in the penitentiary. Shortly after that robbery, he had disappeared from the city. He was arrested in Memphis, Tennessee, on July 31, 1909.[15]

That Mark Townsend was the mastermind behind a premeditated act of private justice that led to Coleman's killing is, admittedly, an inference on the part of the authors, but the evidence overwhelmingly supports such a conclusion. Kincheloe was, according to John Goeppinger, Townsend's personal bodyguard. Shoaf and Maibaum vigorously denied that they were involved and it never came out in direct testimony that they were in the employ of Mark Townsend. Mark Townsend covered his tracks very well in this regard. Maibaum, nevertheless, subsequently skipped bail and fled to Mexico to avoid trial, not exactly the behavior of an innocent man. That Clements and Hope, both from Wharton County, just happened to be in San Antonio at the same time, happened to first bump into Kincheloe and then Shoaf, happened to be armed, and happened to stumble on to Coleman in the back room of the Iron Front Saloon where he was sharing a drink with Maibaum—the narrative offered by the defense—cannot be believed. Moreover, Mark Townsend defended the parties, made bail, and then provided Marion Hope a home and job on a ranch he owned near Nixon in Gonzales County for the rest of his life. The only explanation that fits the facts is that the whole thing was planned, and the only person with the cunning and wherewithal to orchestrate such an event, as John Goeppinger pointed out, was Mark Townsend.

By most accounts Coleman's death was the curtain call to the feud. In the next chapter we will see that this might not have been the case, at least not for Marion Hope.

CHAPTER TEN

The Deaths of Marion Hope, Will Clements, and Jim Townsend

During a three-week span in the summer of 1911, Jim Townsend, Will Clements, and Marion Hope all suffered violent deaths. It was a most extraordinary coincidence. The first to die was Marion Hope. After the murder of Jim Coleman, Hope had moved with his family from Wharton County to Mark Townsend's ranch near Nixon, a few miles southeast of San Antonio, where, it was said, he hoped to live out his declining years in peace and free from the troubles.[1]

On the afternoon on August 11, 1911, he saddled up a large Norman horse and rode out alone along a road to a calf pasture to drive up some calves. Passers-by found him unconscious sometime later, lying in the road, his neck broken. He expired shortly thereafter without ever regaining consciousness. The coroner ruled that his horse had fallen and broke his neck, although a large and visible bruise on the back of his neck could not be explained by the fall. The remains of Marion were brought back to Wharton by train August 19, 1911, for interment and were laid beside the graves of his two children who had predeceased him. Mark Townsend and other close family members accompanied the remains.[2]

The coroner, however, had apparently erred. Years later, in 1972, John Goeppinger volunteered in a private and unrecorded conversation that Marion Hope had actually been murdered, and he knew who did it.[3] He was very wary of naming those involved. He simply said, "They got the drop on him out in the pasture. They broke his neck and made it look like his horse had fallen with him, and that's what the coroner ruled."[4] John Goeppinger's revelation not only explained the large bruise on the back of Marion Hope's neck,[5] but also thrust him into the position as someone more deeply involved in the feud than anyone had assumed, for the suspicion lies close at hand that he actually was a party to Marion Hope's death.

In *Flaming Feuds of Colorado County*, Lillian Reese stresses over and over again that the Reese brothers, Walter and Hub, had long memories and intended to get even no matter how long it took. Herbert had suffered his greatest humiliation at the hands of Marion Hope during the skating rink altercation of 1906. She ends the book with an anecdote wherein she relates the reaction of a close family friend to the news of Marion Hope's death. His cryptic response, to whit that it must have been a mighty fine horse, leaves little doubt that there was much more to the story.[6] Likewise, in the taped interview, John Goeppinger says of the death of Marion Hope: "Marion Hope went out in the pasture there to see about some cattle and he never come back. Nobody knows what happened. (Laughter) Pretty terrible wasn't it."

On August 19, just eight days after the death of Marion Hope, a man named Frank Stelzig, whom one newspaper characterized as a Bohemian shoemaker originally from Schulenburg, ambushed and killed Will Clements with a shotgun from a place of concealment at Pledger in Matagorda County as Clements rode his horse down Main Street.[7] The altercation that led to the shooting clearly had nothing to do with the feud itself, but the subsequent murder trial of Stelzig in June of 1912 occasioned a most unlikely reunion of nearly all those still alive who had been involved in the

Colorado County feud and capable of making the trip to Bay City, and for this reason is important to the story.

The bad blood that had developed between Stelzig and Will Clements came to a head in the summer of 1911. Both parties had opened general stores in Pledger in 1910, a small town that had enjoyed substantial growth and rising prosperity since the arrival of a branch of the New York, Texas, and Mexican Railroad in 1900. Pledger also had a large black population: the descendants of the slaves that once toiled on the large antebellum plantations along the fertile bottomlands of Caney Creek and who now formed a substantial part of the clientele of both stores.

The week before the shooting Frank Stelzig had written the sheriff to complain about Will Clements, who had accused him of encouraging the black clientele to avoid his store. Clements had come into his store, verbally abused him, and then pistol-whipped him.[8] In obvious fear for his life and receiving no reassurance from the sheriff, Stelzig resolved to strike first and waylaid Clements the following week with a shotgun in downtown Pledger.

He was immediately charged with murder and at the examining trial was denied bail. His case, which came up for trial in June 1912, created a sensation and turned into what one newspaper reported as the "hardest fought case Matagorda County has ever known."[9] A detachment of Texas Rangers was dispatched to Bay City where the trial took place to insure that there was no trouble.

The trial put the now-dormant feud back on the front pages. In its effort to establish that Will Clements was a dangerous and violent man, whose threats had to be taken very seriously, the defense subpoenaed 128 witnesses.[10] The subpoena list read like a who's who of former Reese sympathizers. The subpoena list also revealed clearly that the chief base of support for the Reese faction lay among former friends and associates of Bob Stafford. The old-timers had had it right: there was a Stafford/Townsend feud but it only took place after the Stafford brothers were dead and ran concurrently with the Reese/Hope/Townsend feud.

Walter Reese, who travelled from El Paso for the trial, headlined the list of defense witnesses. It also included the three Burttschell brothers; all the Reese cousins and uncles from Lavaca County who had been involved; the brother of Jim Coleman; J. H. Williams of Columbus, whose son had been struck by a stray bullet; the railroad porter who had witnessed the shoot-out at Rosenberg; many former business associates of Bob Stafford including George Little, Frank Auerbach, E. S. Sandmeyer, and the brothers James and Ike Towell, leaders of the drive to establish the White Man's Primary; and, as a kind of grand finale, ex-Ranger captains McDonald and Brooks, who had been so close to the various events.

The parade of witnesses underscored that of all the participants in the feud, Will Clements had one of the highest scores in terms of gunplay and murders committed—a man of violent tendencies whose threats had to be taken seriously. The prosecution, for its part, only produced six witnesses, three of whom were black. All were men who had actually observed the shooting, but had little understanding of the circumstances. The result was predictable: the jury acquitted Stelzig after a short deliberation, for although the shooting was obviously premeditated, Stelzig had good reason to fear for his life.

On the same day as Will Clements's death, Marion Hope's widow moved with her children back to Wharton County from Nixon and took up residence with her father, Jim Townsend. They would have less than a week together. On September 1, 1911, Townsend, who had once again taken up the lawman's trade as a constable, rode up to Gandry's saloon at Louise in neighboring Jackson County, dismounted and entered the establishment with his pistol drawn. Shooting began at once. The proprietor Mr. Gandry was hit three times, once in the leg, once over the left eye, and then in the abdomen. Despite these wounds, he was able to fire one shot himself, hitting Townsend in the temple, inflicting a wound that caused instant death.[11] Gandry succumbed shortly thereafter to his own wounds. The paper remarked that the two had a history of bad feelings, which had grown very intense of late. In the span of three weeks, Marion Hope's widow lost her husband, her father, and an uncle to private justice.

The murder of Marion Hope (if indeed it was murder as John Goeppinger claimed) marked the last instance of private justice directly associated with the feud. His death plus the deaths of two other men, Will Clements and Jim Townsend, in the space of one month caught the attention of many people, including the editor of the *Weimar Mercury*. On the occasion of Will Clements's funeral in Weimar the week after his death, the paper pointed out the surprising coincidence that three of the main players in the notorious Colorado County feud died violent deaths in the span of three weeks.[12] The violence connected with the feud came to an end, but the hard feelings lingered for years to come.

CHAPTER ELEVEN

Postscript

Walter and Herbert Reese, sons of Sheriff Sam Reese, also died untimely deaths, but their deaths were unconnected to the feud. In March 1912 Herbert "Hub" Reese accidentally dropped his pistol, a .32 Colt's automatic. The pistol was supposed to be accident proof, but when it struck the floor it discharged, and struck the right leg just above the knee, inflicting a slight flesh wound. From there it ranged through the testicle, on up through the groin, and lodged somewhere near the upper part of the left hip. The family telegraphed for a specialist from Houston, but before he could arrive on the night train, Hub Reese expired. He was buried in Weimar the following day at the side of his father. Reese was just thirty years of age and, in addition to his wife, was survived by his brother Walter, mother, and three sisters.[1]

Walter Reese followed his brother Hub to the grave in 1919. In the twelve years between his move back to Columbus in 1907 and his death in El Paso as the result of a car accident, Walter Reese led a very unsettled life. He bounced between failed business ventures and various stints as a lawman. He applied at one point to be a Texas Ranger but was turned down.

In 1913 Walter Reese married Ethel Cox. That August the couple had a daughter, Lola Herberta Reese. Her middle name, of course, was in honor of Walter's recently deceased brother.

It was not a happy marriage and led to eventual estrangement with the wife moving away to live with her sister in Chicago for an extended period.[2]

In 1919 Walter took a new job as inspector of police for the El Paso Police Department. When a new police chief abolished that position, he was named captain of detectives. On a November afternoon, Walter drove the car that had been provided to him on a short excursion outside the city. He took along a friend named William Kell. On their way back to El Paso, at about three o'clock in the morning and with rain falling, the car went into a skid and rolled over. Kell was thrown from the car, breaking three ribs and suffering a back injury, but Reese was much more seriously injured. A passing motorist took both injured men to a hospital. Reese was treated and then taken to a hotel. Doctors predicted that he would never regain consciousness.[3]

His mother and sister arrived at his bedside early on the morning of November 8. His wife Ethel, contacted by telegram, soon joined them. They were told that he would be dead in a matter of hours. He had sustained a severe blow to the head, and had serious, irreparable internal injuries. However, the next day he revived somewhat, and was able to speak. Then the long deathwatch began. He lingered for weeks, before finally expiring on December 11, 1919. He was forty years of age.[4]

Walter Reese at least had the pleasure of outliving the old nemesis of the Reese family, Mark Townsend. Marcus Harvey Townsend passed away of natural causes June 18, 1915, at his home in San Antonio. The *San Antonio Express* published a long and glowing obituary outlining his rags to riches story and cataloging his many achievements as a legislator, lawyer, and businessman, chief among them his sponsorship of the bill to preserve the Alamo. At the time of his death, he had risen to be one of the most powerful and respected men in South Texas, with an estate valued at over $250,000, in today's dollars, a millionaire many times over.[5] Predictably, of course, this eulogy, as well as the many others that appeared across the state, neither mentioned the feud, nor alluded to the dark side of Mark Townsend's character that did not shirk from private justice when called for, even when directed against members of his own extended Townsend family.

Keetie (Townsend) Reese, wife of Sheriff Sam Reese, outlived her two sons and died in Austin in 1912, where she had moved to live with her daughter Lillian after the accidental death of her son Herbert. Daughter Lillian never married, and supported herself throughout her life by giving music lessons. She is credited with establishing the Austin Conservatory of Music. In her later years she often returned to Columbus for extended stays and would give piano lessons in a house across the street from the Columbus High School. Her father's loaded Colt pistol always occupied a prominent position atop the piano, which none of her students could fail to notice and which no doubt motivated them to do their best. In 1962 she self-published a book about the feud, *Flaming Feuds of Colorado County*, which was based largely on newspaper clippings and writings put together by her brother Walter before his accidental death in 1919. It is a naively amateurish effort that presents an exceedingly one-sided account of the feud, but one that offers clear insight into the psychology of a family whose honor was wronged, which kept the fires of hatred alive over the years. She died November 23, 1974.

One of the most poignant stories associated with the feud concerned Carrie Estelle Townsend, daughter of Sheriff James Light and Margaret Alice (Cummins) Townsend. She was born April 10, 1882, the same year as John Goeppinger, and thus was twelve when her father died. She married Joseph Winston Stafford in 1905, the only son of John Stafford who had been shot and killed by Larkin and Marion Hope, allies of her father J. Light Townsend. The marriage of a daughter of Light Townsend to a son of John Stafford raised many eyebrows, as it seemed to represent a kind of storybook ending to the feud, with love triumphing over all. It was said they had eloped to avoid the wrath of their families, which only added to the aura of the story.

Mrs. Carrie, as she was affectionately known, was an eccentric and beloved fixture of Columbus until her death in 1971. She had a very stately and dignified bearing, and drove around in a black Buick limousine with a chauffeur dressed in a snappy uniform at a time when only a handful of people in the county owned luxury vehicles and no one else had a chauffeur. For many years she also resided part of the time at the John Stafford mansion south of Columbus (see illustration) and was an old widow alone in a very large house. Carrie and Joe Stafford had one son, Joe Jr., who subsequently married the daughter of John Goeppinger.[6]

The title of this book is taken from the tombstone of Ike Towell (1851–1934), which is to be found in the Odd Fellows Cemetery in Columbus. It reads:

HERE RESTS IKE TOWELL.

AN INFIDEL WHO HAD

NO HOPE FOR HEAVEN

NOR FEAR OF HELL

WAS FREE OF SUPERSTITION

TO DO RIGHT AND LOVE

JUSTICE WAS HIS RELIGION

The epitaph has generated a lot of controversy over the years and even made its way as a heading into a book of poetry by Rita Dove, erstwhile poet laureate of the United States.[7] Ike Towell supported the Staffords in the earlier phase and counted as a Reese supporter after 1898. He came close to disemboweling Larkin Hope in a street brawl in 1888. He and his brother, James Towell, led the push in 1902 to introduce the White Man's Primary in Colorado County, which spelled the end of Townsend domination of county politics.

Ike Towell never hid the fact that he did not believe in a higher deity. When afflicted with a terminal disease as an old man, he commissioned his own tombstone, bought himself a nice suit, went to the barbershop for a shave, then went home and put an end to his life with chloroform. The *Colorado Citizen* (and several other area newspapers) ran a glowing eulogy about Towell, acknowledging that he was an atheist, but crediting him for the courage of his convictions.[8]

John Goeppinger could never settle down to the life of a farmer even though his grandfather gave him a nice farm south of Columbus. By 1911 he had a wife and children and "was about to starve to death." He asked for a job at the switchyards of the Southern Pacific in Glidden a mile west of Columbus and ended up remaining employed there for forty-three years. He retired in 1954. Over the years he came to be regarded as one of the town characters while his renown as an off-color storyteller spread far and wide. His love of hunting continued to get him in trouble. He was arrested for poaching at the ripe old age of eighty-nine. His daughter Mildred (Pete) was a schoolmate of my father. She subsequently married Joe Stafford, Jr., the only son of Joe and Carrie (Townsend) Stafford. My parents were best friends with Joe and Pete (Goeppinger) Stafford until Joe's untimely death in 1944.

His death in 1973 left only Lillian Reese alive, but she passed away the following year. After their deaths no one was left alive with first-hand knowledge of the events of the feud. But through Lillian Reese's book, *Flaming Feuds of Colorado County*, and her childhood friend's taped interview, we gain insight into actual events and, equally important, into a frame of mind that encouraged private justice when family honor was involved.

Conclusion

In 1936 young Howard William Townsend, distant cousin of Sheriff Light Townsend, wrote a term paper for his English class at the University of Texas.[9] Over the years he had heard many stories and anecdotes concerning the feud from various family members who had been involved, and he came to the conclusion that these should be preserved, which was the original intent of his term paper.

When he approached the family with his plan, however, he encountered a wall of silence and hostility. His own father wrote him, "You can't get anyone here, as funny as it seems, to tell any of the stories [*sic.* for the record]. I think they are still all afraid. You be careful of what you write and what you do with it after you write it. Remember, you are playing with dynamite!"[10] His mother also wrote to say, "Carrie Stafford came to your father Friday all up in the air. They do not want you to write it. They do not want it stirred up again as there is still too much hot blood on both sides. And too, they do not want their names messed up again; you will regret it later, so please leave it alone." The coals of hostility, it seems, were still glowing and could easily reignite even in 1936. Reluctantly (and unfortunately for historians), he yielded to the pressure.[11]

Enough time has elapsed in the intervening seventy-five years for the smoldering coals of hatred to die down. The purpose of this book was not, as Carrie Stafford had feared, to stir up old passions. Nevertheless, many will find the true story of events unsettling and painful since many descendants on both sides still make Columbus and Colorado County their home. There does come a time, however, to face the past, to confront both the good and the bad with open eyes. Bill Stein believed that such a time had arrived when he began this project. He also realized that if he did not undertake to write the story, somebody else surely would, for this was the last major Texas feud that had not received serious and unbiased book-length treatment, and several prominent historians had indicated the desire to undertake the project.

Bill also had a family connection to the story. He was a direct descendant of Ben Stafford through his mother's side. He was also kin to Jim Coleman in a very roundabout way. It might be expected, therefore, that Bill would bring a built-in bias to the story in favor of the Stafford family in the first phase of troubles, and the Reese family in the second phase. However, Bill's uncompromising dedication to the principle of historical objectivity—the guiding light of every historian worth his salt—lifted him above any narrow partisan feelings.

Due to his untimely death, Bill was not able to complete the project. One thing he was certain about, however, was that both the families involved and the wider community as a whole suffered as a result of an outmoded and exaggerated code of conduct that had condoned and encouraged private justice. Howard Townsend concludes his short account of the feud with a quote from an unnamed person who had lived through the dangerous days, "All they did was to fill the cemeteries, and no one got any good out of what happened." That pretty much sums it up, but it is proper and fitting to end this book with a quote from Bill Stein:

> In the years immediately after the Civil War, a wave of gun violence swept through Texas. In Colorado County, the violence lasted for nearly fifty years. Though it stretched across all classes and races,

two prominent extended families, the Staffords and the Townsends, became identified in the public mind as purveyors of much of the violence. In later years, and perhaps even at the time, observers believed that a feud existed between the families. In retrospect, it seems clear that there never was a full-scale feud between the Staffords and the Townsends. They had two brief clashes, one nearly twenty years after the other. But, there was no continuing pattern of animosity between the families in the intervening two decades. The Staffords, who made fortunes in the cattle business, frequently used extra-legal and violent means in attempts to control rustling, but there were no attacks on any specific family or any acts of retribution by or against the Staffords for real or imagined wrongs. There was a feud in Colorado County, but it did not start until 1898, and it did not involve the Staffords.[12] The feud started over control of the sheriff's office, and was principally within the Townsend family, including their various kinfolk, people with surnames like Reese, Hope, Clements, and Burford.

By no means does this book mention every murder or violent incident that occurred in Colorado County during the period covered.

Their crazy ideas about what it meant to be a Texan went a long way toward defining the term in the popular culture and the popular imagination for years to come. Their intention was to protect family honor. However, they believed that the right and proper way to do so was to become one of the most dishonorable kinds of human beings, a murderer.

As to who was right and who was wrong, there is an old story about two men who always argued. One day, one of them bet the other that he did not know the Lord's Prayer. He took the bet and rattled off, "Now I lay me down to sleep, I pray the Lord my soul to keep." The first man said, "Alright, you win. I didn't think you knew it." Sometimes everybody is wrong.

Bill Stein

APPENDIX A

Feud Biographies

Brooks, John (1855–1944): Texas Ranger captain John Abijah Brooks was born November 20, 1855, in Kentucky. He joined the rangers in 1883 and became a captain in 1889. He is regarded as one of the "Great" captains. He resigned in 1906. Later, he served two terms in the state legislature and, from 1911 to 1939, served as the county judge of Brooks County, which was named in his honor. He died January 15, 1944. Captain Brooks and eight rangers were detached to Columbus in September 1899 to insure no trouble broke out during the fall term of district court. He was in charge of maintaining the peace during the murder trial of Jim Townsend that had been moved to Bastrop January 1900 on a change of venue.

Brown, Jennie (1845–1942): Jane Elizabeth Townsend was the daughter of Spencer Burton and Louisa Drusilla (Dillard) Townsend, and thus the sister of Keetie Reese and Jim Townsend. She married Hiram Walter Brown on August 1, 1867. She was prepared to testify against her brother Jim Townsend at his trial for murder in Bastrop in 1900.

Burford, Arthur (1876–1900): Arthur Lee Burford was the son of Sheriff William Thomas and Mattie (Pinchback) Burford. He was shot to death in Bastrop, Texas, on January 15, 1900. He had recently graduated from the University of Texas with a law degree. His death was a great shock because he was not considered a party to the feud. When the town of Garwood was laid out in southern Colorado County, his father had a street named "Arthur Street" in his honor.

Burford, Frank (1871–1939): Frank Walker Burford, sometimes called Red, was the son of Robert Phillip Burford, who was a half-brother of Francis Marion Burford. He spent most of his life in Belton, where he practiced law. However, while he was studying law, he lived in Columbus with his relative-by-marriage Mark Townsend, and became principal in the shoot-out at the railroad depot in Rosenberg in 1900.

Burford, Will (1850–1908): William Thomas Burford, son of Francis Marion and Cordelia Ann (Shaw) Burford. He owned a large farm in the Osage community northeast of Weimar. He was a devout Methodist and a prominent Mason. Together with his brother-in-law, he co-founded the Red Bluff Irrigation Company and the town of Garwood. In 1898 Mark Townsend recruited him to run for sheriff of Colorado County after the assassination of Larkin Hope by the Reese faction. He won the election and served as sheriff until 1902. With the introduction of the White Man's primary in 1902 he lost the next election to W. E. Bridge. After losing his bid for reelection as sheriff in 1902, Will Burford retired to a home in Columbus. He died at that home on November 3, 1908, ten years to the day after he had first been elected sheriff. He had been in poor health for several months, though he was only 58 years old. His wife, Martha, who had stood up to the lynch mob at the jail in 1902, lived on until December 9, 1929, when she died at the age of 73. Both were buried in Columbus.

Burttschell, Charles August (1873–1926): son of Frank and Anna (Maertz) Burttschell. He was a brother of Jacob and Henry Burttschell. He married Mary Daniels, the sister of Tom Daniels, in 1889. He was one of the men who was arrested in Bastrop, and then quickly released, when Arthur Burford was killed there in 1900.

Burttschell, Henry (1861–1930): Henry Burttschell was a son of Frank and Anna (Maertz) Burttschell, and thus a brother of Jacob and August Burttschell. He was one of the men who was arrested in Bastrop, and then quickly released, when Arthur Burford was killed there in 1900. On March 14, 1910, Henry shot and killed a man by the name of Max Theumann at a saloon near Eagle Lake as the result of a feud-related disagreement. For most of his life, he operated a farm and ranch near Alleyton. On March 18, 1930, he was driving a wagon to his fields when he collapsed and died.

Burttschell, Jacob (1860–1894): son of Frank and Anna (Maertz) Burttschell and a brother of Joseph, August, and Henry Burttschell. He married Maria Coleman, the sister of Jim Coleman, on January 25, 1881. He was killed by Tucker Hoover on April 30, 1894, who in turn was murdered by Jim Coleman, Jacob's brother-in-law.

Burttschell, Joseph (1859–1910): oldest of the sons of Frank and Anna (Maertz) Burttschell of the Menz community and the leader of the clan. He married Katherine Coleman, the sister of Jim Coleman. He served as county commissioner during the term of Sheriff Reese from 1894 until 1898 and the two became close political allies, business associates, and family friends. Joseph owned a large ranch east of Alleyton and was an investor in the Texas Oil and Mining Company, which was organized in 1901 to explore for oil in Colorado County.

Clements family (1847–1886): Louise Florida "Lou" Townsend was the daughter of Spencer Burton and Louisa Drusilla (Dillard) Townsend, and thus the sister of

Keetie Reese and Jim Townsend. She married Augustus D. "Gus" Clements (1844–1900) on November 29, 1867. Their children were Spencer Burton "Spence" Clements (1870–1892), James Augustus "Jim" Clements (1871–1929), Jennie B. Clements (1872–1891), Alice L. Clements (1872), William D. "Will" Clements (1876–1911), and Hiram E. Clements (1879–1906). Spence lived with the Reese family and died as a young man. Jennie also died young. Will engaged in a gunfight with Sam Reese and probably was the man who fired the bullet that killed him. Hiram was shot and killed by Dr. Joe Lessing, Jr. Jim became a successful farmer in Wharton County. Alice married David Larkin Hope, son of Larkin Secrest Hope, on May 2, 1906.

Clements, Hiram (1879–1906): Hiram E. Clements was the youngest son of Augustus D. and Louise Florida (Townsend) Clements. He was the brother of Spence and Will Clements, and the nephew of Sam and Keetie Reese. He was shot and killed in Columbus by Dr. Joe Lessing, Jr. in 1906.

Clements, Lou (1847–1886): Louise Florida Townsend was born June 26, 1847, the daughter of Spencer Burton and Louisa Drusilla (Dillard) Townsend. Therefore, she was the sister of Keetie Reese and Jim Townsend. She married Augustus D. Clements on November 29, 1867. (See Clements family above) She was the mother of Spence, Will, and Hiram Clements.

Clements, Spence (1870–1892): Spencer Burton Clements was the eldest son of Augustus D. and Louise Florida (Townsend) Clements, and thus was a brother to Will and Hiram Clements. His mother was a sister of Keetie Reese. He lived with the Reese family in Oakland, rather than with his own parents, from his teenage years. He moved to Columbus with the Reeses, living with them until his death from pneumonia.

Clements, Will (1876–1911): William D. Clements was the son of Augustus D. and Louise Florida (Townsend) Clements. His mother was a sister of Keetie Reese and Jim Townsend, thus he was the nephew of Sam Reese and first cousin of Walter Reese. He was allied with the Mark Townsend faction and considered to be one of the most violent men associated with the feud. He most likely fired the shot that killed Sam Reese in 1899, was severely wounded in the Bastrop shoot-out in 1900, was a participant in the Rosenberg shoot-out, was present at the assassination of Jim Coleman in San Antonio in 1907, subsequently killed two men in Wharton county, and was shot and killed himself on August 19, 1911, by one Frank Stelzig at Pledger in Matagorda County.

Coleman, Jim (1876–1907): James Henry Coleman was a son of Thomas Patrick Coleman and his second wife, Julia Parrott. His half-sisters, Maria and Katherine, married brothers Jacob and Joseph Burttschell. He killed Tucker Hoover and was arrested for the murder of Larkin Hope. He participated in the gunfights in Bastrop and Rosenberg, and was severely wounded in the latter. He was shot and killed in San Antonio on May 15, 1906, by a group of men that included Marion Hope, Will Kincheloe, and Will Clements.

Daniels, Tom (1873–1940): Thomas Barnette Daniels was the son of Williamson and Mary E. (Chandler) Daniels. His sister, Mary, married August Burttschell, bringing him into the feuding families. He was one of four men indicted for the murder of Arthur Burford in Bastrop.

Dudley, Molly (1853–?): Mary Lucretia Townsend was the daughter of Spencer Burton and Louisa Drusilla (Dillard) Townsend, and thus the sister of Keetie Reese and Jim Townsend. She married William A. Dudley on June 15, 1871. She was prepared to testify against her brother at his trial for murder in Bastrop in 1900.

Goeppinger, John Henry (1882–1972): was the son of Dora Seymour and Carl Robert Goeppinger. His father was born in Germany and was the recipient of a good education; he was a shrewd businessman who started out as a travelling salesman in Texas but ending up quite wealthy, owning a lumberyard in Columbus and a large ranch in the southern part of the county. His father eloped with the daughter of James Alexander Seymour, a longtime native of the county, but eventually brought his brothers-in-law, Charles and Samuel King, into the business that eventually became the Seymour Hardware and Lumberyard Company, a fixture of Columbus for many years. Although a disagreement concerning fencing led to an early altercation with the Staffords, the Seymour family staunchly supported the Reese faction in the latter phase of the feud. John Goeppinger became close friends with the Reese brothers and their sister Lillian. He was present at the meeting where it was decided to assassinate Larkin Hope in 1898. He was probably involved in the attempted assassination of Will Clements the following year and this was the reason the rangers attempted to arrest him. He escaped arrest and jumped a boat bound for South Africa and was gone a full year. Later he took a job at the Southern Pacific Railroad yards in Glidden, west of Columbus, and worked there until his retirement, some forty plus years later. He also had inside knowledge concerning the death of Marion Hope in 1911, and may have been one of the perpetrators himself. His daughter Mildred married Joe Stafford, Jr., who was the grandson of both Sheriff J. Light Townsend on his mother's side and the murdered John Stafford on his father's side. He requested the interview, which has been transcribed and made available as an appendix, six months before his death. It was conducted on the front porch of his house in Columbus and comes across as a conversation between himself and my father, C. W. "Charlie" Kearney. His daughter

Mildred and my father had been schoolmates and friends so "Goep," as he was called, felt comfortable speaking with my father, who had known many of the people involved from his youth and who had a fair understanding of the outlines of the feud himself.

Hope, Larkin (1855–1898): Larkin Secrest Hope was the son of David and Mary (Townsend) Hope. Larkin Hope served as city marshal of Columbus when he and his brother Marion shot and killed the Stafford brothers at the Nicolai Saloon in Columbus in July 1900. He subsequently ran successfully for constable and was assassinated by the Reese faction with Jim Coleman as the triggerman in August 1898. With the death of his brother Marion at the hands of parties unknown in 1911, the feud came to a close.

Hope, Marion (1859–1911): Samuel Marion Hope was born December 18, 1859, and died in Gonzales County on August 6, 1911. Marion was the son of David and Mary (Townsend) Hope, the brother of Larkin Hope, and the stepbrother of Dr. Joe Lessing, Jr. He married the daughter of Jim Townsend as a second marriage. He served as deputy city marshal and shot John Stafford in July 1890. He was present at the killing of ex-sheriff Sam Reese in 1890, was a participant in the 1906 courthouse shoot-out in Columbus, and was one of the assassins of Jim Coleman in San Antonio in 1907. He spent his last years as foreman of a ranch owned by Mark Townsend near Nixon in Gonzales County where he died in 1911. Although the coroner ruled his death accidental—the result of a horse fall—John Goeppinger later confided that he had been murdered by members of the Reese faction.

Houchins, John Fleming (1857–1900): Ex-sheriff of Lavaca County and nephew of Sam H. Reese. He came to Columbus with a party of twenty-five to thirty armed men after the killing of Sam Reese in March 1899.

Hughes, John R. (1855–1947): One of the most famous of the Texas Ranger captains, Hughes first enlisted in the rangers in 1887. He served mainly along the border between Texas and Mexico and in 1893 was made captain in command of Company D in El Paso. He was later appointed senior captain, with headquarters in Austin. He retired from the force on January 31, 1915, having served as a captain and ranger longer than any other man. After the 1906 shoot-out in Columbus, Captain Hughes answered the call with privates Tom Ross, H. A. Carnes, and J. C. White. The rangers arrived July 18, 1906, and stayed in Columbus for several weeks.

Kincheloe, J. W. (1882–1919): son of George and Jennie (Hope) Kincheloe, who settled in the Sheridan community in the latter part of the nineteenth century. He was related to the Hopes through his mother. He held odd jobs, had served a stint as a lawman, and was apparently living in Live Oak County when Mark Townsend hired him as a bodyguard in San Antonio in 1907. Along with Will Clements and Marion Hope, he was implicated in the killing of Jim Coleman at the Buckhorn Saloon in San Antonio in 1907. He accidentally killed his wife Alma in 1914 and committed suicide in 1919. He is buried in the family plot at the Cheetam cemetery in Sheridan, Texas.

Lessing, Joe, Jr. (1874–1947): Joseph Franklin Lessing, Jr., the son of Joseph and Mary (Townsend) Lessing. His mother was the sister of Sheriff James Light Townsend. He was trained as a dentist and had an office overlooking the courthouse square. His mother had two previous husbands and at least five earlier children, including Larkin and Marion Hope. He married Nuddie Ella Reese, daughter of Sam Reese, and fired the shot from his office window that killed Hiram Clements in the courthouse shoot-out of 1906.

Lessing, Nuddie Ela (1877–1962): Oldest child of Sam and Keetie (Townsend) Reese. She married Dr. Joseph Lessing, Jr., her second cousin. On May 17, 1899, the date of the shooting of Dick Reese and his black driver Dick Gant, she was caught in blackface and man's disguise in the vicinity of the county jail.

Mansfield, Judge Joseph Jefferson (1861–1947): Born in Wayne County, West Virginia, as Beauregard Mansfield. His name was changed to Joseph Jefferson Mansfield for his father, a Confederate colonel who was killed soon after Mansfield's birth. Mansfield came to Texas in 1881, studied law, was admitted to the bar in 1886, and opened a law office in Eagle Lake (11 miles southeast). While in Eagle Lake, he served as mayor, city attorney, and newspaper editor, and in 1888, married Annie Scott Bruce. The couple had three children. In 1892 Mansfield was elected county attorney and moved to Columbus, where in 1896, he was elected county judge. During his tenure as judge, in 1912–13, Mansfield served as Grand Master of the Grand Lodge of Texas Masons. In 1916 he was elected to the United States Congress. As a congressman, Mansfield served as the Chairman of the House Rivers and Harbors Committee, which was responsible for federal funding of flood control on the Colorado River. Mansfield Dam (95 miles northwest), constructed in 1934, was named in his honor. Early in 1947, Mansfield donated this property to Columbus for construction of a public Library. He died in Washington, DC and many dignitaries, including congressman (and later president) Lyndon B. Johnson, attended the funeral in Columbus. Burial was at Eagle Lake.

McDonald, Bill (1852–1918): William Jesse McDonald, legendary captain of the Texas Rangers from 1891 until 1907. He died on January 15, 1918. He commanded rangers in Columbus on several occasions.

Reese, Buster: Thomas John or Thomas Jasper Reese was the son of Sam Reese's brother, John Wesley Reese, and thus a brother of Les Reese. He was one of the men arrested in Bastrop and then quickly released when Arthur Burford was killed in 1900.

Reese, Dick (1852–1899): Richard Burrell Reese was the son of Fleming Sanders and Nancy (Whittington) Reese, and thus the brother of Sam Reese. He was killed on May 17, 1899, while attempting to cross the bridge into Columbus.

Reese, Flem: Asa Fleming Reese was the son of Sam Reese's brother, John Wesley Reese, and thus a brother of Les Reese. He was one of the men arrested in Bastrop and then quickly released when Arthur Burford was killed in 1900.

Reese, Hub (1880–1912): Spencer Herbert Reese was the younger son of Sam and Keetie (Townsend) Reese. He was involved in the Rosenberg shoot-out in 1900 and together with his brother Walter was wounded in the courthouse shoot-out of 1906. He died of an accidental gunshot wound on March 6, 1912.

Reese, Keetie (1858–1944): Keron Blanche Reese, the daughter of Spencer Burton and Louisa Drusilla (Dillard) Townsend married Sam Reese on September 21, 1876. She was the mother of five children, two boys and three girls. She died November 16, 1944.

Reese, Les (1873–1907): Leslie Wilkinson Reese was the son of Sam Reese's brother, John Wesley Reese. He was one of the men indicted for killing Arthur Burford in Bastrop in 1900. It was reported that he shot himself to death accidentally in Houston on November 25, 1907.

Reese, Lillie (1884–1974): Lillian Estelle Reese was the youngest child of Sam and Keetie (Townsend) Reese.

She never married and supported herself by teaching music. In 1962 she published a book about the feud, *Flaming Feuds of Colorado County*.

Reese, Pee Dee (1855–1931): Fleming Sanders Reese, called Pee Dee, was the son of Fleming Sanders and Nancy (Whittington) Reese, and thus the brother of Sam Reese. He was one of the men arrested in Bastrop and then quickly released when Arthur Burford was killed in 1900.

Reese, Sadie (1882–1959): Keron Virginia Reese, popularly known as Sadie, was a daughter of Sam and Keetie (Townsend) Reese. She married James T. Johnston. She died at her daughter's home in Baton Rouge, Louisiana, on November 27, 1959.

Reese, Sam (1859–1899): Samuel Houston Reese, son of Fleming Sanders and Nancy (Whittington) Reese, was appointed sheriff of Colorado County in 1894 to replace Light Townsend, who had died. He had served as deputy sheriff for Townsend, and was married to Keetie Townsend. He was elected sheriff in 1896, but lost a bid for reelection in 1898. He was shot and killed in a shoot-out in Columbus on March 16, 1899, by a group that included Will Clements, Marion Hope, and Mark Townsend.

Reese, John Walter (1879–1919): Elder son of Sam and Keetie (Townsend) Reese, was a central figure in the feud, was a party to the conspiracy to assassinate Larkin Hope in 1898, present at the death of his father in 1898, part of the crowd that ambushed Will Clements and James Burford in Bastrop, an instigator (together with Jim Coleman) of the Rosenberg shoot-out, together with his brother Hub was a participant in the Columbus shoot-out of 1906, and was most likely involved in the death of Marion Hope in 1911. He died on December 11, 1919, of injuries received in an automobile accident in El Paso, Texas. Is listed as a coauthor with his sister Lillian of *Flaming Feuds of Colorado County*, self-published in 1962.

Reese, Walter, Sr.: Walter Gray Reese was the son of Fleming Sanders and Nancy (Whittington) Reese, and thus the brother of Sam Reese. He was one of the men arrested in Bastrop and then quickly released when Arthur Burford was killed in 1900.

Rogers, John (1863–1930): joined the rangers in 1882 and became a captain in 1892. He resigned his commission in 1911, but was reappointed a captain in 1927. He served until his death in 1930. On January 23, 1900, Captain Rogers was ordered to Bastrop in the aftermath of the shooting of James Burford and Will Clements with several rangers to assist Captains Brooks and McDonald who were already there.

Sieker, Captain Lamartine Pemberton (1848–1914): Sieker joined the rangers in 1874 and rose through the ranks to become lieutenant in 1881 and then captain on September 1, 1882. Sieker served as quartermaster of the Frontier Battalion from 1899 until 1905. He also had three brothers who served in the rangers.

Stafford, Carrie (1882–1971): Carrie Estelle Townsend was the daughter of Sheriff James Light and Margaret Alice (Cummins) Townsend, and the sister of Howard Townsend. She was twelve when her father was killed. She married Joseph Winston Stafford, the only son of the slain John Stafford, in 1905. Many regarded it as a storybook marriage since their union joined both the Stafford and Townsend families. Her only son, Joe Jr., married Mildred Goeppinger, daughter of John Goeppinger.

Stafford, John (1849–1890): son of Benjamin Franklin and Annie (Walker) Stafford of Georgia and the youngest of the

Stafford brothers to make the move to Texas. He built a large house south of Columbus. In 1882 he and Warren Stafford were indicted for the murder of a man named Stedham who intended to homestead on public land in the southern part of the county. He was killed, along with his brother Bob, by Larkin and Marion Hope in July 1890. His son Joseph married Carrie Townsend, daughter of Sheriff Light Townsend. After R. E. Stafford established a meatpacking plant in 1883 and a bank and opera house in 1886 in Columbus, John managed the cattle operation.

Stafford, Ben (1847~1914): Benjamin Franklin Stafford was born April 29, 1847, in Glynn County, Georgia, to Robert Earl and Martha (Ratcliff) Stafford, one of fourteen children. After the outbreak of the Civil War, Ben, at only fourteen years of age, was too young to serve. However, four days before his seventeenth birthday, April 25, 1864, he enlisted as a private in Company B of the Fourth Regiment, Georgia Cavalry, which was also known as Clinch's Cavalry. In 1867 he followed, along with several of his brothers and sisters, their older brother Robert Earl to Texas, where they entered, and became quite successful, into the cattle business. Over the next several years, the Staffords and their hired hands defended their interests as vigilantes, acquiring reputations as violent men.

On September 6, 1871, Ben married Annie Walker and, less than a month later, bought a tract of land some ten miles southwest of Columbus. Establishing a home there, he and Annie were eventually joined by six sons and one daughter. However, in December 1871, the Stafford boys participated in a gun battle in downtown Columbus, where Sumner Townsend, on the one side, was seriously wounded, and Ben was shot in the ankle, and thereafter walked with a limp. Indicted for attempted murder, Ben was brought to trial and assessed a small fine. In 1880 he was again indicted, along with his uncle S. W. Ratcliff, for murder of W. W. Guinn, but was acquitted.

In 1886 Ben moved his family to Columbus, but later, circa 1902, relocated to Beaumont, Jefferson County, where he successfully applied for a Confederate Pension in 1907. Prior to 1909, he and Annie moved back to Colorado County, where Annie died on August 31, 1909. Returning to his ranch, Ben remained there until April 17, 1911, when he was admitted to the Texas Confederate Home in Austin. After living in the Home for three years, Ben died May 12, 1914, and was buried that same day in the Texas State Cemetery. Ben Stafford was the great grandfather of Bill Stein, co-author of this book.

Stafford, Warren Decatur (1858–1891): Only surviving son of R. E. and Sarah Elizabeth (Zoucks) Stafford. His arrest in July 1890 by the Hope brothers for drunken and disorderly behavior precipitated the deaths of his father R. E. and uncle John Stafford. He was indicted for murder on two different occasions and died at the age of thirty-three as a consequence of his alcoholism. He was married to Carrie (Casagne) Stafford. The couple had one son, Robert Earle, who died at the age of nineteen in 1903.

Taylor, Creed (1878–?): Thomas Carney Taylor served as a Texas Ranger from 1899 to 1900 and again from 1902 to 1904 and was stationed in Columbus on numerous occasions. He was sheriff of Kimble County in 1905 and 1906, and served as a special ranger in 1917.

Towell, Ike (1849–1934): was born in Obion County, Tennessee. While city marshal of Columbus forty years ago, Mr. Towell had an ordinance passed requiring the railroad company to provide separate waiting rooms for white and black people. He later urged and secured the passage of the state separate carriage for railroads. He organized the White

Man's party in Matagorda County and was involved in the same organization in Colorado County in 1902.

Towell was firmly on the side of the Stafford/Reese faction and later helped to manage Stafford cattle in the county after the deaths of Bob and John in 1890.

He was the bother-in-law of Dr. R. H. Harrison.

Towell instructed that the following be read at his funeral:

> Especially do I want to impress the fact upon the people that one child was born, passed through the years of youth, grew to manhood, lived a tolerably respectable life, reached old age, died, and could be buried without the assistance of clergy. My religion consists of doing right and loving justice. I affirm that all men should tell the truth and pay their debts. I do not believe in any god, devil, ghost, or savior, and I have opposed tobacco, whiskey, gambling, lying, and stealing practically my whole life. If any one of the clergy ever calls my name after death I insist that he speaks the truth about me, a thing I have never known a preacher to do about a dead disbeliever. The clergy have never been able to bribe me with the promise of a beautiful home in a fictitious heaven nor bluff me by their everlasting punishment in a hell of fire and brimstone. (*Colorado County Citizen*, March 1, 1934)

Townsend, Howard (1878–1930): Howard Asa Townsend was son of Sheriff James Light and Margaret Alice (Cummins) Townsend and sister to Carrie Townsend. He was with Arthur Burford when he was killed at Bastrop in 1900. He practiced law in Columbus until his death on April 26, 1930.

Townsend, Jim (1851–1911): James Gaither Townsend was the son of Spencer Burton and Louisa Drusilla (Dillard) Townsend, and thus was the brother of Keetie Reese. He was born October 18, 1851. He was one of two men accused of shooting Dick Reese and Dick Gant at the river bridge in Columbus in 1899. He was killed in a saloon shoot-out near Ganado on August 28, 1911. His sister, Keron Blanche (Keetie), was married to Sam Reese and his daughter, Minnie L., married Marion Hope in 1899.

Townsend, James Light (1845–1894): James Light Townsend was born November 12, 1845, and died on his birthday in 1894, the result of food poisoning. He was the youngest of fifteen children born to Asa and Rebecca (Harper) Townsend. He served as sheriff of Colorado County from 1880 until his death in 1894. Together with his nephew Mark, he presided over a political machine that, by means of strong support among the large black population, had come to control law enforcement in Colorado County. Although there is no indication criminality was involved, Sheriff Townsend grew quite wealthy during his term. Envy of this plus resentment of black support led to much discontent among the white electorate, and this discontent was one of the principal causes of the bloodshed.

Townsend, Mark (1859–1915): Marcus Harvey (sometimes Hervey) Townsend was born March 26, 1859, in Colorado County and died in San Antonio on June 26, 1915. His father, Moses Salon Townsend, was a brother of Sheriff Light Townsend. On December 20, 1883, he married Annie Euphemia Burford, the sister of Sheriff Will Burford. He was an attorney, and was elected to the House of Representatives in 1882 and the State Senate in 1888. He was involved in the shooting of Sam Reese in 1899 and the shooting at the railroad depot in Rosenberg in 1900.

Townsend Mary (Polly) (1832–1912): daughter of Asa Townsend, mother of Larkin and Marion Hope by her first marriage and mother of Dr. Joseph Lessing, Jr. by a subsequent marriage.

Townsend, Moses Salon (1830–1867): He was he fifth child of Asa and Rebecca Townsend. He had many run-ins with the law in Colorado County prior to the Civil War. During the war he served as a lieutenant in Colonel Griffin's regiment. He drowned after the war while attempting to ford a swollen creek west of Columbus. Marcus Townsend was eight years old when his father died and went to live with his grandfather Asa.

Townsend, Spencer (1806–1857): Spencer Burton Townsend was one of the original seven Townsend brothers (and one sister) to move to Texas from Florida and Georgia in the early decades of the nineteenth century. Several of his children and grandchildren were involved in the feud. The death of his son A. Stapleton Townsend in 1867 at the hands of a posse probably led to the Columbus shoot-out in 1871 between the Stafford brothers and Sumner Townsend. Son James (Jim) Gaither Townsend allied with Mark Townsend and was indicted for the murder of Dick Reese in 1899 and his trial on a change of venue to Bastrop precipitated the ambush in which Arthur Burford was killed and Will Clements severely wounded. Daughter Keron Blanche (Keetie) Townsend married Sam Reese and became, by several accounts, one of the chief instigators of the feud after the death of her husband in 1899.

Townsend, Stapleton (1849–1867): he was killed in July 1867 by a Lavaca County posse while attempting to flee arrest for stealing two horses and conspiring to steal two more. Exculpatory testimony by R. E. Stafford led to the exoneration of the men involved, which infuriated the Townsend family and led, by some accounts, to a shoot-out on December 5, 1871, between R. E. Stafford, Ben Stafford, John Stafford, and their cousin Richard R. Ratcliff on the one side and Sumner Townsend on the other. Leander H. McNelly, at the time a captain in the State Police, was summoned to Columbus to put a lid on matters.

Townsend, Sumner (1837–1888): Son of Asa. He was involved in an 1871 shoot-out in Columbus with Ben and Bob Stafford. He had no other involvement in the feud after this episode.

Walker, W. R. "Bob" (dates unknown): City Marshal when Sam Reese was killed (March, 1899) and was a staunch friend and ally of the ex-Sheriff. He had deputized both Sam Reese and his son-in-law Joe Lessing, Jr., which permitted them to legally carry pistols. He was present at the shooting of Sam Reese.

Williams, Johnny (1893–?): John Williams was the son of Henry S. and Mattie Williams. He was shot in the hip by a stray bullet during the March 16, 1899, shoot-out in downtown Columbus.

Wooldridge, Gunger (1872–?): Augustus B. Wooldridge was born about 1872. He was the grandson and namesake of a prominent Oakland plantation owner. His great-aunt was Theresa Ivey, who owned most of the town of Oakland. He served as deputy sheriff and was considered to be partial to the Townsend side. He was present at both the shooting of Sam Reese in 1898 and at the Rosenberg shoot-out in 1900.

Wright, Will (1868–1942): William Lee Wright joined the Texas Rangers in 1898, serving until 1902. He resumed his on-again-off-again career with the rangers in 1917, when he was appointed a captain. He had family connections with Columbus through his great-grandmother Elizabeth

Tumlinson. Ranger Wright served in Columbus on several occasions and gained the respect of all sides.

Yates, Step (1861–1899): Andrew Lynn Yates was the grandson of Will Burford's grandfather's second wife. Along with Jim Townsend, he was accused of shooting Dick Reese and Dick Gant at the river bridge in Columbus in 1899. He died of a fever September 14, 1899, before the matter came to trial.

APPENDIX B

Goeppinger Interviews

1. The Staffords and Townsends

Charlie Kearney[1]: Go an' ask him about some of this shootin' around here. Some of this stuff ought to be recorded.

Goeppinger: You talking about this Stafford business again?

Jim Kearney: Yeah.

Goeppinger: Well, Stafford, he run the bank, and he had the best opera house between Houston and San Antonio, the only one because people had to travel, show people had to travel, and they couldn't make it, ya know, show in one town. So we built this and we had a nice opera house at one time ... Well, then, Bob Stafford was a banker then, and, John Stafford was the cattleman, ya see ... ran the cow people from here to the coast. Ole man Stafford [*sic*. Bob] was the brains and the money. He had a packinghouse. We had a packinghouse here, Jim, down on the river there. Stafford owned it, and they had their own cars, Charlie.

Charlie Kearney: Had an ice plant too.

Goeppinger: Ice plant and they iced 'em up and ship 'em to Chicago and St. Louis, all around ya know. Big business. Well, they had these Columbus goin's [railroad]. Old man Stafford took a notion they made too damn much noise, couldn't sleep. He made 'em move out to Glidden out there. That wasn't nothin' but brush. Cleaned it up and made Glidden a railroading center. That's how come Stafford made the railroad move. You know, right there where Thurmond West[2] live, that was the S. P. [*sic*. Southern Pacific] hospital. One time, it was all the people worked on the Southern Pacific from New Orleans to El Paso went to that hospital. Ole Dr. Harrison,[3] and his family and them, was his doctor there at that time, which is how come ole man Harrison lives here. Well, then the Staffords had this cattle ranch and finally they, they began to get too much, and these old natives around here, ole man Seymour,[4] and ole man Buck Carlton,[5] ole man Oakes.[6] They got Light Townsend[7] to come in here from Tennessee. And they got him to stay a little while. First thing he done work on a section gang, and then they knew they could handle the nigger vote, the niggers could vote like they do now. And ole Light Townsend run for sheriff against ole man Toliver.[8] Light Townsend beat ole Toliver. He done it with the nigger votes. Well, he [Stafford] went t' stealin' the cattle, burnin' up the houses, ya know, it was pretty bad in them days.(26:14) So Light Townsend, he begin to form his opposition, he begin to whittle 'em down, kill 'em out, one at a time. He never killed nobody, he'd have it done. Ole man Light never killed a man in his back, but he had warriors would do it. Now I want to tell ya, and that's the way the feud started between the Townsends and the Staffords. Then they wound up between the Townsends, Hopes, and the Reese's. That's the end of it, that's where I come in, in the Reese part. I ain't gonna tell some of that[9] and I was great friends of Hub [*sic*. Herbert Reese][10] when we was boys.

Charlie Kearney: Well Reese[11] was Sheriff later.

Goeppinger: He was brought in here, Light Townsend brought him in here as his first deputy, from Oakland,

and he was a good 'un. And then after ole man Light got sick and died at his house, with his boots on. He didn't get killed. All the rest of 'em was killed. All was quiet down and then ole John Stafford out there had two children, one named Joe and one named Carrie, a girl. Light Townsend had seven children, but his youngest daughter was named Carrie.[12]

Charlie Kearney: That was Miss Carrie.

Goeppinger: And it went on, Light Townsend hired Larkin Hope[13] and Marion Hope[14] to kill John and Bob Stafford when they laid the cornerstone here at the courthouse. They put ole Warren Stafford[15] in the calaboose.[16] Up there we had a calaboose. Remember up the street there ... and ole man Stafford went, told Light Townsend and said, "I want you to turn my boy out, you got him in that calaboose, we got a big day here, cause he got drunk you locked him up and he can't see nothing." Well we got a big argument come up and ole man Bob went on home, and Townsend told Larkin and Marion Hope, they were two young men, badder 'n hell. He told 'em, "When ole Bob comes out, comes by, start an argument and kill 'im." And then John Stafford, he's up the street ya know, he come back down here when he hears the shootin'. He'll come down to see what it's all about and shoot him. So that's what they done. They killed 'em. (28:50).

Charlie Kearney: Killed 'em in that saloon.[17]

Goeppinger: Right on the corner.

2. **Seymour Ranch story**

    Goeppinger: But anyhow, he come down here and he opened up that lumberyard (07:34.1) and Sam Seymour[18] run it.[19] He come home with his hardware business. Drop in at home and see us every now and then. And it went on thataway and then he go in the cattle business so went down to the edge of Wharton

County and Jackson County and Colorado County, bought a ranch and from the State of Texas, 7,000 acres, paid $2 an acre for it to the government.[20]

Charlie Kearney: He bought it from the state government?

Goeppinger: It was all free land. All you had to do was pay taxes on it.

Jim Kearney: About what year was it? Approximately.

Goeppinger: Well let me see, I'm 90 years old, I was born in '82. It happened in about five years.

Jim Kearney: Around 1880?

Goeppinger: See I'm 90 now January sixth, and they bought this ranch down there. And they run that along down there and they put Charlie Seymour[21] down there, the other Seymour, one would run the lumberyard, he put Charlie Seymour down there running the ranch. (08:47.5) Charlie Seymour was ranch foreman of Seymour ranch. Charlie Tropkick[22] for the Horne Ranch where Tatum and Nada is down there. That was Horne Ranch.[23] Cattle ranch was west of that and then it was open from there to the coast, you see. All right. It went on, they run that ranch down there, Sam Seymour run the lumberyard, and we children drove up went to the little old high school. I never went no further than sixth grade. I'd run off, go out to the farm, ya know. I wanted to stay out there with them nigras. We had six hundred niggers out there.[24] (09:34.2)

Charlie Kearney: Was that the Seymour farm?

Goeppinger: Yeah, that was the Seymour farm. My grandad,[25] he run it and, and my grandaddy lived out there. He had this big farm and he worked his ranch, and we had the lumber business, you know. It was all mixed up together, you know, and so ... He put up the first barbed wire fence, in Jackson, Colorado and another county, what is it?[26]

Charlie Kearney: Wharton County.

Goeppinger: Wharton County, you know, all right. He got in his buggy, rode up to the Stafford Bank, Stafford had a bank here at that time, called old Bob Stafford out. He said, "Bob, I want to tell you something." My dad called Bob out. He says, "I put up, I fenced up seven thousand acres down there. I put nine gates in it, and when your cowpunchers come through there and open and shut them gates so my cattle won't get out." Bob says, "All right, Seymour I'll do my best." Went on about six months, they began to cut the fence, wires get loose, and would then have to patch it, you know. Everybody had a six-shooter in a saddle pocket and a pair of wire cutters—cowpunchers did in them days. In your left hand you had your pistol on your left hand side, and your wire cutters on your right. You always had your pistol in your saddle pocket.

Charlie Kearney: Most everybody carried a pistol?

Goeppinger: Oh yeah (11:09.8), you never left home without your pistol.

Charlie Kearney: Like putting on your pants.

Goeppinger: Puttin' on your pants. And so, it went on a little while and they began to cut his fence. Ole man Charlie Seymour come up and told granddaddy on the farm about it, told him daddy what is goin' on. He says, "All right I'll be down there in a day or two." In them days the Winchesters were the best you could buy, you know, old 44's.

Charlie Kearney: Fit your pistol and your rifle.[27]

Goeppinger: (11:42.5) He went down there and bought 'em two or three 44's, and seven boxes of cotton gin cartridges[28] to the ranch. We had a tough cowpuncher down there with us, one of the toughest in South Texas, named Matt Moore.[29] He called old Matt Moore out, talked

to him, he says, "Matt, I'm gonna give you a new job tonight." He says, "What's that Mr. Seymour?" He says, "You gonna ride that fence from sundown to sunup," he says, "That's your job, ride this pasture fence." He says, "Anybody you see, be sure, you see him down cutting that fence," he says, "Kill 'im and put him in the pocket, Devil's pocket." We had a place about 400 acres down there just thicker than hell you know. (12:27.9) They call this part of it, part of it left in the hills that ranch.
Charlie Kearney: Allen Ranch.
Goeppinger: Yeah, and so Ole Matt he rode around. Finally he got his first man, he says kill 'im, put him in the pocket, tie his reins around the horn on his saddle and head his horse towards Ranche Grande.[30] Ranche Grande was the headquarters for the Stafford Ranch.
Charlie Kearney: Where was that located?
Goeppinger: Where Nada is now, Nada is ole Ranche Grande, ain't that ole Ranche Grande?
Charlie Kearney: Yeah.
Goeppinger: I think that's the place. Anyhow, ole Matt put about four or five of them in the thicket, ya know, say nothing about it. One day on the front gallery, I was six years old. I can remember it just like it was yesterday. I wasn't but between six and seven years old then. I looked up to this big gate, you know, they have a big gate in the pasture, and I saw somebody drive in, in a buggy, had two horses to that buggy. I says, "Granpa, somebody's comin' in the big gate up yonder, and he drivin' two horses." He says, "That's old Bob Stafford, he never, he's the only man who comes down here and has two horses to a buggy and a nigger driver. Big rich man, Stafford, owns that bank up there." (13:57.1) So he drove up there and stopped at the ranch and granpa hollered at him and said get out Bob and come in. Have some coffee

or something like that. He said, "No, Seymour, I want to talk to you." Granpa went out to the gate, didn't have no gun. He went out to the gate and old man Bob Stafford told him, he says, "Jim I want to tell ya," he said, "I've got too many horses coming home without their riders." He says, "All right Bob, I want to tell you something, you stop 'em from cuttin' my fences and all your horses will come home with the riders." [*laughter*]

3. Ike Towell[31]

Charlie Kearney: Now what do you know about ole man Ike Towell?

Goeppinger: Well, I want to tell you something about Ike. Ole man Ike Towell. He fought the Townsends, but he was brave. He's the man that put the niggers ...

Charlie Kearney: Jim Crow law ...

Goeppinger: He started it right in our depot here one night, right here in Columbus, Texas. He walked in there, there was a bunch of niggers in there with some white women by the door. He says, "You black sons-of-bitches get over there, get outta here and get on your horse, and leave (unintelligible) white folks, and (unintelligible)." Jim Crow law had to put in two depots all over and they had to have the same car and (unintelligible) for the niggers to ride in.[32]

Goeppinger: He bought his own tombstone before he died. Put it up. He said, "Here lies the body of old Ike Towell. No chance for heaven, No fear of hell."(41:28) You can go out there and read it.

Charlie Kearney: Ya know he come by the barbershop and he said, "What you all get for shaving a dead man?" Two dollars. He said, "I just saved a dollar and a half." They shaved him and then.

Goeppinger: One time outside Zummwalt's drug store old Ike, ole man Ike Towell, was in there and him and

Larkin Hope got in an argument, got in a fight. Larkin Hope hit him over the head with his pistol, he fell on the sidewalk, and in them days upstairs the roof had two iron posts. He fell right between them two iron posts, they wasn't that far apart, with his face up. Larkin jumped on him over there and beat 'em over the head with his six-shooter. He went with his hand in his pocket, had one of these spring back knives, he got mad enough to get ole Larkin by the neck, ya know, and he stuck that god damn knife in him right up here, and he cut his guts plum out of him. Larkin Hope begin to holler, "Pull him off of me, he's killin' me, he's cuttin' me." Ole man Ike just whittlin' him, cuttin' him. And do you know, they took him up there and put his guts back in and Bob Harrison and he liv's that son-of-a-bitch (unintelligible), but he was just scars all over him. Well, ole man Ike, he stays around there, but he didn't want, he knew he didn't have a chance, but he fought him as long as he could, but he left here and went to Bay City. He went down there on that Bernardo River somewhere and bought a lot of property. But after he sold that he come up here and died up here with Miss Walker.[33] That was his sister. (43:26)

4. **Saloon Story**

Goeppinger: One time ole Bob Foard[34] and a blacksmith, they went out here on Sandmeyer Ranch[35] and went huntin', squirrel huntin', and they got in an argument and come back here to the saloon, and they were drinking in there. Ole blacksmith was a customer, long, tall, (unintelligible). Me and George Little[36] was sittin' on the steps at the saloon, street ya know, we saw him go in Brunson's Saloon.[37] Blacksmith pulled his drawer out and got his pistol, a .45.[38] I punched George Little, I said, "George, what is he doing goin' getting his pistol? I see him taking it out of his drawer." He said, "I don't know, we'll see." He come right by us, had his pistol in his hand. He walked in the saloon there, and he told Bob Foard. Bob Foard called him a liar or something and they got in another argument. Put two bullets in him. Killed him. Bob Foard fell back there ya know like he was goin' dancin', an he killed him dead. Me and George Little sittin' down out there. Larkin Hope[39] come up there and arrested ole blacksmith took him along and put him in jail. Me and George Little sittin' there and we never were a witness … but we lookin' right at it when he shot. (laughter)(1:08:06)

5. **The Killing of Larkin Hope**
   Goeppinger: Well his next time come up to be sheriff, Larkin Hope run against him. Well Larkin Hope knew, I mean Sam Reese knew, that Larkin Hope would beat him because he had the nigger votes. There wasn't but one way to do it, which was to get rid of him. So he had a meeting, [*laughter*] Jim Coleman, Walt [*sic*. Walter] Reese, Hub [*sic*. Herbert] Reese, Sandy Reese, this Miss Lilly [*sic*. Lillian] up here, me. Well, on that summer, Sunday night, at the jail,[40] we finished our supper, shoved our chairs back, started out. Hub said, "Goep[41] where your goin'?" I said, "I am goin' around to ole Ben Stafford's[42] house over there and see a gal named Jesse Strand (?), make a date." I said, "Hub, where are you goin'?" He said, "I'm going down to Traylor's house[43] to see Bob Traylor." He said, "But wait, we got to saddle my horse, saddle old Baldy for us." Well, I didn't ask no questions, we went out and saddled old Baldy. He was a bald faced, single-footin' horse. When he got him saddled Jim Coleman[44] come out of the house, he eat supper with us, he come out of the house Hub handed him, I believe it was, a ten gauge shotgun. He said open the gate there Goep and let him out—the gate going out

to the street. I opened the gate and when he passed I said, "Good luck, Jim, and hold up my hand." (31:12) See him (?) went off down west down there. Well, he turn in and come up between that alley up there.
Charlie Kearney: By Goldsmith's saloon.
Goeppinger: Right there by where that store is, ya know. He got his horse in there.
Charlie Kearney: There at Wynn's.
Goeppinger: He got his horse in there and went up between those buildings. Jim did with his shotgun. Walt Reese come on town, sent ole Tom Schein, a nigger, down to Hope, told him to come to town they wanted to talk to him at the saloon, had to have some beer. Mrs. Hope tried to get him not to go. She begged him. "They just want to hurt you," says Larkin, "Don't go." He says, "I'm goin up there... see what they want." He come up there and just as he passed ole Jim put that buckshot to him, then ole man Larkin empties his gun, six times. But in the meantime, I was sitting on that bridge up there, reason I was on the bridge, I was on the front gallery talkin' to this gal and ole lady Stafford her aunt come out and I wanted to love her a little. [*laughter*] I said, "Jess, let's get out of here." The bridge to town that's where they cleaned the sewer. We were sitting there swinging our feet up towards town, when he shoots him. Jess told me, "Goep, what's goin on up there?" I says, "Nothing," something like that. I didn't know exactly what was going on, but in a little while, we was sittin there, we still on the bridge, I heard that single-footin' horse comin', right there where they got that ... laundry you know? When you cross that river (makes sound like horse steps), but I knew that's Jim, that hoss', I knew him. He passed me and passed close to ... and his horse like jumped out from under him and he picked up that

shotgun, and I said, "Look out there, Jim, this is me, don't shoot me." He crossed the river, went on over to Bernardo, Mrs. Burttschell ... when they went over there and arrested ole Jim over there, she swore on stand over there that Jim had been out there plowing for two or three weeks, had never been to town. [*laughter*] Boy, that's ugly, you put that out there where I can get it. (33:46)

6. **The Killing of Sam Reese**

    Goeppinger: He rode up there one day and there was a hobo[45] there ... Marcus Townsend, he was in there in that grocery store. Ole man Reese rode up there an asked that hobo, but inside of the place was Will Clements, and Will Clements and Gunger Woolridge was in the saloon ... He says, "Well, how ya gettin' along?" He says, "All right, but these fella's are knockin' after me, Mr. Reese." He says, "Well, you're ain't gonna have to take it, ain't ya?" About that time, Gunger Wooldridge and what ya call it started in on Reese, ya know, and then they all went after their guns at the same time an ole Mark Townsend was a crack shot with a .38 pistol, he made one shot and broke Sam Reese's neck out of that grocery store. He put his gun in his pocket and walked on home. Left the rest of them up there to be arrested.

    Charlie Kearney: Be arrested huh. [*laughter*] (38:41)

    Goeppinger: (unintelligible) right there. And this here old fellow that used to run that road, use to run that paint shop, of furniture fixtures down there near the hospital ya know, what was his name?

    Charlie Kearney: Ole, uh, yeah. Well, his boy got drowned in the river.

    Goeppinger: Yeah. He went to get in his wagon, his daddy, he went to get in his wagon, start home, one of those stray bullets, when they shootin' at Sam Reese, killed him.[46] He fell off his wagon, and this John Williams was down there where John Williams[47] run the store down there where that boy got that flower shop, that John Williams when he was a kid he learned to shoot and (unintelligible) and he went and swung around on the gate. He caught a bullet right in his ass.

Charlie Kearney: He was up there at that old Heller place.

Goeppinger: Yeah, right through the cheek. Old man Williams[48] step in and got his Winchester, put it on his shoulder, grabbed his boy in one hand and come right up between 'em. He says, "Now lookee here, I'm taking my boy to the doctor and you sons of bitches better none of you ever raise a gun at me I'll kill the whole outfit." He walked right up to 'em. Nobody bother him. He carried his boy up to the drug store. Ole Doc Harrison, but he didn't break no bones.

Charlie Kearney: Oh yeah, that was some rough times. You know old man Warner told me a lot about that. 'Bout the times here then.

7. **The Rangers after Goeppinger; the Revenant**

Goeppinger: I went to St. Edwards,[49] I stayed up there till Christmas … I was just doin' fine, but ole Billy Dietz. He talk to me had a young priest that came from Notre Dame, named Father Robertson, and he was a ball player, pitcher. Hot dog he was good. He was teachin' 'rithmatic there. He took a big interest in me. They wanted me to stay, ya know. But they let me come home Christmas.

Charlie Kearney: That was a mistake.

Goeppinger: That was the biggest mistake they ever done. (19:26.2) And I got out of there and of course the feud was on. Me and Hub [*sic*. Herbert] Reese got to slippin' around and it wasn't long until I was in trouble again. [*laughter*] The Rangers got me.

Jim Kearney: What did you do to get in trouble?
Goeppinger: Shootin' that's all.[50] So they looked up for me one day and I was gone. I went to Houston. Jim Laurel(?), I knew him down there and I went to work in the S. P. shops.[51] Nobody knew where I was. Well in those days you could go to Houston you could get plum out a, didn't have no automobiles, they had a telegraph, but I don't believe telephones were workin' even. Well I was down there workin', just doing fine. Doin' all right. ... God damn they come down and they was lookin' for me. Ole man Sam... And they located me. And he sent over... I'm missin' who was sheriff, but ole gun [*sic* Gunger] Woolridge[52] and Will Clements[53] come down there one day and they start to put handcuffs on me. I told 'em wait a minute, I want to get some stuff out of my locker. Shit, I went out the back door of that locker and I was gone again. I caught me a freight train right at the end of the yard and went through the top of a reefer, dropped down the reefer and got out in New Orleans. Stayed in there two days. That's a long trip, stayin' in that reefer. Well, I got down in there, I got around, I go down there on that river, bunch of Dagos. Boy that was tough down there on Dago front and the United States government was buyin' mules, sellin' them to England in the Boer War.[54] (21:18.5) Ya remember when the Boer War was?
Charlie Kearney: About 1902, wasn't it? 1902? Right at the turn of the century.
Goeppinger: I helped 'em. Helped load them mules. Went with 'em. Long gone. Two years those sons-a-bitch didn't know where I was. Goddamn, I had some rough old times out there in that water. You know took ya six months-four months to go across that pond ... Why I was over there. It was rough. We kick those old mules in the

head and pull 'em around. [*laughter*] ... know Charlie. I walk in the lumberyard one day two years after an ole man Townsend look at me and say, "Ain't you John Goeppinger?" He says, "By gosh we thought you was dead two years ago." I said, "Well, I'm back again. That's a good 'un ain't it?" [*laughter*]

8. **Shooting of Mark Townsend's Henchman**

One time, I rode in from the country on my horse, tied my horse at the Zummwalt's drug store.[55] That was about 1904. I was married then too. Tied my horse, and ole man George Best[56] was sittin' there on that window. He was a cotton [broker]. He was a big shot too. He was an ole man. Ya know, young men listened to old men in those days. I tied my horse and he says, "Goep, ya see that nigger up yonder." I say, "Yeah." He says, "He's ridin' up and down the street. That's one of Mark Townsend's henchmans, niggers. He gonna ride out of town directly. Reckon can do anything about it?" I says, "Well I don't know, why?" He says, "Ya got the pistol?" I said, "It's in my saddle pocket." Meantime, I go to the saloon and got me a drink. Ole man Best says, "I'll tell ya what do, Walt Reese, come up there and sit down by him, Walt Reese. You go down there to creek, rattlers creek,[57] where that old (unintelligible), go down there to that creek, on this side of the sand bank, they have a lot of huisaches."[58] He says, "Get in them huisaches down near the creek, and when that nigger comes by,[59] you ride out and get in an argument with him. And he says anything to ya, kill him." Well, I done like he told me. I rode on out there, when I got in the huisaches, I began to think, well that nigger may have a pistol too. Best thing you can do is kill the son-of-a-bitch and then argue with him. [*laughter*] He come out singin', I laid him over ya know, one shot, (unintelligible). He fell off his horse on that (unintelligible). I come on town an act like nothing happen, put the pistol back in my saddle pocket. (36:37) Rode up to the drug store in town tied my horse and got me a drink. Ole man Best, he says, "What come of that nigger, see anything of him?" I said, "He's down there in them huisaches where you told me to put him." [*laughter*]

9. **The Killing of Jim Coleman**[60]

   Goeppinger: Mark Townsend afraid they gonna get him, he moved to San Antonio. He carried ole man Will[61] as a henchman. And Kincheloe[62] down in Wharton, you know that Kincheloe is the one that killed Jim Coleman, he's bad son-of-a-bitch. He had old Kincheloe as his bodyguard. San Antonio. Ole Jim Coleman was in (unintelligible) saloon one night. He followed him up there, you know. Lookin' for a shot. Out in front he's sittin' at the table, has a drink or two, ole Jim, an ole Kincheloe walked in, with Light, uh, Townsend, not Light, Mark, he was a lawyer. Mark was a ramrod, the lawyers the brains, Light was the sheriff. Just like the Staffords, Bob was the brains and money and ole John Stafford done the work, ya understand? That's the way, that's just the way. So, ole Jim was sittin' at that table and walked in there and he looked up and seen ole Kincheloe and he went for his gun but Kincheloe—boom, boom, boom—shot him four times. Ole Jim just slumped over the table, bartender run up there and say, "Jim, is there anything I can do to you?" He said, "Hell no, just get out of the way and let me die in peace." [*laughter*]

10. **The Death of Marion Hope**

    Marion Hope went out in the pasture there to see about some cattle and he never come back. Nobody knows what happened. [*laughter*] Pretty terrible wasn't it?[63]

APPENDIX C

Ranger Captain Sieker Report

After the death of Dick Reese on May 17, 1899, a call went out for the rangers. Captain Lamartine Pemberton Sieker, quartermaster of the Frontier Battalion, answered the call and arrived in Columbus by train on May 19, 1899. He found a great many armed men, members of both factions, roaming the streets. Four more rangers, including Will Wright and Creed Taylor, joined Sieker the next day. The five rangers set about disarming men who were not legally entitled to carry guns, and urging those who did not live in town to return home. Sieker subsequently wrote a report that was included in Adjutant General Scurry's June report to Governor Sayers. Of all the ranger reports it is the most succinct and insightful. Below it is reproduced in full:

"The existing troubles in this county date directly from political affairs preceding the late election, but much of the bitter feeling attending the same is due remotely to an old feud of fifty years standing between the Stafford and Townsend factions, but which was virtually ended in 1890 when R. E. and John Stafford were killed by Larkin and Marion Hope, which left the Stafford element without a head. Light Townsend, the leader of the Townsend element, was at that time sheriff, and the late Sheriff Reese was his deputy. The Hopes were nephews of Townsend and Reese was related by marriage. Townsend died in 1894 and Reese was appointed to fill the unexpired term, and elected in 1896 to another term. At that election, the Townsends, Hopes, and Burtshells [*sic*. Burttschell] were all warm supporters of Reese. Lessing, a half-brother of the Hopes, married Sheriff Reese's daughter, and in the summer of 1899 a coldness existed between Larkin Hope and Reese. Lessing became a candidate for constable against Larkin Hope, his half-brother who was then the incumbent of that office. Hope thought Lessing's candidacy was instigated by Reese, and immediately withdrew from the race for constable and announced for sheriff against Reese. Both Hope and Reese were bold, daring, and desperate men. A vigorous campaign was prosecuted for about two months and a deadly fight was expected to occur between them at any time. The Burttschells and their brother-in-law Jim Coleman were active supporters of Reese, and Hope denounced the Reese and the Burttschells in unqualified terms, boldly and openly, [*sic*. New sentence starts at "on"] on the night of August 3, 1898, Hope was assassinated on the streets of Columbus and Jim Coleman is now under indictment charged with this offense. The circumstances of this assassination were most dastardly and Coleman was refused bail by Judge Kennon until only a few weeks ago he reconsidered his former decision and granted bail. There were certain circumstances in connection with the killing of Hope which caused his friends to believe that it was done by Coleman and at the instigation of Reese and the Burttschells. M. H. Townsend, a prominent lawyer and a cousin of the Hopes, and also of Reese's wife, vigorously prosecuted Coleman upon the Habeas Corpus trial and shortly thereafter, Mr. Burford, Townsend's brother-in-law, announced as a candidate for sheriff against Reese. The campaign was bitter and much money was spent on both sides, all the parties being men of considerable wealth. Burford was elected by over six hundred majority, and Reese and his friends both took the result very keenly. M. H. Townsend was the object of their intense hatred, as they thought Burford's election was due his political power and manipulation of the Negro vote, backed by the necessary funds to make it effective. After the election many circumstances, which ought to have been considered in a trivial light, occurred and greatly intensified the existing bitter feeling. One of Burford's deputies, Mr. Clements, was related to the Townsends and also related to Mr. Reese. Reese seemed to take the appointment of Clements as a personal affront, and serious trouble between them became imminent. Mr. Reese, stinging over the result of the election, became very aggressive towards Clements, and serious trouble was only averted by the intervention of third parties on several occasions. After his defeat in the election, Reese and his son-in-law Lessing were both deputized by the city marshal of Columbus, a friend of theirs, and thus all parties were permitted to carry arms. On the evening of March sixteenth Clements was in a verbal altercation with one Ed Scott, a friend of Reese and the Burttschells, who had just been released from jail where he had been confined in the cell with Coleman for several months, and Reese rode up and proposed to arm Scott in order to place him on an equality with Clements. Both Clements and Reese at once drew their pistols and began firing at one another, and M. H. Townsend and Marion Hope, friends of Clements, and City Marshal Walker, a friend of Reese and probably several others drew pistols. About twenty shots were fired, and Reese was killed, also a German farmer Boehme, a non-combatant was killed and a six year old boy was shot through the hips and seriously wounded for life. A few days after the difficulty, about twenty-five or thirty armed men, mostly from Lavaca County, including several brothers of Reese, and headed by ex-Sheriff Jim F. Houchins of Lavaca County, Mr. Reese's nephew. These men were also backed up and encouraged by Reese's friends in this county, but more particularly by the sympathizers of the old Stafford or anti-Townsend faction,[1] who after the killing of Larkin Hope, whom they hated, became warm friends of Reese. The sheriff called to his assistance about an equal number of his friends and partisans, and the people of Columbus became much alarmed at the presence of these two armed bodies of infuriated and dangerous men. The call for rangers was made by the district judge, and they arrived a few days later, under command of Captain McDonald, who immediately took the necessary steps to avert further bloodshed. The Lavaca County men returned home, and the sheriff's posse disbanded and went to their respective abodes. M. H. Townsend, Will Clements, and Marion Hope were all indicted for manslaughter charged with the killing of Reese, and many threats have been made against Townsend's life by members of the combined Reese/Burttschells factions. On May sixteenth one or two of the Reese faction appeared in this county from Sublime in Lavaca County. On the same day Jim Coleman came to Eagle Lake by train and was conveyed in a buggy by one of the Burttschells to Alleyton,[2] within three miles of Columbus. Dick Reese of Orange came to Columbus the night before in the company with another one of the Reese's, and went immediately to Alleyton in the night time, and remained there in the company with Coleman and some of the Burttschells until about nine o'clock at night of the seventeenth when he (Dick Reese) started for Columbus in August Burttschells buggy in company with a Negro driver. There has recently been a great deal of shooting along the Columbus and Alleyton road,[3] and on this occasion the sheriff, Burford, had special deputies A. L. Yates and J. G. Townsend, and probably others, stationed on the road east of the bridge for the purpose, as he Burford claims, of intercepting pistol carriers. When the buggy containing Dick Reese and the Negro came along, deputies Yates and Townsend stepped out in front of them, halted an shot them down, the Negro jumping out the buggy, and Reese falling dead and remaining in the buggy. They were both probably killed instantly by shotgun and pistol shots. The deputies claim that Reese immediately drew his pistol upon being halted, and they at once fired upon him. The horse turned and ran way with the buggy, and when it was found by a disinterested posse about three o'clock in the morning, the dead body of Reese was lying across the buggy seat, and a loaded pistol was on the seat near him. About half an hour after the killing, a girl eighteen years old dressed in male attire and with face and hands blackened, was arrested in front of the jail. She was afterwards found to be the daughter of a member of the Reese faction, and she is supposed to be engaged to be married to the eldest son of the dead ex-sheriff Reese.[4] A few days later she made a voluntary statement to the effect that she had been sent out by members of the family of the ex-sheriff Reese, to visit the premises of M. H. Townsend, J. G. Townsend, Will Clements, and also the jail to see if any men were at those places, and with instructions to return to Mrs. Reese's house by ten o'clock at night and to make there three taps on the south side door where she would be admitted. Upon completion of this round, she was apprehended at the jail and lodged within until morning. On the morning of the eighteenth the friends of Reese were notified by telephone of the occurrence the night before, and the county judge at once upon the solicitation of several disinterested citizens applied to the governor for the rangers to be returned, which was done, and with the result of which, the Adjutant General is familiar. Deputy J. G. Townsend is an uncle of deputy Clements, and a brother of ex-sheriff's Reese's widow. The anti-Townsend elements and many others, who are disinterested, now contend that the troubles will continue as long as Burford occupies the sheriff's office and they persistently demand his resignation. He declines to resign, claiming his life will be in danger, and contends that this is a combined move on the part of the elements opposing him in the late election to accomplish by this means what they failed to accomplish at the polls."

APPENDIX D

Witness List Stelzig Murder Trial

TO THE CLERK OF THE DISTRICT COURT OF MATAGORDA COUNTY, TEXAS:

In the case of the STATE OF TEXAS vs. Frank Stelzig, No. 1339, charged with murder, you will please issue subpoenas in accordance with law, for the June Term, 1912, for the following named witnesses residing in the counties as below set forth:

1. Adam Burttschell residing in Columbus, Colorado County, Texas
2. E.C. Burttschell residing in Columbus, Colorado County, Texas
3. Chas. Burttschell residing in Columbus, Colorado County, Texas
4. Henry Burttschell residing in Alleyton, Colorado County, Texas
5. Willie Braden residing in Columbus, Colorado County, Texas
6. George Best residing in Columbus, Colorado County, Texas
7. Herman Braden residing in Alleyton, Colorado County, Texas
8. Conrad Clothe residing in Alleyton, Colorado County, Texas
9. W.E. Bridge residing in Columbus, Colorado County, Texas

10. J.E. Hester residing in Columbus, Colorado County, Texas
11. Geo. H. Little residing in Columbus, Colorado County, Texas
12. E.S. Sandmeyer residing in Columbus, Colorado County, Texas
13. Joseph Odom residing in Columbus, Colorado County, Texas
14. W. Odom residing in Columbus, Colorado County, Texas
15. Chas. Sronce residing in Columbus, Colorado County, Texas
16. Chas. Bailey residing in Columbus, Colorado County, Texas
17. R.C. Ilse residing in Columbus, Colorado County, Texas
18. W.L. Adkins residing in Columbus, Colorado County, Texas
19. M. Kennon residing in Columbus, Colorado County, Texas
20. E.B. Mayes residing in Columbus, Colorado County, Texas
21. J.W. Harrison residing in Columbus, Colorado County, Texas
22. J.J. Mansfield residing in Columbus, Colorado County, Texas
23. Geo. Gegenworth residing in Columbus, Colorado County, Texas
24. P.B. Martin residing in Columbus, Colorado County, Texas
25. George Martin residing in Columbus, Colorado County, Texas
26. Abe Steiner residing in Columbus, Colorado County, Texas

Appendix D

27. Sam Hamburger residing in Columbus, Colorado County, Texas
28. L.D. Shaw residing in Columbus, Colorado County, Texas
29. Frank Auerbach residing in Columbus, Colorado County, Texas
30. Frank Auerbach, Sr. residing in Columbus, Colorado County, Texas
31. S.K. Gardner residing in Columbus, Colorado County, Texas
32. A. Gardner residing in Columbus, Colorado County, Texas
33. H.J. Lass residing in Columbus, Colorado County, Texas
34. A.A. Gregory residing in Columbus, Colorado County, Texas
35. Lester Holt residing in Columbus, Colorado County, Texas
36. Lige Hightower residing in Columbus, Colorado County, Texas
37. Jos. F. Lessing residing in Columbus, Colorado County, Texas
38. Conrad Byars residing in Altair, Colorado County, Texas
39. Henry Thomas residing in Weimar, Colorado County, Texas
40. Joe Pierce residing in Weimar, Colorado County, Texas
41. Aug. Strunk residing in Weimar, Colorado County, Texas
42. T.J. Wooldrige residing in Weimar, Colorado County, Texas
43. Tom Bouldin residing in Weimar, Colorado County, Texas

44. Clate Bouldin residing in Weimar, Colorado County, Texas
45. C.T. Hancock residing in Weimar, Colorado County, Texas
46. Geo. Herder residing in Weimar, Colorado County, Texas
47. Herman Sachs residing in Weimar, Colorado County, Texas
48. Mark Callison residing in Eagle Lake Colorado County, Texas
49. Arthur McDow residing in Eagle Lake Colorado County, Texas
50. H. Vineyard residing in Eagle Lake Colorado County, Texas
51. Will Loessin residing in La Grange, Fayette County, Texas
52. E. Houchin residing in Hallettsville, Lavaca County, Texas
53. Flem Reese residing in Beeville, Bee County, Banker
54. Stafford Reese residing in Beeville, Bee County, Marshal
55. J.T. Reese residing in Sublime, Lavaca County, Officer
56. J.W. Whittington residing in Yoakum, Lavaca County, Tax Collector
57. Sam Burkett residing in Yoakum, Lavaca County, Marshal
58. J.P. Williams residing in Yoakum, Lavaca County, Stockman
59. S.B. Townsend residing in Yoakum, Lavaca County, Contractor
60. J.W. Reese residing in El Paso, El Paso County, Officer
61. C.H. Webster residing in El Paso, El Paso County, Officer

Appendix D

62. Sam L. Green residing in Houston, Harris County, Lawyer
63. Carey Shaw residing in Houston, Harris County, Banker
64. Dr. R.H. Harrison residing in Houston, Harris County, Doctor
65. Thos. B. Daniels residing in Houston, Harris County, Barber
66. Geo. Daniels residing in Houston, Harris County, Barber
67. John Perry residing in Houston, Harris County, R.R. Conductor
68. Henry Byars residing in Houston, Harris County, Real Estate
69. H. Hanson residing in Houston, Harris County, Real Estate
70. Len McFarlane residing in Houston, Harris County, Dept. U.S. Marsh.
71. S.B. Ehrenwerth residing in Houston, Harris County, Lawyer
72. A.Y. Baker residing in Chapin, Hidalgo, Cty. Treas.
73. J.W. Tobin residing in San Antonio, Bexar, Sheriff
74. W. McDonald residing in Houston, Harris Ex-Capt. Tex. Rangers G.H. & S.A. R.R.
75. J.H. Brooks residing in Falfurras, Starr Ex-Capt. Tex. Rangers Member Legislature
76. J.J. Harrison residing in Victoria, Capitalist
77. Edward Maynard residing in Bastrop, Lawyer
78. John Mathis residing in Brenham, Washington, Lawyer
79. S.H. Zapp residing in La Grange, Fayette, Mail Carrier
80. L.C. Ayars residing in Houston, Harris, Lawyer
81. H.J. Insall residing in Weimar, Colorado, Marshal
82. Tom Coleman residing in Rosenberg, Fort Bend, Farmer
83. Tom Folts residing in Glidden, Colorado, Conductor

84. Louis Burger residing in Eagle Lake, Colorado, Stockman
85. Robert Goldsmith residing in Columbus, Colorado, Saloon-man
86. W.H. Leirmann residing in Columbus, Colorado, Saloon-man
87. Bob White residing in Columbus, Colorado, Saloon-man
88. Willie Wirtz residing in Columbus, Colorado, Saloon-man
89. O.A. Zumwalt residing in Columbus, Colorado, Saloon-man
90. W.R. Sronce residing in Columbus, Colorado, Saloon-man
91. Alvey Harbert residing in Columbus, Colorado, Saloon-man
92. P. Heller, Sr. residing in Columbus, Colorado, Saloon-man
93. Fritz Kollman residing in Frelsburg Colorado, Saloon-man
94. F.R. Walker residing in Columbus Colorado, Saloon-man
95. A. Dugat residing in Columbus Colorado, Saloon-man
96. A. McCormick residing in Columbus Colorado, Saloon-man
97. Henry Walker residing in Eagle Lake Colorado, Saloon-man
98. S.H. Reese residing in Eagle Lake Colorado, Saloon-man
99. Chas. Kuntze residing in Eagle Lake Colorado, Saloon-man
100. Richard Byars residing in Altair, Colorado, Saloon-man
101. Tom Byars residing in Altair, Colorado, Saloon-man
102. T.B. West residing in Columbus, Colorado, Saloon-man

Appendix D

103. L.R. Wooten residing in Columbus, Colorado, Saloon-man
104. L.F. Dicks residing in Columbus, Colorado, Saloon-man
105. Louis Wink residing in Alleyton Colorado, Saloon-man
106. K. Brandon residing in Columbus, Colorado, Saloon-man
107. Henry Buescher residing in Bischer, Colorado, Saloon-man
108. Allie Clapp residing in Skull Creek, Colorado, Saloon-man
109. James Towell residing in Columbus, Colorado, Saloon-man
110. Billie Miller residing in Columbus, Colorado, Saloon-man
111. Joe Franka residing in Columbus, Colorado, Saloon-man
112. John Hastedt residing in Columbus, Colorado, Saloon-man
113. John Brigham residing in Columbus, Colorado, Saloon-man
114. Adolph Franz residing in Columbus, Colorado, Saloon-man
115. M.D. Flowers residing in Eagle Lake, Colorado, Saloon-man
116. Howard Fitzgerald residing in Eagle Lake, Colorado, Saloon-man
117. Dr. Potasht residing in Weimar Colorado, Saloon-man
118. E.A. Scheel residing in Galveston, Galveston, Saloon-man
119. B.F. Grace residing in Burr, Wharton, Farmer
120. C.D. Kemp residing in Wharton, Wharton, Stockman
121. Robt. Koehl residing in Wharton, Wharton, Sheriff
122. Tom Lane residing in Lane City, Wharton, Merchant

123. Will Lane residing in Lane City, Wharton, Farmer
124. Luke ward residing in Lane City, Wharton, Farmer
125. C.M. Shipman residing in Lane City, Wharton, Lumberman
126. Martin Wyland residing in Lane City, Wharton, Hotelman
127. Horace Goode residing in Lane City, Wharton, Farmer
128. Ike Towell residing in Hinkle's Ferry, Braz. Farmer

The testimony of said witnesses is believed to be material to the defense. Frank Stelzig

Sworn to and subscribed before me this 1 day of April A.D. 1912.

N.L. McKinnon

Notary Public, Fayette County, Texas

Endnotes

Introduction
1. Sonnichsen, *I'll Die Before I Run*, Introduction, xvi.
2. It is not generally understood that very strong gun-control laws existed in Texas during the whole period of this story. The Hollywood version of Texas, where practically everyone packed a pistol, is false. Only officers of the law—sheriffs, deputies, sheriffs, marshals, etc.—could legally carry firearms in public.
3. In 1962 Lillian Reese released *Flaming Feuds of Colorado County*. Although factually accurate in respect to the dates of the events and the names of the people involved, it was exceedingly one-sided in its interpretation, which is not surprising since she and her brothers were heavily involved in the feud.

Chapter One
1. Bill Stein and Jim Sewell, "Historical Atlas of Columbus," *NMLJ* 3, no 2 (May 1993): 82–84.
2. "Larkin Hope ... had acquired the reputation of a desperado some years before this occurrence by recklessly shooting, first, an old Negro man, whose daughter he had seduced, and then a paralyzed Mexican, after which he had been elected marshal of the city, a position he held at the time he killed the Staffords. He too relied on the

Negro vote to secure and maintain him in office." (Judge Mansfield memo Report of Thomas Scurry, Adjutant General to Joseph D. Sayers, governor, June 16th 1899.)
3. Ibid.
4. Ibid.
5. "Marshall Larkin Hope and ex-Marshall Ike Towell became involved in a dispute ... Hope was cut seven times ... Hope's recovery is doubtful." (*Weimar Mercury*, December 28, 1889.)
6. Henry Thomas refers to a dispute from the year 1877. See Henry Thomas, "A Sketch of my Life," in *NMLJ* 1, no. 3 (February 1990): 79.
7. *San Antonio Light*, May 22, 1907.
8. *Colorado Citizen*, July 14, 1890.
9. *Galveston Daily News*, July 9, 1890.
10. It is almost impossible to reconstruct for certain what Bob Stafford owned at the time of his death. Stafford was chronically paranoid of public disclosure. He had managed to avoid every census up to that point and because his cattle ranged freely over many counties, it was very difficult for the tax assessor to corroborate what he owned. Since by the terms of his will he left everything to his wife Sarah, there was no legal requirement for an accounting of the estate, and, in fact, Stafford expressly stipulated that there be no public disclosure of his holdings when the will was probated.

    In terms of cattle, E. E. Townsend claimed that Stafford's cowboys branded 25,000 calves in 1884. If correct, his total herd can be roughly inferred from this figure. With a 75 percent calf crop he probably owned about 30,000 cows and 1,000 bulls. Since calves were kept as steers and heifers until they reached the age of two and three, we get an additional 50,000 or so animals, the total easily approaching 100,000 animals. But this was only for Colorado, Jackson, and Wharton counties. In addition to this, we know from other sources that Stafford also owned substantial herds in Refugio County, was a partner with Ike Pryor in the Brush Country, and owned a large herd in the Indian Territory in Oklahoma. Including these figures, the grand total could have easily added up to 150,000 animals or more.

11. State of Texas v. Larkin Hope and Marion Hope, Grand Jury Murder Indictment. September 9, 1890, Colorado County District Court Records, Criminal Cause File No. 2314.
12. Application for change of venue filed by Thomas H. Spooner, District Attorney, on September 11, 1890. Austin County District Court Records, Criminal Cause File No. 2125: State of Texas v. Larkin Hope and Marion Hope.
13. Reese, *Flaming Feuds*, 23.
14. Memorandum by Judge Mansfield attached to Report of Thomas Scurry, Adjutant General, to Joseph D. Sayers, Governor, June 16th, 1899.
15. Reese, *Flaming Feuds*, 35–37.
16. *Colorado Citizen*, October 9, 1890.
17. Ibid.
18. *Colorado Citizen*, October 2, 1890.
19. Causes continued at request of state. Austin County District Court Records, Criminal Minute Book E, 342: (2125 and 2126) State v. Marion and Larkin Hope, Jan 13, 1891.
20. This claim is made by Judge Mansfield of Columbus. See: Memorandum by Judge Mansfield attached to Report of Thomas Scurry, Adjutant General, to Joseph D. Sayers, Governor, June 16th 1899. *Ft. Worth Daily Express*, August 25, 1890.
21. "We the jury find the defendant Larkin Hope not guilty Thomas Johnson Foreman," Austin County District Court

Records, Criminal Cause File No. 2125: State of Texas v. Larkin Hope and Marion Hope, Filed July 18, 1891.
22. Ibid. Court documents list the attorneys as Brown, Lane & Jackson; Kennon, Bell & Shelburn; and Mark Townsend.
23. State v. Larkin Hope and Marion Hope (2125) continued by agreement, January 17, 1892, Austin County District Court Records, Criminal Minute Book E, 390; State v. Marion (2125) and State v. Marion and Larkin (2126) "continued generally," January 9, 1893, Ibid., 394; State v. Marion dismissed at request of the state, July 5, 1893, Ibid., 439; 2126 State v. Larkin and Marion dismissed at request of the state, July 5, 1893. 447: 2125 State v. Marion, July 5, 1893, "Now in this cause comes the state of Texas by her district attorney, and moves the court to dismiss the above case for the following reasons to wit: because at a former term of this court a companion case to this involving the same facts, was tried and the defendant acquitted; that by reason of said acquittal this case has been so weakened that I deem it impossible to secure a conviction at least in this county where the case has been considerably discussed and the sympathy of the public is entirely with the defendant." Same thing said about 2126.
24. Ibid.
25. A law requiring separate coaches passed the Texas Legislature March 19, 1891. (Gammel, *Laws*, V. 10, 44, 45.) City Marshal Ike Towell, however, apparently took it upon himself prior to this date to require separate seating at the Columbus depot, and some have claimed this as the first act of this kind after Reconstruction. Mary Farrar Holland, a Columbus native wrote in 1948:

> The "Jim Crow Law," which required the separation of whites and Negroes in public service institutions, coaches, waiting rooms, etc. ..., originated

in Columbus, Texas. Ike Towell, City Marshal of Columbus, became incensed over the fact that Negroes were taking possession of the waiting room in the Southern Pacific depot while the white ladies were forced to stand outside. He appealed to the city authorities to break up this practice, but his request was refused. Ike Towell took the law into his own hands and proceeded to clear the depot. He had some trouble at first, having to whip two resentful Negroes. After this episode, another waiting room was built for Negroes. Out of this action, what is known as the "Jim Crow Law" was passed by the Texas Legislature in 1891. (Clipped from a "Thesis" by Norma Shaw and appeared in Mary Farrar Holland, *Tales that have been Told*, 96.)

John Goeppinger repeated the claim in his interview and Ike Towell's official obituary also repeated the claim:

Mr. Towell had an ordinance passed requiring the railroad company to provide separate waiting rooms for white and Negro people. He later urged and secured the passage of the state separate carriage for railroads. He organized the White Man's party in Matagorda County and was involved in the organization of the same in Colorado County in 1902. (*Eagle Lake Headlight*, February 24, 1934.)

26. Douglas, *The Cattle Kings of Texas*.

Chapter Two

1. See: Wyatt, *The Seven Townsend Brothers of Texas*, 273; also, Samuel Luck Townsend Memoir, a manuscript in the ANML.
2. Stein, "Consider the Lilly," *NMLJ* 6, no. 1 (Jan. 1996): 6.

3. A complete description of the Townsend settlement is given in the unpublished memoirs of Samuel Luck Townsend. A copy is in ANML.
4. Wyatt, *Seven Townsend Brothers*, 272.
5. "Enough of Austin's original 300 families brought slaves with them that a census of his colony in 1825 showed 443 in a total population of 1,800." (Campbell, "Slavery," *NHT*.)
6. Perhaps the best first-hand account of conflict with Native Americans is by J. H. Kuykendall. See Kuykendall, "Reminiscences of Early Texas, *SWHQ* 7, no. 1 (July 1903): 29–64.
7. For a discussion of the sources and controversy concerning the destruction, see Stein, "Beyond Boosterism: Establishing the Age of Columbus," *NMLJ* 2, no. 2, (May 1992): 77.
8. Recruits included younger brothers Moses, William T. and Spencer Burton Townsend as well as a nephew, who also went by the name Stephen. The nephew was the son of Asa Townsend and the older brother of future sheriff of Colorado County, Light Townsend. (Moore, *Eighteen Minutes*, 99.) According to the rolls compiled by Stephen Moore, only Spencer and the elder Stephen were present at San Jacinto (Moore, *Eighteen Minutes*, 437), but Tula Townsend Wyatt maintains that Stephen, Spencer B., and Moses were all present whereas John T., William, William T., and Thomas R., and John T., were ordered to guard the baggage train at Harrisburg and had missed the battle through no fault of their own. Stephen Townsend's brother-in-law, Joel Robison and another relative, Scion Bostick, are credited with capturing Santa Anna. (Wyatt, *Seven Townsend Brothers of Texas*, 272.)
9. Wyatt, *Seven Townsend Brothers*, 273.
10. Stephen received a 1st class unconditional grant for a league and a labor in 1838. (See Land Certificates,

Colorado County, 19.) Both Spencer and Moses received in 1838, as unmarried men, 1st class unconditional grants for 1/3 leagues. (Land Certificates, Colorado County, 20.) Moses settled his headright on the western bank of the Navidad near the present community of Vienna in southeastern Lavaca County, though at the time it was still part of Colorado County. Stapleton and W. J. Townsend received conditional titles (meaning they had to take possession and live on them) to 640 acres each in 1839. (Land Certificates, Colorado County, 152.) Stapleton and Asa Townsend both received unconditional grants to 640 acres each in 1841. (Colorado County Book of Land Certificates, 153, 156.) Asa located his grant next to land he had already purchased on Harvey's Creek, but sold 300 acres to John Suggs in 1845. (Colorado Bonds and Mortgages, Book C, 184.)

11. A big bow on the high bank of the river offered early settlers high ground and a defensible position on the western side of the river. In this beautiful natural park of majestic live oak trees the town of Columbus slowly took shape on a site that Stephen F. Austin and the Baron de Bastrop had originally surveyed in 1823. For many years the settlement was known simply as Beeson's or Beeson's Ferry, but in 1835 the citizens formally adopted the name Columbus for the fledgling settlement of about twenty-five families. For the best discussion of early Columbus, see Stein, "Consider the Lilly," *NMLJ* 6, no. 2, part 3 (May 1996): 63–72; for chapter-length coverage of the Texas Revolution, see Howell, et al., *Beyond Myths and Legends*, 77–102.

12. Spencer Townsend and Leander Beeson were indicted for the murder of Naham Mixon and locked up in July 1838. They faced trial and were acquitted a month later. (Stein, "Consider the Lilly," Part 3, *NMLJ* 6, no. 2 [May 1996]: 73.)

13. William Bell was granted first class unconditional certificate number 24 on January 22, 1838 for one-third league. (Colorado County Book of Land Certificates, 32.)
14. Asa Townsend was granted third class unconditional certificate number 5 for 640 acres on May 3, 1841. (See Colorado County Book of Land Certificates, 32.)
15. Asa sold off part of his land to Scion Record Bostick who had married his sister Susan and another tract to William Stapleton, a first cousin from his mother's side. The currently maintained Townsend/Stapleton cemetery, sandwiched between the old Weimar road and the railroad tracks near the defunct community of Borden, reminds contemporary wayfarers of their former presence.
16. Tula Townsend Wyatt makes this claim in her genealogical study. See Wyatt, *Seven Townsend Brothers*, 187. The Eighth Census of the United States, 1860, confirms this. Asa Townsend is listed with forty head of horses, the largest number in the county.
17. Asa's brother Stephen also lived in Columbus. In addition to serving as the first sheriff of Colorado County (Tise, *Texas County Sheriffs*, 117), Stephen also briefly owned and operated a ferry that crossed the river where the East River Bridge now stands. The house where Stephen and his family lived, known as the Koliba-Townsend house, survives to this day.
18. Some accounts list him as having served in the Mexican War, but this is clearly a mistake. (See Morris, *Citizens of the Republic of Texas*, 261; Stein, "Consider the Lilly," Part 4, *NMLJ* 6, no. 2, 115.) He is confused on the muster rolls with his younger son, Asa Leonard, who did serve. (See Spurlin, *Texas Veterans in the Mexican War*, 44.)
19. Stein, "Consider the Lilly," Part 3, *NMLJ* 6, no. 1, 72; Stein, Part 4, Vol. 6, No. 3, 116; Wyatt, *Seven Townsend Brothers*, 290.

20. The first commission he served on was to study the feasibility of building a new courthouse and jail, which was duly constructed. (Ibid.) A meeting of the citizens of Columbus was held in Columbus, April 19, 1845, to adopt suitable measures for the annexation of Texas to the United States of America. Townsend was a member of this committee. (*Telegraph and Texas Register*, May 7, 1845.) He joined the Colorado Navigation Association and became a member of its board of directors. The association members were ultimately successful. They hired a crew that cleared the Colorado River of a raft of debris, making the waterway navigable from Colorado County through Wharton and Matagorda counties, thereby reaching the Gulf Coast. (*Texas State Gazette*, November 3, 1849.)
21. Phelan, *A History of Early Methodism in Texas, 1817–1866*, 295, 297. The Caledonia Lodge No. 68 was established in February 1850. Asa Townsend was a charter member and served as treasurer. Brothers Stephen, Stapleton, and William T. also were charter members. (Holland, *Stories That Have Been Told*, 92, 93.)
22. "Townsend transactions." Deed Records, Book A, 330, 331, 344, 345–7. Colorado County Clerk's Office, Columbus, TX.
23. Seventh Census of the United States, 1850, Schedule 1, Slave Schedule, Colorado County, TX.
24. Eighth Census of the United States, 1860, Schedule 1, Slave Schedule, Colorado County, TX.
25. Memoirs of Samuel Luck Townsend, unpublished manuscript in the Archives of the *NML*.
26. Wyatt, *Seven Townsend Brothers*, 187.
27. Memoir of Samuel Luck Townsend, typewritten manuscript in ANML, 14.
28. Boethel states: "A fugitive from justice for nine years, he [*sic*: Spencer Townsend] found refuge in the newly founded 'county town' Petersburg. There he operated a

tavern, threw his weight around in county politics, drinking and horse racing. In 1852 he was the main spokesman for the Petersburg partisans; again he mixed gambling with community efforts, wagering $100 on the contest; he lost." (Boethel, *The Lavacans*, 16.)

29. Spencer Townsend and Leander Beeson were indicted for the murder of Naham Mixon and locked up in July 1838. They faced trial and were acquitted a month later. (See Stein, "Consider the Lilly," Part 3, *NMLJ* 6, no. 2 [May 1996]: 73.)

30. Boethel, *Sand in your Craw*, 39.

31. For an account of the controversey see: Boethel, "When the Poll was Contested," *La Baca*, 56–60.; also, Finkelstein, "Hallettsville wins the Election," *John and Margaret Hallett*, 40.

32. Ibid., 240.

33. Report of AG Thomas Scurry, to Governor Joseph D. Sayers, June 16, 1899, GP [301], ATSL.

34. The quote calls to mind the title to C.L. Sonnichsen's book about the Texas feuds, *I'll Die before I Run*. (New York: Harper & Brothers, 1951.)

35. For the best account of the shoot-out see, Bill Stein, "The Conflict between H.H. Moore and Sheriff Light Townsend," in *NMLJ* 3, no. 2 (May 1993): 58–72.

36. Three years later, on January 18, 1888, a mob of about seventy-five men appeared at the county jail in Columbus and announced its intention to lynch William Washington. Washington was accused of the rape and murder of a white woman near Frelsburg. The Colorado County sheriff, James Light Townsend, met the mob at the door, informed them that Washington had been transferred to a jail in another county, and invited any one of them into the jail to see for himself. No one accepted his offer and the mob left. Two months later, Washington was brought to trial.

He was convicted and sentenced to death. On October 19, 1888, he was hanged at the county farm. (Colorado County District Court Records, Criminal Cause File No. 2187: *State of Texas v. William Washington; Colorado Citizen*, January 5, 1888, February 2, 1888, October 25, 1888, November 1, 1888.)

37. Ibid.; Adjutant General Thomas Scurry to Governor Joseph Sayers, "Report on the homicides in Columbus," February 7, 1900, GP, (301), ATSL.
38. Colorado County Probate Index, Light Townsend.
39. In a later memo to the governor, the respected and neutral Judge Mansfield of Columbus remarked about Sheriff Townsend: "The sheriff's office yielded him, by some means, a very rich harvest as shown by the fortune he acquired during the fourteen years in which he held that place." (Report of AG Thomas Scurry, to Governor Joseph D. Sayers, governor, June 16, 1899, GP [301], ATSL.)
40. Inferred from extant Civil War letters from Moses Salon to his wife housed in the Townsend file of the Archives of the Nesbitt Memorial Library, Columbus Texas.
41. Colorado County District Court Records, CCF No. 127: State of Texas v. Moses [Salon] Townsend; CCF No. 129: State of Texas v. Moses Townsend and Thomas L. Townsend; CCF No. 146: State of Texas v. Moses Townsend, Thomas L. Townsend, Richard Waddell, and Asa Smith; CCF No. 151: State of Texas v. Moses Townsend et al.; CCF No. 152: State of Texas v. Moses Townsend et al.; Criminal Cause File No. 227: State of Texas v. Moses Townsend; CCF No. 250: State of Texas v. Moses Townsend and Asa Smith; CCF No. 256: State of Texas v. Moses S. Townsend; CCF No. 260: State of Texas v. Moses Townsend; CCF No. 261: State of Texas v. Moses Townsend; CCF No. 276: State of Texas v. Moses Townsend; CCF No. 475(a): State of Texas v.

Moses Townsend; CCF No. 475(b): State of Texas v. Moses Townsend; CCF No. 500: State of Texas v. Moses Townsend; Lavaca County District Court Records, CCF No. 127: State of Texas v. Moses Townsend and Leonard Townsend. In one incident, on May 3, 1858, Townsend exchanged gunfire with Thomas Lewis, the man from whom Robert E. Stafford bought his first land in Texas. (see also Colorado County District Court Records, CCF No. 263: State of Texas v. Thomas Lewis.)
42. Ibid., 22.
43. W.W. Bonds v. Ann E, Townsend, Administrix of the Estate of M.S. Townsend, In the Probate Court of Colorado County, TX, November term 1868. Copy of suit in the Townsend/Burford Papers, Woodsen Research Center, Fondren Library, Rice University, Houston, TX.
44. Foard County, located just to the west of Wichita Falls at the southeastern base of the Panhandle, was carved out of lands previously assigned to Cottle, King, Knox, and Hardeman County in 1891. Although Beaver County was the original name proposed, the county was named for Robert Foard because he was the law partner of an influential member of the committee, M. H. Townsend, that reported on the bill to establish the county. ("FOARD COUNTY," HTO accessed January 10, 2016.)
45. "M. H. Townsend, Author of the Bill to Save the Alamo Dies," *San Antonio Express*, June 29, 1915.
46. Starting out with nothing, at the end of his life his estate was valued at $250,000, which in today's dollars would be worth many millions in value. This is not to suggest that either Light Townsend or his nephew Mark systematically defrauded the county, but it does underscore that certain prerogatives went along with the office, which a shrewd person could parlay to financial advantage.
47. One of the in-laws, Scion Bostick, who was married to Mary Elizabeth, the fourth child of the stirps of the clan,

Thomas Townsend, had an extraordinary military career. He was present at the Battle of Bexar (1835), at Gonzales, at the Battle of San Jacinto and is credited with being a member of the party that captured Santa Anna. Later he participated in the Battle of Plum Creek (1840) where the Texans rallied to drive off a large party of invading Comanche warriors, who had raided Victoria and Linnville. Then he volunteered and served for service in the Mexican War in 1846 and, finally, rode with Hood's Texas Infantry in the Civil War.

48. Asa's daughter Mary married David Hope and was the mother of Larkin and Marion Hope. She was also the mother of Dr. Joe Lessing by a subsequent marriage. Dr. Lessing, however, sided firmly with the Reese faction and probably traded shots with his half-brother Marion and most certainly fired the shot that killed his second cousin Hiram Clements. Mary was keenly distressed by this situation, as newspaper accounts of the period make clear. (*Weimar Mercury*, July 21, 1906.)

    Spencer's daughter Keron Blanche Reese, on the other hand, had a niece, Minnie L., married to Marion Hope and a sister, Louise Florida, married to Gus Clements, both on the other side. Unlike her cousin Mary, this fact never seemed to temper her passions, which seethed with self-righteous fury at the wrongs that had been visited on her family while remaining cold to the injuries inflicted by her children and confederates on others.

    It is, of course, virtually impossible to keep all the names and connections straight at first read. A chart has been provided as an appendix for the benefit of the reader to help lessen this situation. The reader should, however, take from the above short sketch how woefully incestuous the feud became in its latter phase.

Chapter Three

1. See: "Bob Stafford to 'My Dear Wife,' Oakland, October 14, 1859," Shropshire-Upton Chapter, United Daughters of the Confederacy Collection (Ms. 25), Archives of the Nesbitt Memorial Library, Columbus; reproduced in "Miscellaneous Letters," *NMLJ* 7, no. 3 (Sept. 1997): 183.
2. *Weimar Mercury*, July 12, 1890; J. Marvin Hunter, ed., *Trail Drivers of Texas* (Nashville: Cokesbury Press, 1925), 708.
3. Memorandum of Judge Mansfield attached to report by Adjutant General Thomas Scurry to Governor Joseph D. Sayers, June 16, 1899. Adjutant General's Reports, Archives of the Texas State Library, Austin, Tex.
4. Stafford apparently left for Texas in late August or early September 1859. He may have gotten the idea to go to Texas from his cousin, Robert Frederick Stafford, who purchased 477 acres in northeastern Lavaca County on August 3, 1859. In a few weeks, Robert E. Stafford had located and arranged to purchase a 354-acre tract near that of his cousin from Thomas M. S. Lewis. Lewis had previously sold the tract, but the purchaser had defaulted on payment. Stafford offered $3000 and seventy hogs for the place, and Lewis accepted. Stafford finalized the deal for his new farm on November 12, 1859, apparently keeping the hogs, but conveying the two slaves to Lewis and agreeing to pay him $600 in cash on January 1, 1861. He beat that deadline by nearly a year, making the payment on or before February 19, 1860.

    (R. E. Stafford to Sarah E. Stafford, October 14, 1859, Shropshire-Upton Chapter, op. cit.; Lavaca County, Texas, Deed Records, Book F, pp. 222, 328, 330; Book G, p. 130.) The speculation about the time of his departure from Georgia is based on his statement in his letter of October 14, 1859, that he had been absent from his family "nearly seven weeks." The statements in the biographical sketch of Stafford that appears in Cox, ed., *Historical and Biographical Record*, 640, that he came to Texas and bought land in Lavaca County in 1856, and that he moved to Colorado County in 1857, are wrong. Though he had praised the agricultural value of the land even before he bought it, within a year he seemingly turned his attention away from raising cotton and corn and toward raising livestock, particularly cattle. On November 20, 1860, little more than a year after buying his plantation, and nine months after he finished paying for it, Stafford sold the place for $4,248 to William Austin. He devoted the substantial profit, it seems, to buying cattle. (Lavaca County, Texas, Deed Records, Book G, p. 569.)

5. Thomas Dixon, *The Klansmen*, 26.
6. Saxton, "The Life of Everett Ewing Townsend," Master of Arts Thesis, 23.
7. Lavaca County, Texas, Deed Records, Book G, 569.
8. Stein "Notes on the Feud," Stein Collection, Archives, NML.
9. For the best description of Bob Stafford's life during this period see: Stein, "Consider the Lilly," Part 7, *NMLJ* 9, no. 1 (January 1999): 31–33. Another source said that bad blood between the Staffords and the Townsends actually began during the war. Stafford wanted one company commander, and the Townsends supported another, Captain Upton, whom the men eventually elected. (Leigh McGee statement, ANML; also, Stein "Notes on the Feud," Stein Collection, ANML.)
10. John Goeppinger interview, "The Seymour Ranch," taped in 1973. In possession of authors.
11. Ibid.

12. Stein, "Consider the Lilly," Part 7, page 32.
13. John Glenn, a young black cowboy, who had been raised by Bob Johnson, also went along. At the end of the trail, Bob Johnson took sick and died. He was quickly buried. When the family heard of his death, they requested that the body be disinterred and returned to Columbus. When everyone else balked at the prospect of bringing the body back down the trail, Glenn volunteered. He set out alone in a wagon with the body salted down in a barrel. He completed the trip in forty-two days with many adventures along the way. (Ibid.) This episode, of course, calls to mind a similar episode in Larry McMurtry's famous epic about the Texas cattle drives, *Lonesome Dove*.
14. Ibid.
15. The amount of money that flowed into the state as a result of the cattle drives was in total quite extraordinary. See Introduction by J. Marvin Hunter, *The Trail Drivers of Texas*.
16. The last reported drive on the Western Trail was made in 1893 by John Rufus Blocker to Deadwood, South Dakota. By then, three to five million cattle had been driven to northern pastures and markets along the route. (Jimmy M. Skaggs, "WESTERN TRAIL," Handbook of Texas Online, accessed August 20, 2013.)
17. *Brenham Weekly Banner* (Brenham, Tex.), May 2, 1879.
18. *Weekly Democratic Statesman* (Austin, Tex.), June 12, 1879.
19. When the author was yet a lad of six years age, he had the privilege of knowing an old cowboy, G. Kloepsel, whom we called "Partner." He was a neighbor and old-timer who liked to come over and sit on our porch and spin yarns from his youth when he worked as a cowboy for the Staffords. He had trailed cattle to Wyoming and other points west. I can still remember his descriptions of

the tall grass prairies where "the grass stood as high as a horse and stretched as far as the eye could see," which he related with awe and wonder.
20. *San Marcos Free Press*, San Marcos, TX, April 3, 1884.
21. Saxton, "The Life of Everett Ewing Townsend," 23.
22. *Colorado Citizen*, Columbus, TX, May 19, 1887.
23. *The Standard*, Clarksville, TX, November 4, 1871.
24. "Mr. Allen is the largest cattle dealer and cattle owner in Texas. It seems that this little affair of a 'tight' took him as much by surprise as it did his friends ... No doubt in a short time he will look back on this unexpected episode and wonder how it happened that for once in his life he was short of cash." (See *Dallas Daily Herald*, August 22, 1874.)
25. "Robert Earl Stafford," *Trail Drivers of Texas*, 708–710.
26. C. S. Broadbent, "Lost Many Thousands of Dollars," *Trail Drivers of Texas*, 592–594.
27. Saxton, "The Life of Everett Ewing Townsend," 23.
28. Saxton, "Life of Everett Ewing Townsend," 32. Shanghai Pierce also called the headquarters of his ranch on the Tres Palacios River, Rancho Grande, which has led to some confusion among writers who have confused the two.
29. *Colorado Citizen*, May 12, 1881.
30. Hunter, *Trail Drivers of Texas*, 179.
31. Members of the Mixon Creekers included George Skipton, Ed Valentin, T. Franks, and James Buckly. (Lavaca County Criminal Case Minutes, 1876, CCF 1694.)
32. These gangs cooperated with each other and found refuge in each others' camps. It was a kind of frontier mafia based on stolen cattle and horses. Their network spread as far west as Kimble County (near present Junction) where a collection of outlaws, desperados, and misfits had collected out of reach of the law that came to be

known as the "Kimble County Confederation." The most notorious of these desperados was John Wesley Hardin. Often acting as fences for other gangs, they traded stolen stock to both Indians and Mexicans, and often sold the stolen cattle to unscrupulous trail bosses moving up the western trail to Kansas, which passed only a few miles east of Junction. The gang operated with impunity until the Texas Ranger frontier battalion organized a concerted raid in 1876 and dispersed the gangs. (See Peter R. Rose, *The Reckoning*, Chapter 6, "The Confederation.")

33. Story related by local rancher and neighbor Travis Wegenhoft to the author.
34. Elizabeth Schoellmann wrote that in 1878, Henry Heine, her grandfather, was killed by cattle rustlers near the Fayette/Colorado County line—the suspected rustlers, the Stafford bunch. (Personal note by Elizabeth Schoellmann, ANML.)
35. Emmett, *Shanghai Pierce*, 31.
36. Henry Thomas, "A Sketch of my Life," *NMLJ* 1, no. 3 (February 1990): 71–91.
37. *Colorado Citizen*, July 14, 1877.
38. Henry Thomas, "A Sketch of my Life," *NMLJ* 1, no. 3 (February 1990): 59.
39. Emmett, *Shanghai Pierce*, 57.
40. Ibid., 191.
41. *New York Times*, September 18, 1876 and reproduced in *A History of Eagle Lake* (Austin: Nortex Press, 1987), 27.
42. Bill Stein, "Consider the Lilly," Part 8, *NMLJ* 10, no. 1 (January 2000): 52, 53. Perhaps inspired by the Stafford example, there was at least one other attack on a black community in Colorado County with cattle and horse thievery as the putative motive. The supposed location was only a few hundred yards from the back fence of the

ranch where the author grew up and, true enough, an examination of the site revealed broken bottles, charred wood, and other objects suggesting that the site had once been occupied by a house (or houses). But the author has not been able to uncover a single report or document from the period to corroborate the story.
43. *Newark Daily Advocate*, January 16, 1900.
44. Mansfield memo; See Note 3.
45. Reese, *Flaming Feuds*, 29.
46. Henry Thomas also alludes to troubles between the Townsends and Stafford in 1877 as a result of disputes over cattle, but he does not identify the Townsend in question. (See Thomas, "A Sketch," 90.) Bill Stein notes in a footnote that it was Asa Townsend, but this is not certain. Earlier in his "A Sketch," 73, Thomas mentions that Thomas "Tupp" Townsend, son of Asa, was a noted cowman, so this might be the source of the conflict.
47. For a complete account of the event with all relevant citations, see Bill Stein, "Consider the Lilly," Part 8, *NMLJ* 10, no. 1 (January 2000): 23–24.
48. *The Colorado Citizen*, December 7, 1871.
49. Colorado County District Court Records, Book E, p. 484, CCF 923, "Ben Stafford pleads guilty"; p. 483, CCF 920, Feb. 14, 1873, "Ratcliff pleads guilty, fined $25 plus costs"; p. 305, CCF 922, "Stafford pleads guilty, fined one cent"; p. 320, CCF 921, June 15, 1872, "Stafford found not guilty."
50. Stein, "Consider the Lilly," Part 8, *NMLJ*, 10, no. 1, 23, 24.
51. "Application for a new trial by John Stafford," Colorado County District Court Records, CCF 949, June 12, 1872.
52. Bill Stein, "Prime Circuit: The Glory Days of the Stafford Opera House," *NMLJ* 1, no. 4 (March 1990): 103–125.

53. "State of Texas v. Ben Stafford and Silas W. Ratcliff," Colorado County District Court Records, Minute Book H., pp. 47, 347, 417, 488, 560. p. 320, CCF 921, June 15, 1872.
54. For a complete description of the lynching see, Stein, "Consider the Lilly," Part 9, *NMLJ* 10, no. 3 (June 2001), 145, 146. For a report of the arrest of Warren Stafford and his two accomplices see, *Dennison Daily News*, November 8, 1879.
55. Ibid., 147, 148.
56. Reese, *Flaming Feuds*, 29, 30.

Chapter Four

1. Statements of Judge Mansfield as addendum to AG Scurry's report to the governor, June 10, 1899, GP, Box 301-177, ATSL.
2. Lillie Reese also devotes some space to what she called the Reese's "very happy family life." Her father habitually kissed his wife and children goodbye when he left in the morning, and he expected all his children to be home when he returned from whatever occupation he had been pursuing each day so he could kiss them all again. Then, he and the children would play a game together. The family often spent evenings playing music. Sam Reese played the violin and Keetie sang and danced. Each of the five children learned to play one or more instruments. Lillie herself became proficient on the piano and the violin. (Reese, *Flaming Feuds of Colorado County*, 65–66, 79.)
3. Reese identifies the man who slapped Hub Reese as "Waugh." He probably was Andrew Miller Waugh (1869–1939), a one-time mayor of Eagle Lake and, in later years, an attorney in Houston. (see *Colorado County Citizen*, June 22, 1939; *Eagle Lake Headlight*, June 23, 1939.)
4. *Weimar Mercury*, November 7, 1896.

5. Statement of Judge Mansfield as addendum to AG Scurry's report to the governor, June 10, 1899, GP, Box 301-177, ATSL.
6. Ibid.
7. *Colorado Citizen*, November 17, 1892, November 12, 1896, September 9, 1897; *Weimar Mercury*, November 17, 1894.
8. *Colorado Citizen*, May 12, 1898.
9. *Colorado Citizen*, July 14, 1898.
10. *Galveston News*, August 4, 1898, March 29, 1899; *Weimar Mercury*, July 7, 14, 1898; *Eagle Lake Headlight*, July 7, 1906; AG Thomas Scurry to Governor Sayers, Report on Columbus homicides, February 7-12, 1900, Sayers, GP, RG 301, Archives, TSL; H. Townsend, "Townsend-Reese Feud," 3, ms, typescript, ANML, copy in possession of the authors; Stein, "Feud Notes," ANML.
11. Lessing was also the half-brother of Hope and the nephew of Keetie Reese, which is to say his wife was also his second cousin.
12. Statement of Judge Mansfield as addendum to AG Scurry's report to the governor, June 10, 1899, GP, Box 301-177, ATSL.
13. *Colorado Citizen*, September 2, 9, 16, 1897; October 7, 1897; November 4, 11, 1897.
14. *Austin Statesman*, October 28, 1874; AG Scurry to Gov. Sayers, June 10, 1899, RG 301, ATSL; *Galveston Daily News*, August 4, 1898, March 29, 1899; *Weimar Mercury*, July 6, 7, August 13, 1898, October 7, 1899, March 17, 1900; *Eagle Lake Headlight*, July 7, 1906; *Colorado Citizen*, August 11, 18, 1898; Stein, "Colorado County Feud," *NHT* online; Colorado County CCF 1210, 1220, 1232, 1233.
15. *Weimar Mercury*, May 5, 1894; Galveston Daily News, May 1, 1894; Colorado County CCF 2561.

Chapter Five

1. *Colorado Citizen*, November 17, 1898, November 24, 1898, December 1, 1898.
2. *Weimar Mercury*, September 9, 1898.
3. Both Judge Mansfield and Ranger Captain Sieker state unequivocally in their respective reports that both sides had expended "large sums of money sides to secure the black vote," but that Mark Townsend outspent the Reese candidacy by a wide margin. Judge Mansfield suggested that Townsend had passed out, "perhaps $5,000," an enormous amount of money, which, by today's valuation, would translate into at least $100,000. (Statements of Judge Mansfield and Captain Sieker as addendums to AG Scurry's report to the governor, June 10, 1899, GP, Box 301–177, ATSL.)
4. Mrs. Wetteroth and Mrs. Longnecker, interviews, January 2, 1944, typescripts, ANM, copies in possession of the authors.
5. Report of AG Thomas Scurry to Governor Joseph D. Sayers, June 10, 1899, GP, (RG 301), ATSL.
6. Report of AG Scurry to Governor Sayers, June 10, 1899, GP, Box 301–177.
7. After the death of Mark Townsend in 1915, Red Bluff Irrigation was sold to the Lehrer family and was henceforth known as the Garwood Irrigation Co.
8. Statement of Judge Mansfield as addendums to AG Scurry's report to the governor, June 10, 1899, GP, Box 301–177, ATSL.
9. Report of AG Thomas Scurry to Governor Joseph D. Sayers, June 16, 1899, GP, (RG 301), ATSL.
10. *Colorado Citizen*, March 24, 1899.
11. After the appearance of the Reese book in 1962, Ray Hoagland, who had married into the Townsend family, interviewed Genevieve Sandmeyer Montgomery and asked her to comment on the accuracy of the Reese book.

She had grown up in Columbus, her father had managed the Stafford bank, and she had known all the parties involved. Quoting her from his notes, Hoagland wrote, "I have spent much time in the Burford home and never had the occasion to see him inebriated." When Sam Reese was killed, Lillian Reese lived across the street from the Yates family, who were friends of the Burfords. She would periodically for a long time thereafter hang the bloody clothes taken from her father's body on the fence to irritate the Yates family. (Ray Hoagland notes, Townsend/Burford Papers.)

12. Statement of Judge Mansfield as addendums to AG Scurry's report to the governor, June 10, 1899, GP, Box 301–177, ATSL.
13. Statements of Captain Sieker as addendums to AG Scurry's report to the governor, May 18, 1899, GP, Box 301–177, ATSL.
14. Ibid.
15. M. Kennon Judge 25th Judicial District to Governor Sayers, telegram, 9:45 AM, March 20, 1899, GP, ATSL.
16. The account of the way McDonald defused the tense scene, including the passages quoted, is in Paine, *Captain Bill McDonald: Texas Ranger*, 243–249. Also see *Weimar Mercury*, January 19, 1907; for McDonald's brief report to the adjutant general, see McDonald to Scurry, March 22, 1999, ACO papers, RG 401; also see, AG Scurry to Sayers, *Report of the Adjutant General of the State of Texas for 1899–1900* (Austin: Von Boeckmann, Schutze, & Company, State Printers, 1900), 21; *Galveston Daily News*, March 31, 1899.
17. For examples of rangers involved in law enforcement during this period, see: Reports of Captain Brooks for August 1899, Company F, Records of Scouts, AG Record Group 401, ATSL.
18. *Weimar Mercury*, April 1, 1899

19. *Colorado Citizen*, August 25, 1898, September 1, 1898.
20. "Jim Coleman Granted Bail," *Weimar Mercury*, May 7, 1899.
21. A. G. Scurry's Report to Governor Sayers, June 10, 1899.
22. "Pistol carriers [in and around Columbus] ... have become numerous and bold of late." (*Galveston Daily News*, May 19, 1899.)
23. Walter Reese published a rebuttal in the *Weimar Mercury* that explicitly denied that there had been any shooting at the bridge previous to the death of Dick Reese. (*Weimar Mercury*, June 3, 1899.)
24. Nuddie Ela (Reese) Lessing: see feud biographies.
25. Captain Lamartine Sieker: see feud biographies.
26. *Colorado Citizen*, May 25, 1899; *Weimar Mercury*, May 20, 1899.
27. *Weimar Mercury*, May 27, 1899; Monthly Reports, Company E, May 1899, Adjutant General's Records (RG 401) Archives Division, Texas State Library, Austin; Report of Thomas Scurry to Joseph D. Sayers, June 10, 1899,
28. The Reese version of events was published in the *Weimar Mercury*, May 27, 1899.
29. Judge Mansfield's report was attached as an addendum to A. G. Scurry's report to the governor and is cited in several places in this study.
30. *Colorado Citizen*, May 25, 1899; A. G. Scurry to Governor Sayers, June 10, 1899, GP, RG 301, ATSL; Reese, *Feuds of Colorado County*, 40.
31. A. G. Scurry's Reports, J. C. Taylor, June 14, 1899, ATSL.
32. Ibid.
33. "Adjutant General Scurry arrives in Columbus ... trying to arrange a peaceful solution of the troubles. He ordered more rangers, who will arrive tonight." (*Weimar Mercury*, June 24, 1899.)

34. A. G. Scurry's report to Governor Sayers, June 16, 1899.
35. A. G. Scurry to Governor Sayers, *Report for 1899–1900*, 24; *Weimar Mercury*, May 27, 1899; Monthly Reports, Company E, May, 1899, AG, RG 401, Scurry to Sayers, June 10, 1899, GP, RG 301, ATSL.
36. A. G. Scurry to Governor Sayers, June 16, 1899; W. L. Wright to Scurry, June 10, 1899, AG, RG 301, ATSL.
37. Ibid.
38. Bill Stein, "Biographical Notes," in Stein Feud Notes, ANML.
39. Ibid.
40. Ibid.
41. Ibid. The information on Keetie's mental state comes from an interview with Wetteroth taken on December 28, 1943. The transcript survives but the name of the interviewer has been lost. Other women who knew Keetie and gave interviews include Leigh McGee and a "Mrs. Longnecker" and a "Mrs. Hohn." Copies are in the Archives, NML.
42. Wright to A. G. Scurry, June 19, 1899, AGP, RG 401, ATSL.
43. *Colorado Citizen*, June 22, 1899.
44. After moving to Collin County in Northeast Texas in 1876, Brooks worked as a ranch hand and a miner for a time. Joining the ranger service in 1883, he came up through the ranks. In 1889, he became captain of Company F in the Frontier Battalion. From East Texas to the Mexican border, he and his men had many difficult assignments, including the Townsend-Reese troubles. In the 1880s and 1890s, his company helped police the oil-boom towns in eastern Texas. He and his men were also forced into gunfights with fence cutters in Brown County and the Conner Gang in East Texas. Fighting the Conner gang was particularly bloody, with one ranger

killed and three wounded, including Brooks who lost several fingers on his left hand. (Spellman, *J. A. Brooks, Texas Ranger*.)
45. *Weimar Mercury*, January 20, 1900.
46. Ibid., February 24, 1900.
47. A. G. Scurry, *Report for 1899–1900*, 24; Record of scouts, Company E, 1900, AGR, RG 401, ATSL; *Weimar Mercury*, September 16, 23, 30, October 7, 1899, July 7, 1906; *Colorado Citizen*, September 21, 1899; *Eagle Lake Headlight*, July 7, 1906.
48. *Bay City Tribune*, August 3, 1900; *Weimar Mercury*, August 11, 27, 1898, August 4, 11, September 8, 1900; *Bastrop Advertiser*, August 4, 1900; *Galveston Daily News*, August 1, 1900. The local lore on "Hell's Acre" came from an interview with a Leigh McGee who lived through the Townsend-Reese Feud era, copy in possession of the authors.

Chapter Six

1. *Colorado Citizen*, June 22, 1899; January 11, 1900; January 18, 1900.
2. *Weimar Mercury*, January 20, 1900.
3. "Sept 22,--Three more rangers arrived last night from Alice and reported to Captain Brooks, who has eight men in his charge. Captain McDonald also came up from Houston, but left again on the evening train." (*Weimar Mercury*, Sept 30, 1899.)
4. Reports of Captain Brooks for 1900, Monthly Returns of Company F, AGR (RG 401), ATSL.
5. Ibid.
6. Ibid.
7. Prior to 1870 there had been little or no restriction on the right to keep and bear arms in Texas. The first

comprehensive gun control was passed by the Twelfth Legislature and dates to August 12, 1870:

If any person ... shall have about his person a bowie knife, dirk, butcher knife, or fire-arms, whether known as a six-shooter, gun or pistol of any kind, such person so offending shall be deemed guilty of a misdemeanor, and on conviction thereof shall be fined in a sum not less than fifty nor more than five hundred dollars at the discretion of the court or judge trying the same; provided that nothing contained in this section shall apply to locations subject to Indian depredations; and provided further that this act shall not apply to any person or persons whose duty it is to bear arms on such occasions in charge of duties imposed by law. (Gammel, *Laws*, VI, 63.)

The 1870 law, however, was restricted to carrying weapons into schools, churches or any kind of public assembly. The following year, the legislature strengthened the law by eliminating the public assembly provision. Henceforth, it was illegal for all but law enforcement personnel and "civil officers" to carry weapons in public.

There was, however, one large loophole in the law. The law could not be construed to "prohibit persons travelling in the State from keeping or bearing arms in their baggage." (Gammel, *Laws*, VI, 927–929.)

The Twelfth Legislative session was dominated by so-called "Radical Republicans" and was determined to put an end to the rampant violence and mayhem that had plagued the state for a number of years. For the most part, gun violence was directed at the freedpeople and at Reconstruction authorities.

Interestingly, when conservative Democrats regained control of state government at all levels with the election of 1874, the gun laws put in place in 1870 and 1871 were not repealed. They continued to be the law of the land until 1887 when, astonishingly, they were actually renewed and strengthened. The new law increased the penalty for a first offense by mandating a jail term in addition to a fine for, "not less than twenty nor more than sixty days." (Gammel, *Laws*, IX, 805.) These laws endured more or less as written until 1995 when they were relaxed to permit private citizens to carry arms in public. Thus, for the whole span of this story, from 1871 until 1911, rather strict gun laws were obtained, and their enforcement, or lack thereof, becomes an important part of the story.

8. When he was killed in 1900, Arthur Burford had a fiancée, identified in one source as a girl from San Marcos. A letter written shortly after the killing by one of Sheriff Burford's granddaughters, Verna Belle Burford, mentions two women, one identified as Carrie and the other as Mrs. Brown. In November 1900, a woman named Carrie Brown from San Marcos visited one of Arthur Burford's sisters in Colorado County. Burford's fiancée was apparently Caroline Belvin Brown, whose father, Ossian Tignor Brown, was a prominent attorney in San Marcos. She was born August 27, 1878, and thus was 21 when Burford was killed, certainly a marriageable age. Her maternal grandfather had once been president of Coronal Institute, where Burford went to school. More than five years after Burford's death, on June 14, 1905, Carrie Brown married Samuel S. Shelley. The unlucky girl endured his death on August 1, 1913. She remained a widow for just over two years, marrying Hugh Foley on November 23, 1915. He died on June 24, 1937, after

which she moved back to the family home in San Marcos, where her sister Mary, who had never married, already lived. Caroline Foley died on December 22, 1952. (See O. T. Brown Biographical File, San Marcos Public Library; *Bastrop Advertiser*, January 20, 1900; San Marcos Record, December 26, 1952; *Weimar Mercury*, November 24, 1900; Letter of Verna Belle Burford to Fay Florence Burford, January 19, 1900, Small Manuscripts Collection [ms. 5], ANML. A substantial archive of family material at the San Marcos Public Library makes no mention of Arthur Burford, nor does her brief obituary in the local newspaper.)
9. Bill Stein, "Notes on the Feud," Stein Collection, ANML.
10. Arthur Burford to Mrs. W. T. Burford, January 14, 1899, General Collection, Bill Stein, "Notes on the Feud," Stein Collection, ANML; Record of Scouts, Company F, Texas Rangers, AGR (RG 401), ATSL; AG Thomas Scurry, *Report of the Adjutant General of Texas for 1899–1900* (Austin: Von Boeckmann, Schutze & Company, 1900), 24; *Bastrop Advertiser*, January 20, 1900; *Colorado Citizen*, January 18, 1900.
11. A. G. Scurry, *Report for 1899–1900*, 24; *Bastrop Vidette*, January 19, 1900; *Bastrop Advertiser*, January 20, 1900; *Colorado Citizen*, January 18, 1900; *Weimar Mercury*, January 20, 27, August 11, 1899; *Galveston Daily News*, January 16, 1900; *Austin Daily Tribune*, January 16, 1900; *Houston Daily Post*, January 16, 18, 1900; Texas Rangers, Records of Scouts, Company E, Company F, 1900, AGR (RG 401), ATSL.
12. Bill Stein, "Notes on the Feud," Stein Collection, ANML; A. G. Scurry, *Report for 1899–1900*, 24; *Houston Daily Post*, January 16, 18, 1900; Texas Rangers, Records of Scouts, Company E, Company F, 1900, AGR (RG 401), ATSL.

13. *Weimar Mercury*, January 20, 27, August 11, 1900; Adjutant General Scurry, *Report for 1899–1900*, 24; *Colorado Citizen*, January 18, 1900; *Houston Daily Post*, January 16, 18, 1900; Texas Rangers, Records of Scouts, Company E, Company F, 1900, AGR (RG 401), ATSL.
14. *Weimar Mercury*, January 17, 20, 27, August 11, 1900; Adjutant General Scurry, *Report for 1899–1900*, 24; Stein, "Notes on the Feud," Stein Collection, ANML.
15. Bill Stein, "Notes on the Feud," Stein Collection, ANML; *Weimar Mercury*, January 17, 20, 27, August 11, 1900; Texas Rangers, Records of Scouts, Company E, Company F, 1900, AGR (RG 401), ATSL.
16. Bill Stein, Ibid.; Adjutant General Scurry, *Report for 1899–1900*, 24; *Weimar Mercury*, January 17, 20, 27, 1900.
17. Texas Rangers, Record of Scouts, Company E, Company F, 1899, AGR (RG 401), ATSL; Adjutant General Scurry, *Report for 1899–1900*, 24; Stein, "Notes on the Feud," Stein Collection, Archives, NML.
18. *Bastrop Advertiser*, January 20, 1900; Records of Scouts, Company E, 1900, Company F, 1900, AGR (RG 401), ATSL.
19. Texas Rangers, Record of Scouts, Company E, Company F, 1900, AGR (RG 401), ATSL; Bill Stein, "Notes on the Feud," Stein Collection, ANML.
20. Thomas Barnette Daniels, the son of Williamson and Mary E. (Chandler) Daniels, was born May 21, 1873, and died in Harris County, Texas, on December 21, 1940. His sister, Mary, married August Burttschell, bringing him into the feuding families. He was one of four men indicted for the murder of Arthur Burford in Bastrop.
21. Leslie Wilkinson Reese, born May 3, 1873, was the son of Sam Reese's brother, John Wesley Reese. He was one

of the men indicted for killing Arthur Burford in Bastrop in 1900. He shot himself to death—accidentally, it was reported—in Houston on November 25, 1907.
22. *Bastrop Advertiser*, January 20, 1900; *Colorado Citizen*, January 18, 1900; *Weimar Mercury*, January 20, 1900, January 27, 1900, February 3, 1900, February 10, 1900, February 24, 1900; Records of the District Court, Bastrop County, Texas, Minute Book E, pp. 68; Records of Scouts, Company F, 1900, AGR (RG 401), ATSL. Dr. Harrison, evidently, brought a gun back to Bastrop with him, for he too was arrested for carrying a pistol on January 15. (see Records of Scouts, Company F, 1900, AGR (RG 401), ATSL.)
23. *Weimar Mercury*, February 24, 1900.
24. *Weimar Mercury*, January 20, 1900, January 27, 1900, February 3, 1900, February 10, 1900; Records of the District Court, Bastrop County, Texas, Minute Book E, pp. 70, 72, 73; Records of Scouts, Company E, 1900, AGR (RG 401), ATSL.
25. *Weimar Mercury*, January 17, 1900.
26. Texas Rangers, Record of Scouts, Company E, Company F, 1890, AGR (RG 401), ATSL; John W. Reese and Lillian E. Reese, *Flaming Feuds of Colorado County*, 29.
27. The rangers ordered to Richmond included Captain J. A. Brooks of Alice, Captain J. R. Rogers of Cotulla, M. H. Wright, A. Y. Old, W. A. Old, T. C. Taylor, H. G. DuBose, and Chas. Sandherr. (*Weimar Mercury*, Saturday, March 24, 1900.)
28. Records of the 37th Judicial District Court, Bexar County, Texas, Criminal Minute Book P, pp. 347–348; Records of the District Court, Fort Bend County, Texas, Criminal Cause File No. 3775: *State of Texas v. Jim Coleman*, Criminal Minute Book M, pp. 200, 214, 261; *Galveston Daily News*, March 12, 1900. The fact that the cause file is still in Fort Bend County is further

evidence that the Hope murder case never made it to San Antonio. In those days before copy machines, when a case was transferred to another court, the relevant cause file would normally be sent along with it.

29. See, for instance, "A Texas Steer Responsible for Feud in which Many Lost Lives" in *Newark Daily Advocate*, Newark, NJ, January 16, 1900; also, "Rangers Will Attend Trial," in *Atlanta Constitution*, Atlanta, GA, January 22, 1900.
30. *The Bastrop Vidette*, January 18, 1900.
31. *Bastrop Advertiser*, January 20, 1900, page 3.
32. The younger Arthur Burford, who became known to most people as Bill Burford, was moderately crippled and never acquired much education. When he was young, his parents moved to California, taking his younger brother with them. Bill remained behind in Columbus, living with his grandmother, Mattie Burford. He spent his adult life operating a small grocery store in a nook in a successful Columbus hardware store and lumberyard. He died on October 27, 1956, and was buried in Columbus. (*Colorado County Citizen*, November 1, 1956.)
33. *Weimar Mercury*, February 10, 1900.
34. Ibid., February 17, 1900.
35. *Colorado Citizen*, January 25, 1900; *Weimar Mercury*, January 27, 1900, February 3, 1900; Twelfth Census of the United States (1900) Schedule 1, Fort Bend County, TX; Minutes of the City of Columbus, Texas, January 22, 1900.
36. Ibid.
37. AG Scurry report to Governor Sayers, June 10, 1899. (Box 310–177, GP, ATSL.)
38. *Weimar Mercury*, August 27, 1898, August 4, 1900; Twelfth Census of the United States (1900) Schedule 1, Colorado County, Texas. In those days, people did not have

to go to law school to become a lawyer. They could learn the law under the tutelage of a practicing attorney.
39. Gunger Woolridge statement, *Weimar Mercury*, August 4, 1900
40. *Weimar Mercury*, August 4, 1900.
41. See, for instance, *Bastrop Vidette*, January 19, 1900. "A Bloody Tragedy Enacted."
42. "Walter Reese's Statement," unidentified clipping in Scrapbook of John Walter Reese, Lillie Reese Papers (Ms. 85), Archives of the Nesbitt Memorial Library, Columbus.
43. *Weimar Mercury*, August 11, 1900.
44. *Weimar Mercury*, August 18, 1900.
45. *Weimar Mercury*, November 24, 1900.

Chapter Seven
1. Normally sheriffs were elected every four years, but for some reason there was an extraordinary election held at the two-year mark in 1900, perhaps to set the clock at zero for the new century.
2. "To the Editor of the Post, Card from Sheriff Burford," clipped in *Weimar Mercury*, January 27, 1900.
3. *Weimar Mercury*, November 17, 1900.
4. As an example, the November 1, 1902, edition of the *Weimar Mercury* reported the following: "An impudent Negro man was badly beaten at the Opera saloon last Saturday evening ... Will Vester, a white farmer of this region, split his skull open with an ax handle ... a punishment he richly deserved."
5. For more on this see: Barr, *Reconstruction to Reform: Texas Politics, 1876–1906*; Hine, *Black Victory: The Rise and Fall of the White Primary in Texas*; Rice, *The Negro in Texas, 1874–1900*. For more on the Wharton County White Man's Association, see: Williams, *A History of*

244   *No Hope for Heaven, No Fear of Hell*

Wharton County, and White Man's Union Association, The Constitution and By-Laws of the White Man's Union Association of Wharton County, Texas. (Wharton County, n.p., 1936.)

6. *Weimar Mercury*, June 21, 1902.
7. *Weimar Mercury*, June 7, 1902; June 21, 1902. Resolution of the Democratic Convention summer 1902 read: "Whereas, we believe it to be for the best interests of Colorado County that the White voters of the county irrespective of party should control its politics and policies. Therefore, be it ordained that the Democratic Party henceforth do not make nominations for county and precinct offices, but that the right to the selection of such offices be relegated to the white people of said county." (See Resolution of the Democratic Primary Convention, reproduced in *Weimar Mercury*, June 21, 1902.)
8. *Weimar Mercury*, June 21, 1902.
9. *Shiner Gazette*, October 26, 1898.
10. *Weimar Mercury*, November 17, 1900, July 27, 1902, November 1, 1902, November 8, 1902; Twelfth Census of the United States (1900) Schedule 1, Colorado County, Texas. An analysis of the election returns printed in the newspaper reveals that there were 3,499 voters in 1900 and 2,289 in 1902. The 1920 census of Colorado County enumerated 12,521 people who were described as white, 9,650 who were described as black, and 30 who were described as Hispanic.
11. Between two and three o'clock on the morning of October 4, 1902, a black man broke into the telephone office at Eagle Lake and, with a drawn knife, attempted to assault the operator, Lena Harris. Her screams roused a nearby man, who raced to the office. The black man fled. Soon, City Marshal Kinard had identified a suspect, Davis "Utt" Duncan, a nineteen-year-old drayman. Officers went to Duncan's home but found it empty.

However, Kinard left two men to watch the house. Shortly afterward, when Duncan returned home, they apprehended him. Harris identified Duncan as her assailant. She had seen him in town for years, though she had never learned his name. Kinard, fearing a lynch mob might form, rushed him off to jail in Columbus on an early morning freight train.

Sheriff Burford, meanwhile, had been notified of the crime, and had gone to Eagle Lake to investigate. He arrived from Columbus shortly after Duncan had been put on the freight train. He quickly realized that trouble was in the air, and telephoned the Columbus mayor, Williams, to warn him to expect a lynch mob. When the next passenger train into Columbus arrived at Eagle Lake around noon, Burford was at the depot. So were dozens of armed men. The sheriff went towards the engine, planning to cut it loose and leave the train in Eagle Lake. However, a number of men restrained him, and the train left with the mob on it, about one hundred men. Burford borrowed a horse and set out for Columbus. Needless to say, he would be too late. At Columbus, Williams had raised a posse and stationed it at the jail. He, or someone, notified the governor, who in turn had ordered a militia unit, the La Grange Light Guards, to go to Columbus. When the mob arrived at the jail, they demanded entrance. Williams and the posse stood firm. The sheriff's wife, Mattie Burford, announced that she had the keys, and that she would not surrender them or leave the premises until her husband returned. Her presence stymied the mob for a while, as many of them were reluctant to risk injury to a woman. However, at about 5:30, with the Light Guards expected soon, a number of men swarmed to one side of the jail, attempting to break in with cold chisels and sledge hammers. While the posse diverted their attention to this assault, a few men went to the other side of the jail, and, with no one to deter them, easily broke in. The mob soon had control of the facility. However, they were unable to enter the cellblock. The thick iron door that blocked their way was impenetrable with the tools they had. So, using what was described as "persuasion of a most convincing character," they induced a man who knew the combination to open the door. They found Duncan cowering in a corner, tightly wrapped up in a blanket. They took him to the "Grove," an area in the north part of Columbus that was privately owned but commonly used as a park, and hanged him from a tree. On their walk through the streets with Duncan, a group of local woman cheered, "Hurrah for the men of Eagle Lake." Sheriff Burford and the Light Guards arrived at the site about an hour and a half later. The county had Duncan's body cut down and buried that night. (*Weimar Mercury*, October 11, 1902; "Lynching at Columbus," unidentified clipping in Scrapbook of John Walter Reese, Lillie Reese Papers [Ms. 85], Archives of the Nesbitt Memorial Library, Columbus.)

12. On August 29, 1904, a black man named Oscar Lee Tucker was working in a cotton field with a number of younger persons. He noticed particularly a teenage white girl named Minnie Schultz. Tucker sent the rest of the workers to the house, and in their absence, proposed that he and Schultz have sexual relations. She refused him abruptly and began moving away from him. He chased her down, and the two struggled for some moments. She repeatedly bit him, prompting him finally to release her and run away. She reported the incident to her father, and he alerted the authorities. Tucker was quickly arrested, identified by Schultz, and confined in the calaboose in Weimar. As it was a very hot day, the city marshal, Henry J. Insall, left the front door of the calaboose open and went

to lunch. Tucker, who never actually raped the girl and who was locked in a cell, seemed in little danger. However, when Insall returned, he found Tucker dead. Someone had lured him to the front of the cell, placed a rope around his neck, and strangled him against the bars. There was no condemnation of the lynching in the local newspaper. Instead, the killers must have smiled with pride when they read that their act was "undoubtedly the coolest, quietest piece of work of this kind ever heard of, as it was done in the heart of the city in broad open daylight, and yet so quietly was it done that no one suspicioned anything, until the negro was found dead." It was another example of the kind of murder that found wide acceptance in the community. (*Weimar Mercury*, September 3, 1904.)
13. *Colorado Citizen*, November 6, 1908; *Weimar Mercury*, November 6, 1908; *Colorado County Citizen*, December 12, 1929.
14. Minutes of the City of Columbus, Texas, January 5, 1903.
15. *Weimar Mercury*, May 13, 1905.
16. Ibid., May 27, 1905.
17. Ibid.

Chapter Eight

1. "Coleman testimony," *San Antonio Gazette*, May 23, 1907.
2. *Colorado County Citizen*, June 30, 1906.
3. *Weimar Mercury*, February 10, 1906.
4. *Galveston News*, July 1, 1906.
5. *Colorado Citizen*, July 6, 1906.
6. *Weimar Mercury*, July 7, 1906.
7. Ibid.
8. *Weimar Mercury*, July 21, 1906.
9. Ibid.
10. Ibid. After Hiram Clements was killed, his wife, Natalie, and three children, lived with the family of David Larkin Hope

in San Antonio. Hope's wife was Alice L. Clements, Hiram's sister. (Thirteenth Census of the United States [1910], Schedule 1, Bexar County, Texas.)
11. The Reese brothers and J. F. Lessing were released on bond signed by J. Burttschell, J. J. Odom, Hamburger, W. R. Scronce, H. B. Tanner, and S. K. Seymour. (*Weimar Mercury*, July 21, 1906.)
12. Bond was signed by J. Burttschell, J. J. Odom, Hamburger, W. R. Scronce, H. B. Tanner, and S. K. Seymour, which gives a good picture of the friends of the Reese supporters in Columbus. (*Weimar Mercury*, July 21, 1906.)
13. The Reese brothers and J. F. Lessing were released on bond signed by J. Burttschell, J. J. Odom, Hamburger, W. R. Scronce, H. B. Tanner, and S. K. Seymour. (*Weimar Mercury*, July 21, 1906.)
14. *Weimar Mercury*, May 12, 1906.
15. Ibid., July 28, 1906.
16. J. W. Towell to Governor S. W. T. Lanham, Columbus Texas July 21, 1906. Cover Letter and Draft Resolution of Town meeting. Governor's Reports Texas State Archives.
17. *Weimar Mercury*, July 21, 1906.
18. Captain Hughes to Adjutant General Hulen, July 18, 1906
19. *Weimar Mercury*, September 8, 1906.
20. J. W. Towell to Governor S. W. T. Lanham, Columbus, Texas, July 21, 1906. Cover Letter and Draft Resolution of Town meeting. (Governor's Reports Texas State Archives.)
21. *Weimar Mercury*, July 28, 1906.
22. Ibid., August 11, 1906.
23. *San Antonio Light*, August 11, 1906, City of Columbus petitions to discorporate.
24. A kind of offshoot to the feud flared again on March 14, 1910. The scene of the action was Eagle Lake. Henry

Burttschell killed Max Theumann, who lived at Lakeside and who engaged in rice farming. Burttschell was a planter and a large landholder who lived near Alleyton, about eight miles from Eagle Lake. The editor of the *Eagle Lake Headlight* said the trouble related to the Reese-Townsend feud. Theumann had supported the Townsends while the Burttschells had supported the Reeses. Clearly, however, the bad blood between the two had other causes as well, which the feud had exacerbated. Theumann was sitting on a porch outside Brosig's Saloon. Burttschell walked up the other side of the street, carrying a double-barreled shotgun, with a pistol in his pocket. The killer stopped in front of Al L. Baring's Saddlery and Harness Store, which was diagonally across the street from the saloon. Then, he fired both barrels at Theumann. The spray of shot hit the victim on the right side, ranging from his head to his thigh. After being shot, Theumann staggered through the saloon and exited by a back door only to fall into a closet behind the saloon. He died about an hour later. Meanwhile, Burttschell found Eagle Lake's City Marshal, H. S. Vineyard, and surrendered, handing the marshal a doubled-barreled shotgun and pistol. Theumann was armed with only a butcher knife, found when responders tried to dress his wounds. When he died, Theumann was about forty years old and left a wife and seven children.

Chapter Nine
1. *Weimar Mercury*, November 16, 1907.
2. *Houston Chronicle*, April 20, 1907.
3. *Weimar mercury*, April 20, 1907.
4. *Houston Chronicle*, clipped by *Weimar Mercury*, April 20, 1907; *Eagle Lake Headlight*, April 20, 1907. *Weimar Mercury*, April 20, 1907.

5. Reese, *Flaming Feuds*, 156.
6. Ibid., December 10, 1904.
7. J. W. Kincheloe: see feud biographies.
8. *San Antonio Gazette*, May 19, 1907, May 20, 1907, May 21, 1907, May 22, 1907, May 23, 1907; *San Antonio Light*, May 22, 1907; *Weimar Mercury*, May 25, 1907.
9. *San Antonio Gazette*, May 20, 1907, May 21, 1907, May 23, 1907; *Weimar Mercury*, May 25, 1907; *San Antonio Light*, May 22, 1907.
10. "Tragedy in Iron Front Saloon Makes Another Chapter in Celebrated Columbus Feud," unidentified clipping in Scrapbook of John Walter Reese, Lillie Reese Papers (Ms. 85), Archives of the Nesbitt Memorial Library, Columbus, Texas.
11. "Umscheidt's Verdict Says Two or More Fired at Coleman," *San Antonio Gazette*, May 25, 1907.
12. *San Antonio Gazette*, May 23, 1907.
13. *Eagle Lake Headlight*, May 25, 1907.
14. *San Antonio Light*, n.d., clipped by *Weimar Mercury*, Aug. 11, 1906.
15. 37th Judicial District Court, Bexar County, Texas, Criminal Minute Book R, 66, 78–79, 353, 604; *San Antonio Gazette*, May 20, 21, 23, 1907; *San Antonio Light*, November 6, 1907, January 10, 1908, August 1, 4, 1909, October 19, 21, 1909; *Eagle Lake Headlight*, May 25, June 1, 8, 1907; *Weimar Mercury*, May 2, 25, June 1, 8, 1907. The authors found the watch fob information in the *Weimar Mercury*, June 1, 1907.

Chapter Ten

1. *Weimar Mercury*, August 8, 1911.
2. *Weimar Mercury*, August 18, 1911.
3. My wife and I stopped by Goeppinger's house for a visit one day. I wanted to introduce my wife to him. He was

sitting in the front seat of his old car that he was no longer permitted to drive. We sat in the back seat. In the course of this conversation he volunteered that Marion Hope had been murdered and he knew who did it.
4. Goeppinger admission, 1978, as related to Jim and Paulina Kearney in 1978 while sitting in the back seat of his car.
5. According to Goeppinger, Marion Hope was struck against the back of his neck with the barrel of a Winchester with such force that it broke his neck, thus explaining the large bruise.
6. Reese, *Flaming Feuds*, 170.
7. *Eagle Lake Headlight*, August 26, 1911.
8. Stelzig wrote:

Mr. Frank Rugely Sheriff Bay City 8/14/11

On account of business rivalry here Will and Jim Clements seem jealous of my success in winning the trade and have threatened me on two occasions and I deem it best to notify you of the situation. Some time ago Will Clements and Jim's son Spence come into my store and Will accused me of influencing his niggers to quit him; called me names and, with his hand on his gun, said if I wanted anything to come on. Again, last Saturday Will and Jim came to the store when I was alone and made the same accusation; both grabbed me, and Will struck me on the head. I jerked loose from there, and Will pulled his gun while Jim held a large knife and said if I wanted anything to get my gun and come on. I am sure I have not said anything to injure their business and I believe their object is to threaten and intimidate me until they run me out of business. I think the main object in obtaining the appointment of deputy was to have the privilege of carrying a gun so he could use it in this way. I would like for you to investigate this matter and have these men put under peace bond to avoid further trouble.

Yours truly,
Frank Stelzig "State of Texas v. Frank Stelzig, Murder," Matagorda County Criminal Case Files, Cause 1339, June Term, 1912.
9. *Eagle Lake headlight*, June 22, 1912.
10. Witness Subpoena List, Matagorda County Criminal Case Files, Cause 1339, June Term, 1912.
11. *Eagle Lake headlight*, September 2, 1911.
12. *Weimar Mercury*, September 8, 1911.

Chapter Eleven
1. *Weimar Mercury*, March 9, 1912.
2. Stein, Feud Notes. ANML, Columbus, Texas.
3. *El Paso Times*, November 8, 9, 12, 14, 1919; *Colorado Citizen*, November 14, 21, 1919; December 19, 1919; *Eagle Lake Headlight*, November 15, 1919; "Walter Reese Loses His Long Fight for Life," unidentified clipping in Scrapbook of John Walter Reese, Lillie Reese Papers (Ms. 85), ANML.
4. *Colorado Citizen*, November 21, 1919, December 19, 1919; *Eagle Lake Headlight*, March 19, 1910; Davidson, Inquest Minute Book, 1902–1922, 34. "Reese Now Has Slight Chance to Beat Death," unidentified clipping in Scrapbook of John Walter Reese, Lillie Reese Papers (Ms. 85), ANML.
5. *San Antonio Express*, June 29, 1915; *Eagle Lake Headlight*, July 3, 1915.
6. Joe Jr. and my father Charles Kearney were great friends from childhood on.

7. Rita Dove, *Museum* (Pittsburg: Carnegie-Mellon Press, 1983), 11.
8. *Colorado County Citizen*, March 1, 1934.
9. This Howard Townsend was a distant cousin of the son of Sheriff Light Townsend of the same name who was at the side of James Burford when he was killed in Bastrop in 1900.
10. Howard William Townsend, "The Townsend-Reese Feud of Colorado County," Term Paper, English 242, University of Texas Austin, 1936. Paper in possession of ANML.
11. He did, however, produce an account of the feud for his term paper based on various newspaper accounts but without any personal reminiscences that could be considered inflammatory and biased. As a consequence, the document has limited historical significance since this material is readily available from other sources. It is nevertheless a telling document for the very reason that the author describes vividly the hostility he encountered when he announced his plans, and thus provides, perhaps unwittingly, a window into the post-feud psychology that seemed to grip not only the families involved, but the wider community as well.

    Columbus has always been regarded as a very clannish place and not particularly welcoming to outsiders. The feud and its legacy, I believe, contributed to the town's poor reputation. It certainly depressed business for many years. In defense of the town, however, those of us who grew up there became initiated into the dark secrets of the past as a kind of birthright, whether desired or not, in a way that was not possible for an outsider to acquire. We knew the families of those involved, were familiar with the undercurrents of hostility that dated back generations and had their roots in the troubles, but were still very much alive. We were aware of these things even if the particulars of the troubles, which were at the root of it all, were only known in rough outline.

12. On this point I came to disagree with Bill. It is true that no one with a Stafford name was involved in the latter stage to which he alludes, but former supporters and close business associates of the Staffords were very much involved in the second phase. The Stelzig witness list, reproduced as Appendix D, was unknown to Bill at the time of his death. I feel certain had he known of it, he would have conceded that the Reese/Hope/Townsend feud was also, concurrently, the Stafford/Townsend feud, and the title of this book, therefore, is justified.

Appendix B

1. Charles Wesley Kearney (1906–1988) was the father of James C. Kearney. He grew up in Columbus and was familiar with the story and many of the people involved. John Goeppinger had approached my father originally about the interview.
2. Thurmond West (1907–1988) was a prominent citizen of Columbus. He operated a pharmacy for many years.
3. Robert Henry Harrison (1826–1905) was a renowned physician, Civil War veteran, and horse breeder. He moved to Columbus after the war and served as head of the Southern Pacific hospital located at Glidden two miles west of Columbus. He treated many of the victims of the feud and was considered partial to the Reese side of the feud.
4. Goeppinger is referring to his grandfather, James Alexander Seymour (1828–1904).
5. William H. Carlton (1840–1900), called "Buck," was a Confederate veteran and prominent citizen of Columbus.

Endnotes

6. He is probably referring to Thomas Jefferson Oakes (1833–1900). He was part of a large extended family by that name in the county.
7. James Light Townsend: see feud biographies.
8. James A. Toliver (1841–1911) served as sheriff of Colorado County from 1876 until 1880 when Light Townsend defeated him. The Tolivers were an old and established family in the county.
9. Here Goeppinger could well be referring to the murder of Marion Hope in 1911.
10. Herbert Reese: see feud biographies.
11. Sam Reese: see feud biographies.
12. Carrie (Townsend) Stafford: see feud biographies.
13. Larkin Hope: see feud biographies.
14. Marion Hope: see feud biographies.
15. Warren Stafford: see feud biographies.
16. Calaboose: term for a holding cell that was located in the center of Spring Street at the southeast corner of the courthouse square. It was used for temporarily incarcerating prisoners when court was in session or for jailing drunks and other disorderly persons; not to be confused with the county jail, which was located on Milam Street one block south of the square.
17. The Nicholai saloon, where the shootings occurred, was located cattycorner to the Stafford bank at the intersection of Milam and Spring streets.
18. Sam K. Seymour (1861–1951) was John Goeppinger's uncle. He was the father of Sam K. Seymour, Jr. (1895–1988) who was one of the most prominent citizens in Columbus after WWII until his death in 1988.
19. Goeppinger is referring to his father, Robert Carl, who was a German immigrant. He was highly educated, spoke several languages, had a knack for business, and was obviously very ambitious. He had originally eloped with

a Seymour daughter, to the chagrin of his father-in-law, but later set his brothers-in-law up in business. He established what later became the Seymour Lumber and Hardware Store, a fixture in Columbus for over a century. Mr. Sam K. Seymour became quite an important figure. He was chairman of the Colorado County Democratic Party, chairman of the local draft board, commander of the Veterans of Foreign Wars, and chairman of the Lower Colorado River Authority. The power plant at La Grange is named after him.
20. A large part of the Gulf Plain portion of Colorado County remained in the public domain until the 1880s. Much of the land was given to the railroads as incentive for laying track, but it was also possible for individuals to purchase it from the state.
21. Charles Lewis Seymour, Sr. (1866–1909), brother of Sam K. Seymour, brother-in-law of John Goeppinger's father, Carl Robert, and hence John Goeppinger's uncle.
22. Tropkick: no reference found to this name.
23. Horne Ranch: Probably the ranch of T. W. Horne. Several Horne descendants are buried in Garwood.
24. The Seymour farm, as opposed to the ranch, was just south in the valley of the Colorado River and hence good farmland. Black tenant farmers, who lived in shotgun houses on the farm, worked the land. The number six hundred is clearly an exaggeration, but is probably accurate as to the total number of black tenant farmers in the river bottom south of Columbus.
25. Goeppinger's grandfather was James Alexander Seymour (1828–1904). He owned a large river bottom farm south of Columbus.
26. First barbed wire fence: this is a very interesting claim. R. E. Bob Stafford counted as a free-range man, hence the controversy.

27. They are referring to the fact that both Colt (pistols) and Winchester (rifles) made a weapon that took a 44/40 cartridge.
28. Cotton gin cartridges: old-fashioned term for the first rifle cartridges that could be loaded quickly and safely into the breech of a rifle or pistol.
29. Matt Moore: It is not clear whom Goeppinger is referring to. There was a notorious gun hand named H. H. Moore in South Texas at the time. Sheriff Light Townsend killed him in 1894 in the Dee Braddock affair.
30. Rancho Grande: Interestingly there were two headquarters called Rancho Grande in the general area. Shanghai Pierce located the headquarters to his ranch on the Tres Palacios River in Wharton County. Bob Stafford's headquarters, also called Rancho Grande, was located on the east bank of the Colorado River in Colorado County near present Nada, Texas.
31. Ike Towell: see feud biographies.
32. Jim Crow Laws: this discussion throws light on the development of restrictive segregation laws between blacks and whites in the late nineteenth century. Senator W. H. Pope of Marshall introduced the first legislation in Texas to require the railroads to provide separate coaches for blacks and whites in 1887. The legislation passed the Senate, but failed to make it out of committee in the House. (Daniell, *Personnel of State Government*, 199.) The reasons for its failure were largely technical: railroad companies regarded the legislation as an additional expense and a scheduling nightmare since the black population was unevenly distributed across the state. They lobbied vigorously and successfully against passage. Several newspapers took up their point of view. (See, for instance, *Galveston Daily News*, October 7, 1890.) It should be noted that the call for separate coaches in

Texas on the railroads was part of a general movement across the country. In 1887 legislatures in Missouri and Kentucky, to take two examples, took up similar laws under consideration. A law requiring separate coaches finally passed March 19, 1891, over the objections of the railroads (Gammel, *Laws*, V. 10, 44, 45) and in 1925 was expanded to include busses and streetcars (Gammel, *Laws*, V. 25, 387). Thus, during the tenure of Ike Towell as City Marshal of Columbus, 1886–1888, discussion of these matters was current and in the press. Several municipalities across the state apparently took it upon their own initiative to pass ordinances regulating seating in depots prior to the 1891 law. According to Goeppinger, the City of Columbus was the first to do so and Marshal Towell vigorously enforced the ordinance. Ike Towell's obituary reinforces this claim:

"Mr. Towell had an ordinance passed requiring the railroad company to provide separate waiting rooms for white and Negro people. He later urged and secured the passage of the state separate carriage for railroads. He organized the White Man's party in Matagorda County and was involved in the organization of the same in Colorado County in 1902." (*Eagle Lake Headlight*, February 24, 1934)

Another source, however, states that Towell took it upon himself to enforce separation at the local train station:

The "Jim Crow Law" which required the separation of whites and Negroes in public service institutions, coaches, waiting rooms, etc., originated in Columbus, Texas. Ike Towell, City Marshal of Columbus, became incensed over the fact that

Negroes were taking possession of the waiting room in the Southern Pacific depot while the white ladies were forced to stand outside. He appealed to the city authorities to break up this practice, but his request was refused. Ike Towell took the law into his own hands and proceeded to clear the depot. He had some trouble at first, having to whip two resentful Negroes. After this episode, another waiting room was built for Negroes. Out of this action, what is known as the "Jim Crow Law" was passed by the Texas Legislature in 1891. (Clipped from a "Thesis" by Norma Shaw and appeared in Mary Farrar Holland, *Tales That Have Been Told*, 96.)

This led to resentment among the black population and undoubtedly contributed to his defeat in the 1898 election when Larkin Hope used the black vote to defeat him. Bob Stafford was a big supporter of Ike Towell and his last earthly remarks, to whit, calling Larkin Hope a "Nigger loving son-of-bitch" make sense in this context.

33. Mrs. Walker: Bettie Glass Walker (1861–1954) Daughter of Isaac and Artimissa (Glass) Towell. She married William Robert Walker, January 3, 1883. Ike Towell was living with her in Columbus at the time of his death.
34. Robert Levi Foard, Jr. (1871–1897) was the adopted son of Robert Levi and Georgiana (Sherrill) Foard. He was killed by a man named Brack L. Smith in a bar room altercation in Columbus in 1897.
35. Sandmeyer Ranch: A large ranch of several thousands of acres located on Skull Creek at the edge of the prairie southwest of Columbus. Julius Sandmeyer, the owner, was the business manager of the Stafford Bank in Columbus.

36. George Little: most likely George Huff Little Jr. (1875–1947). He was the son of George Huff Little, Sr. who worked as a ranch foreman for R. E. Bob Stafford for many years.
37. Brunson's saloon: founded in 1887 by August Brunson, a German immigrant, was a grand two-story structure located on Milam Street on half block north of the courthouse square. It was considered the home turf of the Reese/Stafford crowd. Herbert Reese married the daughter of Brunson at a later date. The building is owned by the Live Oak Art center at the present.
38. Under the gun laws of the day, it was illegal for all but officers of the law to "have about their person or horse" weapons of any kind. This led to the practice of stashing weapons in places where they could be quickly retrieved, such as saloons. Under the laws of the period this was considered legal.
39. Larkin Hope: see feud biographies. Larkin Hope was a constable in 1897 when the shooting took place.
40. The Reese family had quarters at the jail.
41. Goep: John Goeppinger's nickname.
42. Ben Stafford: see feud biographies.
43. Traylor's home: The home of Charles Wesley (1847–1925) and Laura Virginia (Perry) Traylor, long-time residents of Columbus.
44. Jim Coleman: see feud biographies.
45. Hobo: Goeppinger is referring to a man by the name of Ed Scott who had recently been released from the county jail where he was a cellmate of Jim Coleman. This apparently precipitated the argument.
46. Goeppinger is referring to Charles Boehme, a German farmer from the north part of the county. He was in town shopping when the gunfight broke out. He was driving his wagon when he was hit. Still clutching the reins and

a whip, he fell from the seat into the street. His pregnant wife Bertha and two of their eight children were in the wagon with him. As Boehme fell, the team broke and ran, taking the wagon and his terrified family careening through the streets. Joseph Gloger, who made furniture in a store nearby, stepped into the street and stopped the wagon. Boehme died where he fell, perhaps not ever knowing exactly what had happened to him. Bertha Boehme, realizing that her husband had been killed, collapsed in a dead faint. (*Colorado Citizen*, March 23, 1899.)

47. Johnny Williams was the son of Columbus merchant and city alderman Henry S. Williams and was hit with a stray bullet in his left hip during the shoot-out.
48. Ibid.
49. St. Edwards: a private Catholic School in Austin.
50. The shooting to which Goeppinger refers is almost certainly the one that occurred March 28, 1899, when unknown assailants fired a shot into the house of Will Clements, missing him, but the bullet lodged in a doorstop.
51. The Southern Pacific Railroad had a large yard and facility in Houston that included repair shops.
52. Gunger Woolridge: see feud biographies.
53. Will Clements: see feud biographies.
54. Boer war: The Second Boer War, also known as the Second Anglo-Boer War and the South African War, 11 October 1899–31 May 1902, was the first major international conflict of the twentieth century. The war was fought between the British Empire and the two independent Boer republics of the Orange Free State and the South African Republic (Transvaal Republic). After a protracted hard-fought war, the two independent republics lost and were absorbed into the British Empire.

55. Zumwalt's Drug Store: Oscar Abraham Zumwalt (1870–1951) owned and operated a drug store in Columbus for many years.
56. George Best: Columbus native and cotton broker (1848–1929) is buried in the Odd Fellows cemetery in Columbus.
57. Rattler's Creek: actually Ratcliff's Creek, a small creek and drainage south of Columbus.
58. Huisache: a kind of brush similar to mesquite that is native to South Texas.
59. Mark Townsend owned a farm just south of Columbus along the old Speaksville road. The road crossed Ratliff's Creek south of Columbus about half a mile.
60. Jim Coleman: see feud biographies.
61. Ole man Will: most likely Will Clements, who was present at the shooting of Jim Coleman. See feud biographies.
62. J. W. Kincheloe: see feud biographies
63. Marion Hope died at the Mark Townsend Ranch near Nixon on August 11, 1911. The coroner ruled that his large Norman horse had fallen with him and broken his neck and that the death was accidental. John Goeppinger confessed in a private conversation that Marion Hope had in fact been murdered, but he refused to name the perpetrators. He hints at the true nature of his death several times during the taped interview. The feud could be said to end with the deaths of Marion Hope, Will Clements, and Jim Townsend, all violent deaths and all in a four-week period in the summer of 1911.

Appendix C

1. This is a very important point and corroborates that the second phase of troubles that commenced with the assassination of Larkin Hope in 1898 never completely parted

company from the ill will and hatred that accompanied the deaths of the Stafford brothers in 1890. Former Stafford friends and supporters became the bedrock of support for Sam Reese and his sons.
2. This observation underscores the importance of the release of Jim Coleman in the shooting of Dick Reese and his driver. The Townsend/ Burford faction was (rightfully) afraid of Jim Coleman, who was a known killer and who had sworn revenge on Mark Townsend, and the deputies most certainly believed that it was Coleman whom they were firing upon when they shot Dick Reese in the dark.
3. This was the claim made by Sheriff Burford to justify the posting of deputies Step Yates and Jim Townsend at the bridge. That there had been, in fact, shooting was contradicted by Walter Reese in a letter to the *Weimar Mercury* on May 21, 1899.
4. Actually Ranger Seiker got this part incorrect. The girl was, in fact, Nuddie Ela (Reese) Lessing, a daughter of Sheriff Sam Reese.

Bibliography of Sources Used

Books

"Honorable M. S. Townsend." *Memorial and Genealogical Record of Southwest Texas*. Chicago: Goodspeed Bros., 1894. 162–163.

"Samuel Marion Hope." *The History of the Southwest*. Vol. 2. Lewis Publishing Co., 1907, 370, 371.

Arnn, John Wesley III, *Land of the Tejas; Native American Identity and Interaction in Texas, A.D. 1300 to 1700*. Austin: University of Texas Press, 2012.

Barr, Alywn. *Reconstruction to Reform: Texas Politics, 1876–1906*. Austin: University of Texas Press, 1971.

Boethel, Paul. *History of Lavaca County*. Austin: Von Boeckmann-Jones, 1959.

Boethel, Paul. *La Baca*. Columbus: Butler Printing, 1993.

———. *The Lavacans*. Columbus: Butler Printing, 1991.

Brewer, J. Mason. *Negro Legislators of Texas*. Austin/New York: Jenkins Publishing Co., 1970.

Brice, Donaly E., and Barry Crouch. *The Governor's Hounds; The Texas State Police, 1870–1873*. Austin: University of Texas, 2011.

Colorado County Historical Commission. *Colorado County Chronicles from the Beginning to 1923*. 2 Vols. Austin: Nortex, 1986.

Cox, James, ed. *Historical and Biographical Record of the Cattle Industry and the Cattlemen of Texas and Adjacent Territory*. St Louis: Woodward and Tiernam Printing Co., 1895.

Dale, Edward Everett. *The Range Cattle Industry*. Norman: University of Oklahoma Press, 1960.

Davis, Joe Tom. "Columbus: A Walk Into a Proud Past." in *Historic Towns of Texas*, volume 2. Austin: Eakin Press, 1996, 88–173.

Douglas, C. L. *The Cattle Kings of Texas*. Dallas: Baugh, 1939; rpt., Fort Worth: Branch/Smith, 1968.

Emmett, Chris. *Shanghai Pierce: A Fair Likeness*. Norman: University of Oklahoma Press, 1953.

Finkelstein, Mrs. Dave. *John and Margaret Hallett*. Hallettsville Tribune, 1951.

Gammel, *Laws*, Vol. 6, 292, 297. Columbus incorporated.

Graham, J. O. *The Book of Wharton County, Texas*. Wharton: Philip Rich, 1926.

Harris, Charles H. III, and Louis R. Sadler. *The Texas Rangers and the Mexican Revolution: The Bloodiest Decade, 1910–1920*. Albuquerque: The University of New Mexico Press, 2004.

Harris, Charles Houston. *The Texas Rangers and the Mexican Revolution*. Albuquerque: University of New Mexico Press, 2004.

Hine, Darlene Clark. *Black Victory: The Rise and Fall of the White Primary in Texas*. New York: KTO Press, 1979.

Historic Wharton County. 3 Volumes. D. Armstrong Company, Inc., 1968.

History of the Cattlemen of Texas. Introduction by Harwood P. Hinton. Reprint of a privately printed 1914 edition. Austin: Texas State Historical Association, 1991. Ike Pryor, 171–173.

History of Eagle Lake. Eagle Lake Historical Committee. Austin: Nortex Press, 1987.

Holland, Mary Farrar. *Stories That Have Been Told.* Ann Arbor: Edwards Brothers, Inc., 1948.

Howell, Kenneth W., et al. *Beyond Myths and Legends: Narrative History and Texas.* Wheaton, IL: Abigail Press, 2009.

Howell, Kenneth W., ed. *The Seventh Star of the Confederacy: Texas during the Civil War.* Denton: University of North Texas Press, 2009.

———. *Still the Arena of Civil War: Violence and Turmoil in Reconstruction Texas 1865–1874.* Denton: University of North Texas Press, 2012.

Hunter, Marvin J., Editor and Compiler. *The Trail Drivers of Texas.* Austin: University of Texas, 1985. Mrs. Ike T. Pryor, 895–897; R. E. Stafford, 708–710; Ike Pryor, 173–182.

McCoy, Joseph G. *Historic Sketches of the Cattle Trade of the West and Southwest.* Kansas City: Ramsey Millett and Hudson, 1874; rpt. Columbus, Ohio: Long's College Book Co., 1951.

Moneyhon, Carl H. *Texas After the Civil War: The Struggle for Reconstruction.* College Station: Texas A&M University Press, 2004.

———. *Edmund J. Davis: Civil War General, Republican, and Reconstruction Governor.* Fort Worth: Texas Christian University Press, 2010.

Moore, Stephen. *Eighteen Minutes: The Battle of San Jacinto and the Texas Independence Campaign.* Dallas: Republic of Texas Press, 2004.

Morris, Harry Joseph. *Citizens of the Republic of Texas.* Dallas: Texas State Genealogical Society, 1979.

Paine, Albert B. *Captain Bill McDonald: Texas Ranger.* New York: J. J. Little & Ives Company, 1909.

Phelan, Macum. *A History of Early Methodism in Texas, 1817–1866*. Nashville: Cokesbury Press, 1924.

Reese, John Walter, and Lillian Estelle Reese. *Flaming Feuds of Colorado County*. Salado, Texas: The Anson Jones Press, 1962.

Report of the Adjutant General of the State of Texas for 1899–1900. Austin: Von Boeckmann, Schutze, & Company, State Printers, 1900.

Rice, Lawrence. *The Negro in Texas, 1874–1900*. Baton Rouge: Louisiana State University Press, 1971.

Rose, Peter R. *The Reckoning: The Triumph of Order on the Texas Outlaw Frontier*. Lubbock: Texas Tech Press, 2012.

Sefton, James E. *The United States Army and Reconstruction, 1865–1877*. Baton Rouge: Louisiana State University Press, 1967.

Smallwood, James M. *Time of Hope, Time of Despair: Black Texans During Reconstruction*. Port Washington, NY/London: Kennikat Press, 1981.

Smithwick, Noah. *Evolution of a State: Recollections of Old Texas Days*. Austin: Gammel Book Company, 1900.

Sonnichsen, Charles Leland. *I'll Die Before I'll Run*. New York: Harper & Brothers, 1951. Reprint, New York: The Devin-Adair Company, 1962. Reprint, Lincoln: University of Nebraska Press, 1988.

Siringo, Charles A. *Riata and Spurs: the Story of a Lifetime Spent in the Saddle as Cowboy and Detective*. Boston and New York: Houghton Miffin company, 1927.

Spellman, Paul N. *Captain J. A. Brooks: Texas Ranger*. Denton: University of North Texas Press, 2007.

Spurlin, Charles D. *Texas Veterans in the Mexican War: Muster Rolls of Texas Military Units*. Victoria, TX: Erickson Books, 1984.

Stephens, A. Ray. *Texas: A Historical Atlas*. Norman: University of Oklahoma Press, 2010.

Sterling, William Warren. *Trails and Trials of a Texas Ranger*. Norman, Oklahoma: University of Oklahoma Press, 1959.
Tise, Sammy. *Texas County Sheriffs*. Albuquerque, New Mexico: Oakwood Printing, 1989.
War of the Rebellion. Series I, Vol. 15, "Insurrection of Germans in Colorado County," 220.
Wharton, Clarence. *Wharton's History of Fort Bend County*. San Antonio: Naylor Press, 1939.
White Man's Union Association, The Constitution and By-Laws of the White Man's Union Association of Wharton County, Texas. Wharton County, n.p., 1936.
Williams, Annie Lee. *A History of Wharton County*. Austin: Von Boeckmann-Jones, 1964.
Wyatt, Tula Townsend. *The Seven Townsend Brothers of Texas, 1826–1838: A Genealogy*. Austin: Aus-Tex Duplicators, Inc., 1974.
Yelderman, Pauline. *The Jay Bird Democratic Association of Fort Bend County*. Waco: Texian Press, 1979.

Articles and Chapters

Bostick, Sion. "Reminiscences of Sion R. Bostick." *The Quarterly of the Texas State Historical Association* 5 (July 1901–April 1902): 85–95.
Brice, Donaly. "Finding a Solution to Reconstruction Violence: The Texas State Police." In Kenneth W. Howell, ed., *Still the Arena of Civil War: Violence and Turmoil in Reconstruction Texas, 1865–1874*. Denton: The University of North Texas Press, 2012, 187–213.
Broadbent, C. S. "Lost Many Thousands of Dollars." *Trail Drivers of Texas*, 592–594.
Cambell, Randolph. "SLAVERY," *HT Online*, accessed January 4, 2014.

Campbell, Randolph B. "Reconstruction in Colorado County." *Nesbitt Memorial Library Journal* 5, no. 1 (January 1995): 3–28.

Crouch, Barry A. "'Unmanacling' Texas Reconstruction: A Twenty-Year Perspective." *SWHQ* 93 (1980): 25–302

———. "Guardian of the Freedpeople: Texas Freedmen Bureau Agents and the Black Community." *Southern Studies* 31 (1992): 185–201.

———. "Hidden Sources of Black History: The Texas Freedmen's Bureau Records as a Case Study," *SWHQ* 83 (1980): 211–226.

———. "The Freedmen's Bureau in Colorado County, Texas, 1865–1868." Part 1, *Nesbitt Memorial Library Journal*, Vol. 5, no. 2 (May 1995): 71–104; Part 2, *Nesbitt Ibid.*, Vol. 7, no. 3 (September 1997): 147–176; Part 3, Ibid., Vol.8, no. 1 (January 1998): 3–32.

———. "A Spirit of Lawlessness: White Violence; Texas Blacks, 1865–1868." *Journal of Social History* 18, no. 2 (Winter 1984): 218, 219.

Elliot, Claude. "The Freedmen's Bureau In Texas," *SWHQ* 56 (1952): 1–24.

Hinton, Don Allon. "COLUMBUS, TX." *NHT*.

Kuykendall, J. H. "Reminiscences of Early Texas", *SWHQ* 7, no. 1 (July 1903): 29–64.

Leffler, John. "FOARD COUNTY." *HT Online*, accessed August 22, 2013.

Long, Christopher "WHITEMAN'S UNION ASSOCIATIONS," *HT Online*, accessed August 22, 2013.

McCallum, Henry D. "Barbed Wire in Texas." *SWHQ* 61, no. 2 (October 1957): 207–219.

Moneyhon, Carl H. "RECONSTRUCTION," *HT Online*, accessed May 08, 2014.

Odintz, Mark. "COLORADO COUNTY," *NHT*, vol. 2: 224–226.

Powers, Anthony S. "GARWOOD, TEX." *HT Online*, accessed August 18, 2013.

Richardson, T. C., and Harwood P. Hinton "RANCHING," *HT Online*, accessed August 22, 2013.

"Robert Earl Stafford." *Trail Drivers of Texas*, 708–710.

Shook, Robert W. "The Federal Military in Texas, 1865–1870," *Texas Military History*, 6 (Spring 1967).

Skaggs, Jimmy M. "CATTLE TRAILING," *HT Online*, accessed August 20, 2013.

———. "WESTERN TRAIL," *HT Online*, accessed August 20, 2013.

Smallwood, James. "SLAVE INSURRECTIONS," *HT Online*, accessed May 08, 2014.

———. "Black Education in Reconstruction Texas: The Contributions of the Freedmen's Bureau and Benevolent Societies," *East Texas Historical Journal* 19 (1981): 17–40.

———. "Charles E. Culver: A Reconstruction Agent in Texas: The Work of Local Freedmen's Bureau Agents and the Black Community," *Civil War History* 27 (1981): 350–361.

———. "Early 'Freedmen Schools', Black Self-Help and Education in Reconstruction Texas: A Case Study," *Negro History Bulletin* 41 (1978): 790–793.

———. "The Freedmen's Bureau Reconsidered: Local Agents and the Black Community," *Texana* 11 (1973): 309–320.

Stein, Bill, and Bobbie Elliot. "Index to District Court Criminal Cause Files, 1876–1900." *Nesbitt Memorial Library Journal* 8, no. 2 (May 1998): 79–112.

Stein, Bill, and Jim Sewell. "Historical Atlas of Columbus." *Nesbitt Memorial Library Journal* 3, no. 2 (May 1993): 73–102.

Stein, Bill. "COLORADO COUNTY FEUD," *HT Online*, accessed June 20, 2010.

Stein, Bill. "Beyond Boosterism: Establishing the Age of Columbus." *Nesbitt Memorial Library Journal* 2, no. 2 (May 1992): 71–90.

———. "Distress, Discontent, and Dissent: Colorado County, Texas, During the Civil War," in Howell, ed., *The Seventh Star of the Confederacy*, 301–316.

———. "Capsule History of Colorado County." *Nesbitt Memorial Library Journal* 3, no. 1 (January 1993): 45–50.

———. "Conflict between H. H. Moore and Sheriff Light Townsend." *Nesbitt Memorial Library Journal* 3, no. 2 (May 1993): 58–72.

———. "Consider the Lilly: The Ungilded History of Colorado County, Texas," *Nesbitt Memorial Library Journal*, Part 1, Vol. 6, no. 1, (Jan. 1996): 3–34; Part 2, 35–52; Part 3, Ibid., Vol. 6, no. 2 (May 1996): 63–94; Part 4, Ibid., Vol. 6, no. 3 (September 1996): 115–150; Part 5, Ibid., Vol. 7, no. 1 (January 1997): 3–60; Part 6, Ibid., Vol. 7, no. 2 (May 1997): 75–142; Part 7, *Nesbitt Memorial Library Journal*, Vol. 9, no. 1 (January 1999): 3–40; Part 8, Ibid., Vol. 10, N. 1 (January 2000): 3–62; Part 9, Ibid., Vol. 10, N. 3 (June 2001): 135–182.

———. "Digest of the Book of Land Certificates." *Nesbitt Memorial Library Journal* 3, no. 3 (Sept. 1993): 123–167.

———. "Distress, Discontent, and Dissent: Colorado County, Texas, during the Civil War," in Howell, ed., *The Seventh Star of the Confederacy*, 301–316.

———. "Index to District Court Criminal Cause Files, 1837–1875." *Nesbitt Memorial Library Journal* 4, no. 2 (May 1994): 74–114.

———. "Prime Circuit: The Glory Days of the Stafford Opera House." *Nesbitt Memorial Library Journal* 1, no. 4 (March 1990): 103–125.

Thomas, Henry Calhoun. "A Sketch of my Life." *Nesbitt Memorial Library Journal* 1, no. 3 (February 1990): 71–91.

Ward, Hortense Warner. "HIDE AND TALLOW TRADE," *HT Online*, accessed January 4, 2014.

Weddle, Robert S. "LA SALLE EXPEDITION," *HT Online*, accessed June 1, 2010.

Werner, George C. "GALVESTON, HARRISBURG AND SAN ANTONIO RAILWAY," *HT Online*, accessed April 6, 2010.

Newspapers Cited

Austin Daily Tribune, Austin, TX
Austin Statesman, Austin, TX
Bastrop Advertiser, Bastrop, TX
Bastrop Vidette, Bastrop, TX
Bay City Tribune, Bay City, TX
Brenham Weekly Banner, Brenham, TX
Colorado Citizen, Columbus, TX
Dallas Daily Herald Dallas, TX
Del Rio News, Del Rio, TX
Denison Daily News, Denison, TX
Eagle Lake headlight, Eagle Lake, TX
Flakes Daily Bulletin, Galveston, TX
Galveston Daily News, Galveston, TX
Galveston News, Galveston, TX
Galveston Tri-Weekly News, Galveston, TX
Galveston Union, Galveston, TX
Herald and Planter, Hallettsville, TX
Houston Daily Post, Houston, TX
Houston Daily Union, Houston, TX
Houston Mercury, Houston, TX
Houston Telegraph, Houston, TX
Lavaca Herald, Hallettsville, TX
New York Times, New York, NY
Newark Daily Advocate, Newark, OH
San Antonio Express, San Antonio, TX

San Antonio Gazette, San Antonio, TX
San Antonio Light, San Antonio, TX
San Marcos Free Press, San Marcos, TX
San Marcos Record, San Marcos, TX
The Houston Telegraph, Houston, TX
The Reformer, Austin, TX.
The Standard, Clarksville, TX
The Telegraph and Texas Register, Galveston, TX
The Texas State Gazette, Austin, TX
The Weekly Constitution, Weatherford, TX
Tri-Weekly Houston Union, Houston, TX
Weekly Democratic Statesmen, Austin, TX
Weimar Mercury, Weimar, TX

Archives and Collections

Austin County Cemetery Records. Austin County Historical Commission, Bellville, TX.

Burrell, Velva Whitley. Manuscript. Archives of the Nesbitt Memorial Library, Columbus, TX.

Captain McDonald to Adjutant General Thomas Scurry, March 22, 1899, General Correspondence, Adjutant General's Record Group (RG 401).

Letter of Arthur L. Burford to Mattie Pinchback Burford. January 14, 1900. Small Manuscripts Collection (MS 5). Archives of the Nesbitt Memorial Library, Columbus, TX.

Lillie Reese Papers (MS 85). "Tragedy in Iron Front Saloon Makes Another Chapter in Celebrated Columbus Feud." Unidentified clipping in Scrapbook of John Walter Reese, Archives of the Nesbitt Memorial Library, Columbus, TX.

Lillie Reese Papers (Ms. 85). "Walter Reese to Lillie Reese, June 27, 1917, July 4, 1917." Archives of the Nesbitt Memorial Library, Columbus, TX.

McGee, Leigh. "Remarks concerning the Feud." Archives of the Nesbitt Memorial Library, Columbus, TX.

Minutes of the Columbus Meat and Ice Co. Stein Collection. Archives of the Nesbitt Memorial Library, Columbus, TX.

Monthly Reports, Company E, May 1899, Adjutant General's Records (RG 401) Archives Division, Texas State Library, Austin.

Records of Scouts, Company E, 1899, Report of Columbus Detachment, June 1899, July 1899, Adjutant General's Records (RG 401), Archives Division, Texas State Library, Austin

Records of Scouts, Company F, 1900, Adjutant General's Records (RG 401), Archives Division, Texas State Library,

Reports of Captain Brooks for 1899, Monthly Returns of Company F, Adjutant General's Record Group (RG 401).

Reports of Captain Brooks for 1900, Records of Scouts, Company E, 1900, Adjutant General's Records (RG 401), Archives Division, Texas State Library, Austin.

Schoellmann, Elizabeth, Personal note in Archives of Nesbitt Memorial Library, Columbus, TX.

Stein, Bill. "Notes on the Feud." Stein Collection. Archives of the Nesbitt Memorial Library, Columbus, TX.

Thomas Scurry to Governor Joseph D. Sayers, June 10, 1899, Governor's Papers, Joseph D. Sayers, (RG 301) Archives Division, Texas State Library, Austin

Towell, J. W. to Governor S. W. T. Lanham, Columbus Texas July 21, 1906. Cover Letter and Draft Resolution of Town meeting. Governor's Reports Texas State Archives.

Townsend/Burford Papers, Woodsen Research Center, Fondren Library, Rice University, Houston, TX.

Townsend, Howard. "The Townsend Reese Feud in Colorado County, ca. 1950. Typewritten manuscript.

Townsend, Samuel Luck. Memoir Manuscript. Archives of the Nesbitt Memorial Library, Columbus, TX.

Wetteroth, Mrs. and Mrs. Longnecker, interviews, January 2, 1944. typescripts, Archives of the Nesbitt Memorial Library, Columbus, TX.

U.S. Government Documents

Seventh Census of the United States, 1850, Schedule 1, Slave Schedule, Colorado County, TX.

Eighth Census of the United States, 1860, Schedule 1, Slave Schedule, Colorado County, TX.

Ninth Census of the United States, 1870, Schedule 1, Colorado County, TX.

Tenth Census of the United States, 1880, Schedule 1, Colorado County, TX.

Twelfth Census of the United States, 1900, Schedule 1, Colorado County, TX.

Courthouse and City Government Documents

Austin County District Court Records, Bellville, TX.

Bastrop County District Court Records, Bastrop, TX.

Bastrop County Criminal Minutes Book E

Bexar County District Court Records, San Antonio, TX.

Bexar County, Texas, Criminal Minute Book, San Antonio, TX.

Colorado County Bonds and Mortgages, Columbus, TX.

Colorado County Deed Records, Columbus, TX.

Colorado County Land Certificates, Columbus, TX.

Colorado County Livestock Brand and Marks Book, Columbus, TX.

Colorado County Tax District Court Records, Columbus, TX.

Colorado County Tax Records, Columbus, TX.
Fort Bend County District Court Records, Richmond, TX.
Lavaca County Criminal Case Minutes, Hallettsville, TX.
Lavaca County Deed Records, Hallettsville, TX.
Matagorda County District Court Minutes, Bay City, TX.
Minutes of the City of Columbus, Texas, May 8, 1899, June 5, 1899, July 3, 1899, July 10, 1899, July 28, 1899, August 17, 1899, August 21, 1899, September 4, 1899, September 11, 1899, October 2, 1899, December 4, 1899, January 2, 1900, January 5, 1903, City Hall, Columbus, TX

Thesis and Dissertation

Thompson, Ester L. "The Influence of the Freedmen's Bureau on the Education of the Negro in Texas." Master of Arts Thesis, Texas Southern University (Houston, TX), 1972.

Saxton, Lewis H. "The Life of Everett Ewing Townsend." Master of Arts Thesis, Sul Ross State Teacher's College (Alpine, TX), August 1, 1948.

Interview

Goeppinger, John. Conducted by James C. Kearney and Charles W. Kearney in 1976. Transcribed by Tracey Wegenhoft. In the possession of the author.

Index

–A–
Alamo and Goliad, twin disasters, 25
Allen, Poole, & Co, 45
Auerbach, Frank, 68, 70, 148
Auerbach's Meat Market, 71
Austin Conservatory of Music, 127, 153
Austin County, 15
Austin, Moses, 23
Austin, Stephen F., 23, 25
Austin, William, 41
Austin's colony, 23

–B–
Bank, R.E. Stafford & Co., 57
Bastrop shoot-out, 103–108
Bay City, TX, 147
Bellville, 15
black vote, 7; and Townsend control of, 11; and support among, 17; and Sheriff Townsend, 31; and role in 1898 sheriff's race, 77; appealed to by Mark Townsend, 77; and generous amounts of cash, 77
Boehme, Bertha and Carl, 82
Boer War, 87
Borden community near Weimar, 27
Bostick, Sion, 27

Bouldin, Thomas, 136
Braddock, Dee, 32
Bradshaw, Dee, 63
Bridge, W. E., 64, 119, 122, 123, 129, 131
Brooks, Captain John A., 96, 97, 100, 102, 105, 107, 148
Brunson saloon, 70, 78, 81, 82, 92
Burford, Annie E., 36
Burford, Arthur, 101, 102, 103, 104, 108, 109, 110, 111, 113
Burford, Frank "Red," 113, 226; and Rosenberg shoot-out, 114–116
Burford, Sheriff William "Will" T., mentioned: 75, 87, 88, 90, 92, 93, 96, 101, 105, 113, 122, 124, 125, 127, 141; and 1898 election results, 77; personal integrity of, 78; devout Methodist, 78; owns farm near Osage community, 78; lacks law enforcement experience, 79; allows himself to be managed by M. H. Townsend, 79; partners with Mark Townsend in Red Bluff Irrigation Co., 79; appoints Will Clements first deputy, 80; on the scene of slain Sam Reese, 83; deputizes two men, 88;

runs for reelection in 1900, and White Man's primary, 119
Burttschell clan, 81
Burttschell, August, 106
Burttschell, Henry, 106
Burttschell, Jake, 71, 72, 73
Burttschell, Joseph, 66, 71, 89
Byars, Dick, 68

–C–

calaboose, 8
Carnes, H.A. (Texas Ranger), 132
Chisholm Trail, 46
Clapp, Eliza, 29
Clayton, Nicholas, 56
Clements, Alice, 131
Clements, Augustus D. "Gus," 80
Clements, Hiram, 128; discovered mortally wounded, 128; descended from Spencer Townsend line, 130; twenty-four years old, married and with a baby girl, 130; killed by Dr. Lessing, 131
Clements, James "Jim," 127, 131, 135
Clements, Spencer, 80
Clements, Will, mentioned 3, 75, 81, 86, 92, 93, 95, 96, 99, 102, 104, 108, 111, 127, 128, 131, 135, 143, 145, 149; daughter of Florida "Lou" Townsend and Gus Clements, 80; loud and aggressive, 80; appointed first deputy by Will Burford, 80; altercation with Ed Scott, 81; emerges unscathed, 82; has a .45 Colt pistol, 83; charged with manslaughter for death of Sam Reese, resumes position as chief deputy sheriff, 85; is shot at while home, 86, 87; is wounded, at Bastrop,

101–106; names his assassins, 106; participation in Rosenberg shoot-out, 111–116; habit of violence, 136; arrives in San Antonio, 138; murdered by Stelzig, 146–148
Coleman, Jim, mentioned: 71, 72, 74, 81, 87, 88, 95, 98, 99, 108, 109, 112, 113, 127, 141, 143, 145, 148, 157; swears revenge on Tucker Hoover and kills him, 73; agrees to kill Larkin Hope; provided an alibi, 74; cellmate of Ed Scott, 75; faces *habeas corpus* hearing, 86; infuriated at Mark Townsend, sociopathic, 87; addiction to alcohol and opiates, 87; makes threats against Mark Townsend in open court, 87; released on bond, 87; intends to kill both Sheriff Burford and Mark Townsend 87; something afoot, 88; arrested in Bastrop, 106; bail set, 107; and Rosenberg shoot-out, 113–117; his assassination, 135–145; moves to San Antonio, 136; arrested for carrying a pistol, 137; shadowed by private detectives, 138; is shot by Hope, Kincheloe, and Clements, 139
Colonization Law in 1825, Mexican, 22
colonization, Anglo-American, 22
Colorado Citizen (newspaper), 44, 47, 50, 54, 66, 82, 95, 119, 95
Colorado County, 18, 21, 40, 41, 42, 43, 45, 57, 61, 73, 79, 84, 97, 98, 99, 100, 102, 103, 110, 111, 112, 113, 115, 117, 119, 121, 122, 124, 126;

Index 281

private justice and lawlessness in, 19
Columbus and the "Runaway Scrape," 25
conspiracy, Machiavellian, 16
courthouse, Colorado County, new in 1890, 6
Cox, Ethel, 151
Cummins Creek, 23, 24

–D–

Daniels, Tom, 106
Dove, Rita, 155
Dickson, Sheriff Hamilton of Wharton County, 32
Dunovant, Captain William, 79

–F–

Fayette County, 21
First Methodist Church in Columbus, 27
Flaming Feuds of Colorado County, 53, 62, 83, 111, 115, 123, 146, 153
Florida Chapel, 24
Foard and Thompson Law Firm in Columbus, 35
Foard, Major Robert, 35
Franz Saloon, 128, 129
Frazar store, 52
Frazar, James Underwood and Newton Ford, 52
Frontier Battalion, Company B of Texas Rangers, 85

–G–

Gandry's saloon, 148, 149
Gant, Dick, 89
Garwood, TX, 79, 127
Gegenworth store, 71
Georgia, 21
Glidden, TX, 106, 127, 128, 130, 135, 155, 182
Gloger, Joseph, 82

Goeppinger, John, mentioned: 75, 83, 87, 128, 131, 138, 142, 143, 145, 146, 149, 153, 154, 155; Goeppinger interview, references to: #1, 13, 31; #3, 120; #5, 67; #6, 69, 125; 74; #7, 83, 131; #8, 86; #12, 138
Gonzales Road, 26
Grace, Sam, 136
Groin, T. J., 43
"grove" in Columbus, 6

–H–

Harrison, Dr. R. H., 83, 106, 116
Harvey's Creek, 26
Hester, Constable John, 129
Hill, T.A., 79
Hood's Texas Brigade, 42
Hoover, Tuck, 72, 73
Hope brothers, 16, 18
Hope, David Larkin, 136
Hope, Larkin, mentioned: 3, 7, 8, 9, 10, 11, 12, 13, 15, 17, 39, 61, 66, 67, 70, 74, 75, 86, 87, 95, 99, 108 ; hopes to rejoin lawman's trade, opens a grocery store, frequent saloon visitor, 66; growing rift, 67; a loose cannon, 68; withdraws from constable's race, 69; assassinated, 70
Hope, Marion, 3, 8, 9, 10, 11, 12, 13, 15, 73, 81, 83, 84, 85, 92, 96, 99, 125, 127, 136, 143, 145; in partnership with his brother, 66; arrested for killing of Sam Reese, 85; and the skating rink shoot-out, 128–131; half-brother to Dr. Lessing, 130; mother beside herself with grief, 131; moves to Lane City, 135, 149, 154; bodyguard for Mark Townsend, 138;

shoots Jim Coleman, 139; indicted for murder of Coleman, 141; defended by Mark Townsend, 141; ruled accidental death, 145; probably murdered, 146
Hope, Mary (Townsend), 8
Hope, Molly, 71
Hoskins, R. J., 43
Houchins, Jim F., 84
Houston, Sam, and Texas Army, 25
Hudson (Texas Ranger), 85
Hughes, Captain John R., 132

–I–
Ilse, Henry, 49
Indian threat, 23
Indianola, 45
Insall, Henry J., 78
Iron Front saloon, 138

–J–
Jackson County, 45, 46, 53, 148
Jaybird/Woodpecker feud, 2
Johnson, Bob, 32
Juergen saloon, 82

–K–
Kell, William, 152
Kennon, District Judge Mumford, 85, 87, 132
Kimble County Confederation, 48
Kincheloe, J.W., 138, 139, 140, 141, 142, 143

–L–
La Bahia road, 23
Lane City, 127, 135, 136, 138
Lanham, Governor, 132
Lavaca County, 21, 40, 45, 48, 54, 61, 62, 84, 87, 88, 92, 93, 95, 117
Lessing, Dr. Joe, mentioned: 68, 81, 88, 111; role in skating rink shoot-out, 129–131; half brother of Marion Hope, 130; shoots and kills Hiram Clements, 130; rifle discovered later, 131
Lessing, Mrs. Joe, 112
Lessing, Nuddie Ela (Reese), 88
Little, George, 44, 148
Louise, TX, 148
Lunn Brothers, 51

–M–
Maibaum, Frank, 138–143
Mansfield, Judge, 53, 65, 90
Marlboro District of South Carolina, 26
Masonic lodge at Columbus, 27
Masons, 22
Matagorda County, 135, 136, 146, 147
McCain Detective Agency, 127
McCormick, Judge, 15
McDonald, Captain Bill, mentioned: 85, 90, 97, 106, 148; arrives in Columbus, 89; ordered away, 92; adopts strategy to persuade, cajole, and threaten, 93
McNelly, Captain Leander H., 55
Memphis Commercial Appeal, 117
Mixon Creekers, 48
Moore, H. H., 32, 63
Morgan Shipping Lines, 45

–N–
Nada, TX, 41
Navidad River in Lavaca County, 26
Negro vote, cultivation of, 13
Neuman, Edna, 138
Nicolai Saloon, 10
Nixon, TX, 145

Index

–O–
Oakland, 40, 54, 61, 62, 77, 80
Odd Fellows Cemetery, Columbus, TX, 154
"Old Three Hundred," 23

–P–
Petersburg in Lavaca County, 30
Pierce, Abel H. "Shanghai," 49, 50, 51
Pinchback, Mary and John, 43
Prairie Point, 40
Pryor, Ike, 47

–R–
rally, anti-Townsend, 14
Rancho Grande, 41, 46, 47
Ratcliff, Richard R., 55
Ratcliff, William, 40,
Red Bluff Irrigation, 79, 127, 162
Reese faction, 18, 84
Reese, Buster, 106
Reese, Dick, 75, 89, 90, 91, 93, 95, 96, 99, 109, 111; killed, 88
Reese, Fleming, 106
Reese, Herbert "Hub," mentioned: 63, 72, 75, 78, 106, 112, 115, 123, 125, 127; and the skating rink shoot-out, 127–129; roughed up by Marion Hope, 127; marries Ivy Ilse, 135; has a long memory, 137; accidentally shoots himself, 151
Reese, Keron Blanche (Keetie), mentioned: 61, 62, 70, 77, 80, 88, 93, 99, 112, 127; rushes to her slain husband, 82; keeper of the flame, 84; undercuts rangers, 93; "eggs on" supporters of Reese, 94; moves away, 119; outlives her two sons, 153
Reese, Les, 106
Reese, Lillian, mentioned: 12, 53, 62, 63, 74, 82, 83, 111, 123, 135, 146, 156; establishes Austin Conservatory of Music, 127, last one alive, 153
Reese, Lola Herberta, 151
Reese, Nudie, Ela, 130
Reese, Sam Houston, mentioned: 32, 61, 62, 64, 66, 67, 68, 69, 71, 72, 75, 77, 78, 85, 87, 88, 89, 95, 99, 103, 109, 111, 119, 122, 123, 130, 151, 153; profiled: 61–75; and Dee Braddock affair, 32; farmer and stockman in the Navidad River bottom, embarks on a career in law enforcement, offered a position in Columbus, 62; accomplished musician, 63; role of sheriff, 64; quarrels with Mark Townsend, 68; and election results 1898, 77; and lack of deference to black voters, 77; defeated and bitter, 78; destroys records, 78; settles into new routine, 78; becomes aggressive toward Will Clements, 81; killed, 81; faces a conspiracy to kill him, 83; death evokes parallels to Stafford brothers, 84
Reese, Walter, mentioned: 53, 62, 70, 72, 74, 75, 78, 94, 95, 103, 105, 111, 112, 113, 137; attempts to help his father, 82; arrested, 92; and Bastrop shoot-out, 103–108; shoot-out at Rosenberg, 112–117; takes a job in a detective agency, 127;

and skating rink shoot-out, 128–131; purchases a livery stable in Columbus, 136; had a long memory, 146; travels to trial from El Paso, 148; dies, 151, 152; puts together a scrapbook before his death, 153
Reese/Stafford crowd, 85
Rosenberg, TX, 127, 136, 137, 148; shoot-out at, 112–117
Ross, Tom (Texas Ranger), 132
Round Top, 24, 26
Runaway Scrape, 25

–S–

San Antonio Light, 141, 152
Sanders (Texas Ranger), 85
Sandmeyer, E.S., 148
Santa Anna, 25
Sayers, Governor J. D., 53, 85, 89, 92, 94, 100, 107
Schoelmann, Elizabeth, 49
Scott, Ed, 81
Scurry, Adjutant General, 79
Secrest, Constable Larkin, 52
Settlement, Anglo in Texas, 23
Sheriff's office, role of, 2
Shoaf, George, 138, 139, 140, 141, 142, 143
shoot-out of January 1871, 6
Shropshire, James, 77
Sieker, Ranger Captain Lamartine, 17, 18, 84, 89, 90, 98
Silver King saloon, 138
Siringo, Johnny, 51
slave plantations, location of in Colorado County, 41
Sonnichsen, C. L., 1
South Carolina, Marlboro District, 21
Southern Pacific Railroad, 127
Stafford Bank, 5, 56, 57

Stafford brothers, 18, 83, 84; and run-ins with the law, 58
Stafford faction, background on, 13
Stafford name, 18
Stafford Opera House, 10, 56, 57, 104, 121, 128, 129
Stafford refrigeration and meatpacking, 12
Stafford Station, 12
Stafford, "Colonel," 11
Stafford, Benjamin "Ben," 40, 43, 55
Stafford, John, 10, 11, 13, 15, 16, 17, 40, 43, 55, 56, 153, 154; constructs house south of town, 56; involvement in murder of Stedham, 58; and murder case dismissed, 58
Stafford, Joseph Winston, 153
Stafford, Mariba, 40
Stafford, Mildred (Pete) (Goeppinger), 155
Stafford, Myra, 47
Stafford, R.E. "Bob," mentioned: 5, 6, 7, 9, 10, 12, 13, 15, 16, 17, 18, 148; and H. H. Moore, 32; profile: 39–59; born in Glynn County, Georgia, 39; education, 39; marries Sarah E. Zouks, 39; moves from Georgia, 40; settles at Oakland, 40; three brothers and a sister follow, 40; and family history, 40, 41; and early knowledge of stock business, 41; sells his farm, 41; and Civil War service 41, 42; and medical discharge, 42; buys out other herds, 42; partners with James F. Wright, 42; drives cattle, 43; not always above board, 44;

Index

sells breeding stock, 44; partners with Allen, Poole, & Co., 45; buys out competitors, 45, 46; profits from panic of 1874, 45–46; owns 175,000 head of cattle, 47; forms Stafford Bank, 47; and "Mixon Creekers," 48; deals with turmoil of Reconstruction, 48; earns a reputation, 48; fights prairie turf wars, 49; feuds with Abel H. "Shanghai" Pierce, 49, 50, 51; supports open range, 52; and attitude toward the freedpeople, 52, 53; and Eagle Lake bottom race war, 52; and "Horrible Murders in Texas," 52; punishes suspected rustlers, 52; and Bony Cotton and Lewis Evert killed, 52; and "conflicting interests on the prairie," 53; and A. Stapleton Townsend murder, 54; infuriates Townsend clan, 54; and 1871 shoot-out with Sumner Townsend in Columbus, 54, 55; moves to Columbus, 56; commissions opera house, 56; establishes bank, 57; builds packing plant, 57; and county politics, 57, 58; resolves to unseat Light Townsend as sheriff, 59

Stafford, Robert Frederick, 40

Stafford, Warren, 7, 9, 10, 18, 58; and lynching of two black men, 58; and murder of J. W. Stedham, 58; and murder case dismissed, 58

Stafford, William "Bill," 40

Staffords and Townsends, animosity between, 17

Stapleton, William, 23, 27

State Police, 48

Stedham, J. W., 58

Stein, Bill, 17, 157, 158, 159

Stelzig, Frank, 146; complains to the sheriff of Will Clements, 146; waylays Clements with a shotgun, 146; subpoenas former Reese and Stafford crowd, 147; acquitted of murder, 147

Stevens, Constable Charles, 137, 139

Stringer, Jesse, 74

Sutton-Taylor feud, 48

–T–

Taylor, Creed (Texas Ranger), 89

Texas Rangers, attend the *habeas corpus* hearings to preserve order, 85

Texas War of Independence, 21

Toliver, Sheriff, 52

Towell, Ike, mentioned: 9, 68, 120, 148, 154; history of epitaph, 155

Towell, J.W., 132, 133, 148

Townsend faction, 13, 15, 83, 88

Townsend family, 6; and troubles in Colorado County, 13; has Florida roots, 24; and Battle of San Jacinto, 25; receives headright grants, 26; and family legacy, 37

Townsend, Foard, and Thompson Law Office, 102, 129

Townsend, A. Stapleton, 54, 62

Townsend, Asa, mentioned: 38, 53, 54, 70, 80, 130; profiled: 26–29; and Masonic Lodge Columbus, 27; and First Methodist Church at Columbus, 27; and Borden

Community, 27; and William Bell Headright, 27; and public service, 27; and military record, 27; is breeder of fine race horses, 27; purchase of home in Columbus, 27; and Indian scare, 27; in 1850 and 1860 censuses, 27, 28; and wife Rebecca, 28; is father of eight sons, 28; is patriarch of family, 28

Townsend, Carrie, Estelle, 153, 154, 155, 156

Townsend, Constable A.M., 73

Townsend, E.E., 41, 44

Townsend, Florida "Lou," 80

Townsend, Hampton, 28

Townsend, Howard William, 156

Townsend, Jack, 28

Townsend, James "Jim", 3, 80, 127, 135, 145, 148, 149

Townsend, Light Stapleton, 40

Townsend, Lynn, 28

Townsend, Marcus (Mark) Harvey, mentioned: 7, 12, 15, 16, 17, 38, 64, 67, 68, 69, 70, 75, 80, 84, 89, 92, 95, 96, 99, 102, 111, 112, 113, 114, 115, 116; 119, 124, 125, 126, 133, 135, 138, 140, 141, 143, 145, 152, 153, 162, 165, 167, 168, 171; profiled: 34–38; and Machiavellian ambition, 34; father Moses Salon, 34; begins reading law while still a teenager, 35; joins the law firm of Foard and Thompson in Columbus, 35; wins a seat in the Texas House of Representatives; 35; authors a resolution to purchase the Alamo, 35; wins a seat to State Senate from the Eleventh District, 36; marries Annie E. Burford, 36; presides over Townsend machine, 36; reacts to assassination of Larkin Hope, 36; eulogized in all the major newspapers of the state, 36; supports Larkin Hope, 66; appeals to black voters personally, 77; retires from State Senate, 79; founds Red Bluff irrigation, 79; plats the town of Garwood, 79; and shoot-out with Sam Reese, 81; a crack shot with a .38 pistol, 83; arrested for killing of Sam Reese, 85; presents the State's case against Coleman, 87; agrees to leave Columbus, 93; moves to San Antonio, 127; lead attorney for Southern Pacific Railroad, 127; presides over a far-flung business empire, 127; takes note of Jim Coleman's presence in San Antonio, 137; decides to strike preemptively, 138; represents Marion Hope, 141; was the mastermind, 142

Townsend, Margaret, Alice (Cummins), 153

Townsend, Matthew, 28

Townsend, Moses Salon, 28; is oldest of Asa's sons, 34; is farmer in Oakland, 34; has quick temper and criminal record, 34; is lieutenant in Griffith's Brigade during the Civil War, 35; drowns after the war, 35

Townsend, Moses, 25, 26, 53

Townsend, Rebecca, 28

Townsend, Samuel Luck, 29

Townsend, Sheriff J. Light, mentioned: 7, 8, 11, 12, 13, 14, 15, 17, 36, 38, 53, 59, 61,

Index

62, 65, 77, 102, 119, 154; profiled: 30–34; service as sheriff, 30; as a private in the Civil War, 31; and black vote, 31; and party affiliation, 31; suffers food poisoning, 31; kills Bob Johnson, 32; shoots Dee Braddock, 32; kills H. H. Moore, 32; deals with mobs intent on lynching black prisoners, 33; and the "boodle," 33; is resented by conservatives, 33; and personal rise to affluence, 34

Townsend, Spencer Burton, mentioned: 22, 23, 26, 37, 61, 80, 130; profiled: 29–30; and Texas Revolution, 29; member of Texas Rangers in East Texas under Eliza Clapp, 29; and Battle of San Jacinto, 29; and Mexican prisoners, 29; focuses on Lavaca County, 29; and criminal record, 29, 30; becomes spokesman for Petersburg in contest with Hallettsville, 30; and quick temper, 30; has four children involved in the feud, 30

Townsend, Steven, 23, 25, 26

Townsend, Sumner, 28, 53, 54, 55, 56

Townsend, Thomas "Tupp," 53

Townsend, Thomas and Elizabeth Stapleton, 21, 27

Townsend, Thomas Roderic, 22, 23

Townsend, William T., 25, 26, 28

Townsend, William Wallace, 40

Townsend's Settlement, 24

Townsend/Burford crowd, 85

Tres Palacios Bay, 45

Tumlinson, John, 24

–U–

Umscheid, Justice of the Peace Joseph, 141

Upton, John Cunningham, 42

–W–

Walker, Columbus City Marshal, W. R. "Bob," 81

Weimar, 52, 73, 77, 78, 96, 108, 119, 120, 124, 149, 151

Weimar Mercury (newspaper), 108, 110, 115, 116, 120, 131, 132, 133, 141, 149

Wharton County, 45, 46, 53, 121, 122, 127, 135, 138, 143, 145

White, J.C. (Texas Ranger), 132

William Bell headright on Harvey's Creek, 27

Williams, "Bub," 137

Williams, Johnny, 82

Williams, J.H., 148

Williams, Henry, S., 82

White Man's Primary, 122, 148, 155

White Man's Union, 121

Wooldridge, A. R. "Gunger," 81, 86, 110, 113, 114

Wright, James F., 42

Wright, Will, 89

Western Trail, 46

–Y–

Yates, Step, 64, 66, 88, 89, 92, 95, 96, 99

–Z–

Zouks, Sarah E., 39

Zumwalt Drug Store, 129